CONTENTS

CHAP.   PAGE

I. HANDLING A ROYAL ENFIELD 1
II. THE AMAL CARBURETTOR 17
III. ALL ABOUT LUBRICATION 35
IV. CARE OF LIGHTING EQUIPMENT 56
V. GENERAL MAINTENANCE 88
    INDEX 161

INTRODUCTION

Welcome to the world of digital publishing ~ the book you now hold in your hand, while unchanged from the original edition, was printed using the latest state of the art digital technology. The advent of print-on-demand has forever changed the publishing process, never has information been so accessible and it is our hope that this book serves your informational needs for years to come. If this is your first exposure to digital publishing, we hope that you are pleased with the results. Many more titles of interest to the classic automobile and motorcycle enthusiast, collector and restorer are available via our website at www.VelocePress.com. We hope that you find this title as interesting as we do.

NOTE FROM THE PUBLISHER

The information presented is true and complete to the best of our knowledge. All recommendations are made without any guarantees on the part of the author or the publisher, who also disclaim all liability incurred with the use of this information.

TRADEMARKS

We recognize that some words, model names and designations, for example, mentioned herein are the property of the trademark holder. We use them for identification purposes only. This is not an official publication.

INFORMATION ON THE USE OF THIS PUBLICATION

This manual is an invaluable resource for the classic motorcycle enthusiast and a "must have" for owners interested in performing their own maintenance. However, in today's information age we are constantly subject to changes in common practice, new technology, availability of improved materials and increased awareness of chemical toxicity. As such, it is advised that the user consult with an experienced professional prior to undertaking any procedure described herein. While every care has been taken to ensure correctness of information, it is obviously not possible to guarantee complete freedom from errors or omissions or to accept liability arising from such errors or omissions. Therefore, any individual that uses the information contained within, or elects to perform or participate in do-it-yourself repairs or modifications acknowledges that there is a risk factor involved and that the publisher or its associates cannot be held responsible for personal injury or property damage resulting from the use of the information or the outcome of such procedures.

WARNING!

One final word of advice, this publication is intended to be used as a reference guide, and when in doubt the reader should consult with a qualified technician.

PREFACE

THE AIM OF THIS HANDBOOK is to provide in a concise and non-technical form *all* vital information necessary to enable you to maintain your Royal Enfield in a high state of efficiency. By carefully observing the maintenance instructions given in this handbook you will obtain maximum mileage and performance, combined with minimum fuel consumption, depreciation, and repair bills, factors of no little importance today.

Royal Enfield motor-cycles (manufactured for over 50 years) need no introduction, as they have a well-established reputation for attractive appearance, economy, precision steering, good all-round performance, and reliability. Their successes in reliability trials are a byword.

The present edition of THE BOOK OF THE ROYAL ENFIELD deals comprehensively with the maintenance and overhaul of all except one of the popular 1946–58 single-cylinder four-stroke O.H.V. models. These machines comprise—

1. The 1946–54 346 c.c. Model G.
2. The 1946–8 499 c.c. Model J.
3. The 1946–55 499 c.c. Model J2.
4. The 1949–58 346 c.c. "Bullet."
5. The 1953–8 499 c.c. "Bullet."
6. The 1954–8 248 c.c. "Clipper" (to February, 1958).
7. The 1956–7 346 c.c. "Clipper" (Model G de luxe).
8. The 1958 346 c.c. "Clipper."

All maintenance instructions for 4, 5, 8 also apply to 1959–62 machines. Most of the instructions given are dated. Instructions not dated apply to all 1946 and subsequent models. *Note that the* 1958 346 *c.c.* "*Clipper*" *is, except for the provision of a cast-iron cylinder head and coil ignition, practically identical with the* 1949–58 346 *c.c.* "*Bullet," and most instructions given for the* 346 *c.c.* "*Bullet" therefore apply.*

In conclusion I most sincerely thank The Enfield Cycle Company, Limited, of Redditch (phone: Redditch 4222), Worcestershire, for their very generous assistance in supplying technical data, and some copyright illustrations.

W.C.H.

FLOYD CLYMER'S MOTORCYCLIST'S LIBRARY

The Book of the
ROYAL ENFIELD

A PRACTICAL GUIDE ON THE HANDLING AND MAINTENANCE OF ALL 1946 TO 1962 ROYAL ENFIELD FOUR-STROKE STANDARD SINGLES, EXCEPT THE 1957–62 "CRUSADER" TYPE MODELS WITH UNIT CONSTRUCTION ENGINE AND GEARBOX

BY

W. C. HAYCRAFT
F.R.S.A.

ANNOUNCEMENT

By special arrangement with the original publishers of this book, Sir Isaac Pitman & Son, Ltd., of London, England, we have secured the exclusive publishing rights for this book, as well as all others in THE MOTORCYCLIST'S LIBRARY.

Included in THE MOTORCYCLIST'S LIBRARY are complete instruction manuals covering the care and operation of respective motorcycles and engines; valuable data on speed tuning, and thrilling accounts of motorcycle race events. See listing of available titles elsewhere in this edition.

We consider it a privilege to be able to offer so many fine titles to our customers.

FLOYD CLYMER
Publisher of Books Pertaining to Automobiles and Motorcycles

2125 W. PICO ST.   LOS ANGELES 6, CALIF.

CHAPTER I

HANDLING A ROYAL ENFIELD

THIS CHAPTER IS MAINLY FOR NOVICES and deals with the handling of a Royal Enfield motor-cycle rather than the technique of driving on the road and the cultivation of road sense. It is assumed that you are the owner of a brand-new four-stroke single-cylinder O.H.V. model or else have just bought a good second-hand mount and are about to get on the road.

FIG. 1. TYPICAL OF THE ROYAL ENFIELD FOUR-STROKE SINGLE-CYLINDER O.H.V. RANGE—THE 499 C.C. "BULLET"

The 346 c.c. "Bullet" is similar; both have a light-alloy cylinder head and connecting-rod. The 346 c.c. and 499 c.c. "Bullets" will clock 75–80 and 85–90 m.p.h., and petrol consumptions average about 80–85 and 70–75 m.p.g. respectively. 1958 "Bullets" have Burgess silencers. The other 1958 O.H.V. singles are: the 248 c.c. "Crusader," and the 346 c.c. "Clipper."

Before Getting on the Road. The law insists that prior to riding on the public highway you shall comply with certain preliminaries. Various forms can be obtained from a money-order Post Office and must be carefully and truthfully filled in. Here are some vital preliminaries which you must attend to—

1. Take out an insurance policy to cover *third-party* risks, and make sure that you get the all-important "Certificate of Insurance." If you buy a brand new machine you cannot obtain the certificate until the machine has

been registered and a registration number allocated to it. In the meantime, obtain an insurance "cover note." Should you buy a Royal Enfield on hire-purchase terms, you will almost certainly be required to take out a full comprehensive insurance policy. Such a policy is, incidentally, always advised for a valuable machine. Note that passengers are *not* insured.

2. Obtain the registration book and registration licence (Form R.F.1/A for renewal; Form R.F.1/2* for original registration or change of ownership). All except the 248 c.c. coil-ignition "Clippers" are taxed at the rate of £3 15s. per annum (£1 5s. extra if a sidecar is attached). The 248 c.c. models are taxed at £1 17s. 6d. per annum.

3. Keep the registration book in a safe place, and return it to the Registration Authorities for amendment if you change your address, if you attach a sidecar, or if you sell the machine. Insert the registration-licence disc in a waterproof holder (facing the *near-side*) fitted to the handlebars, the front forks, or the front down-tube.

4. Obtain a "provisional" (six months) or an annual (*see* page 16) driving-licence (Form D.L.1), and *sign* the driving licence as soon as you get it. Note that you are not eligible for an annual driving-licence until you are 16 (for Group G) and have complied with one of the following conditions—

(*a*) You have held a licence (other than a provisional or visitor's licence) authorizing the driving of vehicles of the class or description applied for *within a period of* 10 *years ending on the date of coming into force of the licence applied for*, or

(*b*) You have passed the prescribed driving test (this includes a test passed whilst serving in H.M. Forces) *during the said period of* 10 *years*.

The fee for a driving test is 20s.

5. If you are not eligible for an annual driving-licence, attach "L" plates to the front and rear of the machine. They must not obscure the index letters or registration numbers.

6. Where a pillion rider is carried, see that the passenger sits *astride* a proper pillion seat securely *fixed* to the machine and is the holder of a current annual driving-licence covering Group G if you hold only a "provisional" licence.

7. Use an "ignition suppression" type sparking-plug or terminal cover if the machine was originally registered after 1st July, 1953, so that interference is not caused to radio or television sets.

8. See that a red reflector (of 1½ in. minimum diameter) is fitted to the rear of a solo motor-cycle in addition to (or combined with) the tail lamp or stop-tail lamp. Where a sidecar is attached, this must carry an additional red reflector at the rear at the same height as the reflector on the motor-cycle, and an extra tail lamp must also be provided.

* On Royal Enfields the frame and engine numbers which require to be included on Form R.F. 1/2 are situated on the near-side of the head lug and the near-side of the crankcase (just below the cylinder base), respectively

HANDLING A ROYAL ENFIELD

The Riding Position. The standard riding position on a new machine is generally found to be satisfactory for a man of average build, but to suit those not of average physique, a combined adjustment of the handlebars, footrests, and some of the handlebar controls can be made. See that the riding position *is* really comfortable. The footrest hanger-bosses and shafts are designed so that the hangers can be moved to alternative positions on their shafts. The handlebars are readily adjustable after slackening the securing nuts. The gear-change pedal (*see* page 145) and the rear-brake pedal are also adjustable.

LAYOUT AND USE OF CONTROLS

It is assumed that you understand the functions of the various controls provided on a motor-cycle and have an elementary knowledge of the basic principles of the four-stroke engine, including carburation and ignition. Basic principles are beyond the scope of this handbook, which deals specifically with Royal Enfield machines.

Familiarize Yourself With Controls. If you are unaccustomed to the Royal Enfield control layout you should before attempting to start up or get on the road, familiarize yourself with the disposition of the various levers, pedals, and switches. Also reflect on their functions, and the effect of operating them with the engine running and while riding.

The handlebar controls on 1946 and later four-stroke single-cylinder overhead-valve models are shown in Figs. 2–5. There are certain slight variations on different models and these are referred to beneath the control-layout illustrations. For lighting-switch positions, *see* page 73.

The controls (most of which are on the handlebars) may conveniently be divided into three groups: (1) the engine controls, (2) the motor-cycle controls, and (3) the electrical controls. There are also two instruments, the ammeter (*see* page 60) and the speedometer.

Hints on Use of Controls. Those handling a Royal Enfield "Clipper," "Bullet," Model G, J, or J2 should note the following important points—

1. All handlebar controls (including the throttle twist-grip) are operated by *inward* movement.

2. The throttle twist-grip (controlling engine speed) has a full movement of approximately *one-quarter* of a complete turn. With the throttle-stop adjusted to give a good tick-over, the throttle slide does not close completely. When starting a Royal Enfield from cold it is important to use only a very small throttle opening (about one-sixteenth to one-eighth of the total twist-grip movement), otherwise a quick start may not be possible. The best position is determined by experiment.

3. The air lever (which enables the mixture of air and petrol to be varied) must be kept completely closed for starting from cold, or one-third to one-half open when starting from warm. At all other times the air lever should be kept fully open. It is, however, sometimes desirable to keep the air lever

only three-quarters open until the engine attains its normal running temperature, when it should be fully opened.

4. The ignition lever (omitted on 250 c.c. "Clippers," 1956-8 "Bullets" with automatic ignition-advance) moves the contact-breaker base and should always be kept fully, or nearly fully, advanced while riding. Should pinking occur, however, the ignition lever can be temporarily retarded, but note that such retardation reduces the power output of the engine. When starting up it is advisable to move the ignition lever to about the *three-quarter full advance* position.

5. Do not use the exhaust-valve lifter (Models G, J, J2, 350 c.c. "Clipper") or the decompressor (350 c.c., 500 c.c. "Bullets") for any purpose other than starting and stopping the engine. When descending steep hills with difficult surfaces, however, it is permissible to use it, provided that the throttle twist-grip is shut right back and the air lever is kept wide open.

6. An ignition switch is provided only on 250 c.c. coil-ignition "Clipper" models which have no exhaust-valve lifter or decompressor fitted. Note that the ignition switch must always be switched off when the machine is not being ridden. The function of the ignition switch is to enable the engine to be started and stopped.

On 1954 and early 1955 250 c.c. models with Miller rectifier lighting and ignition equipment, the ignition switch is combined with the lighting switch on the headlamp and has six positions (*see* page 73); three of these concern the ignition with all lights off. These are consecutively—

IGN and CH (ignition and charge). In this position the battery is being trickle-charged (about 2 amp at normal speeds) during daylight running, and current passes through the coil and contact-breaker to provide ignition.

OFF. In this position the battery and generator are both disconnected, and the ignition (and lighting) is switched off.* An ignition key is provided to lock the switch in this position.

EM IGN (emergency ignition). In this position the engine can be started even if the battery is delivering no current (*see* page 73), but note that the battery must remain in the circuit.

On 1955-8 250 c.c. models with Lucas rectifier lighting and ignition equipment the lighting switch (*see* page 73) is placed on the fork head but a separate ignition switch is mounted on the outside of the tool box. It has these three positions—

IGN. Ignition switched on.

OFF. Ignition switched off; the switch can be locked off with the ignition key.

EMG (emergency ignition). For starting with a flat battery (*see* EM IGN).

* Note that when the switch is moved to the "PARK" position (*see* page 73) at night, the ignition coil is disconnected and it is impossible to start or run the engine.

7. A warning light is incorporated in the ammeter and shows *red* when the ignition is switched on and the engine is stationary with the contact-breaker points closed (a situation likely to cause the battery to discharge). The ignition must be switched off or the engine started immediately the warning light shows *red*. A dim red-glow with the engine running is normal. Failure of the bulb does not affect the ignition system.

8. The clutch lever (which disconnects and re-connects the drive from the engine to the rear wheel) must always be used fully and progressively

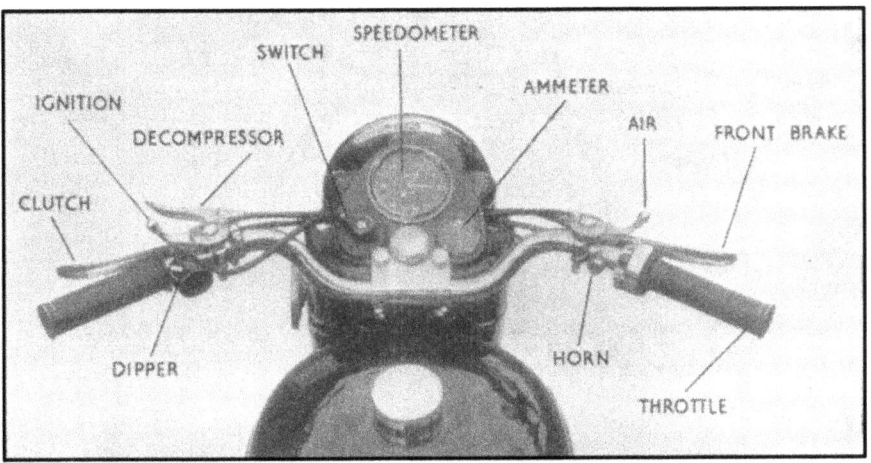

FIG. 2. LAYOUT OF HANDLEBAR CONTROLS ON THE 1954–8 350 C.C., 500 C.C. "BULLETS" AND THE 1956–8 350 C.C. "CLIPPERS"

The following should be noted. On the 1956–7 350 c.c., 500 c.c. "Bullets," automatic ignition-advance mechanism is embodied on the Lucas magneto, and the ignition lever shown is therefore omitted. On the above-mentioned "Bullets" the horn push is also combined with the dipper switch on the near-side. On the 1956–7 350 c.c. "Clipper" the layout shown applies except that the decompressor is replaced (in the same position) by an exhaust lifter.

during engagement of the clutch. It is used when starting and stopping the machine, and during each gear change.

9. The foot gear-change pedal on the off-side of the gearbox provides four gear ratios and "neutral" which lies between first and second gears. All upward gear changes are made by downward movement of the pedal with the toe, and all changes down by upward movement with the toe. The gear-change pedal always returns to the same (horizontal or slightly downward) position after each gear change, ready for the next change to be made. It is necessary during each gear change to make a *full* movement of the gear-change pedal.

10. On all except 250 c.c. Royal Enfield four-stroke singles a most ingenious and useful neutral finder is fitted (*see* Figs. 7 and 8). To obtain neutral quickly from fourth, third, or second gears it is only necessary to

disengage the clutch and press the neutral finder right down against its stop with the machine still on the move. First gear may afterwards be engaged by *one* upward movement of the foot gear-change pedal. Neutral

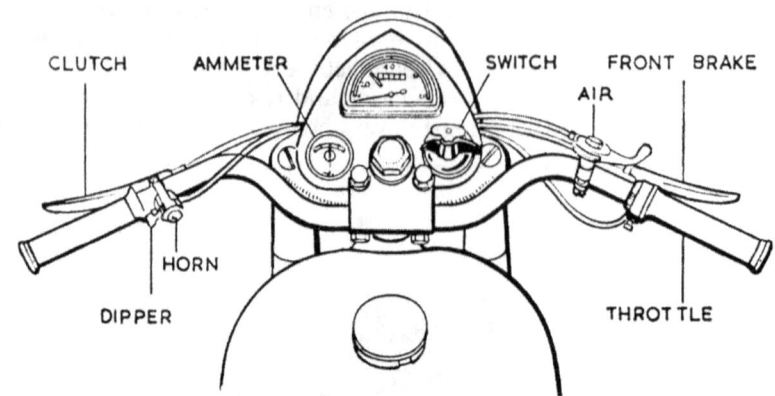

FIG. 3. LAYOUT OF HANDLEBAR CONTROLS ON THE 1954-8 250 C.C. "CLIPPER"

On 1954-5 models with Miller equipment a combined ignition and lighting switch is used on the casquette, but on 1955-8 models with Lucas equipment the ignition switch is separately mounted on the front of the off-side tool box.

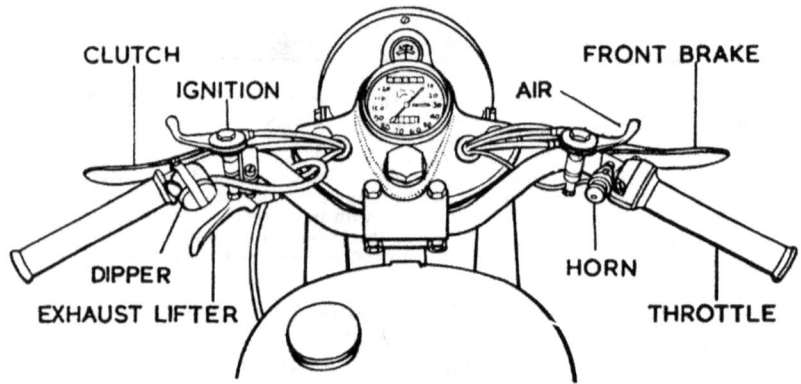

FIG. 4. LAYOUT OF HANDLEBAR CONTROLS ON THE 1953 350 C.C., 500 C.C. "BULLETS" AND THE 1953-5 MODELS G, J, J2

On the 1953 350 c.c., 500 c.c. "Bullets" a decompressor is used instead of the exhaust lifter shown, and the lever protrudes in front, instead of at the rear, of the handlebars as shown.

can be obtained from first gear by engaging second gear (depressing the foot gear-change pedal) and then pressing the neutral finder right down. An alternative method is to depress the foot gear-change pedal *very lightly*. A full depression will result in second gear being engaged. A gear-change indicator is provided to show clearly which gear is engaged, but you should never look down at it while riding.

The Petrol Taps. Twin petrol taps of the push-and-pull type are provided on 1946–55 Models G, J, J2 and the 1949–53 "Bullet" models. They are located beneath the petrol tank, one on each side. Normally it is desirable to use only the tap on the off-side; keep the near-side tap closed

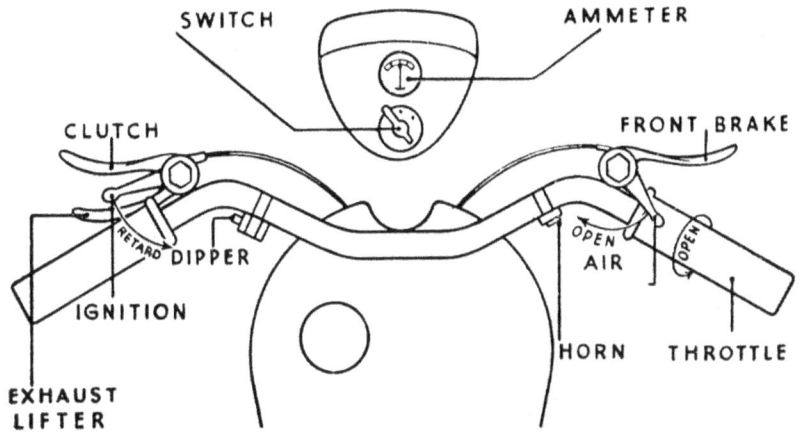

Fig. 5. Layout of Handlebar Controls on the 1949-52 350 c.c. "Bullet" and the 1946-52 Models G, J, J2

On the 1949–52 350 c.c. "Bullet" a decompressor is provided (in the same position) instead of the exhaust lifter shown.

until such time as you are obliged to make use of the reserve fuel supply. To open or close either petrol tap, pull the knob outward or push it inward respectively.

On the 1954-8 350 c.c., 500 c.c. "Bullets" and the 250 c.c., 350 c.c. "Clippers" a single petrol tap of the two-level type is provided beneath the petrol tank on the near-side. To turn on the petrol push the hexagonal button (marked "ON"), and to turn off the petrol push the round button (marked "OFF"). Above the tap proper there is a small reserve lever which enables a reserve supply of petrol to be maintained or drawn upon, according to whether the reserve lever is moved fully anti-clockwise or clockwise respectively. The lever performs this function in a most ingenious manner as described below.

Referring to Fig. 6 (which shows two taps), in the tap shown on the left, the reserve lever has been moved fully anti-clockwise, and the hole at the base of the vertical tube (which projects into the tank filter) is shut, thus compelling the petrol to enter the tap body via the top orifice of the tube, and a reserve petrol-supply is automatically maintained within the tank up to the level of the top of the vertical tube.

Referring to Fig. 6 (right-hand tap) the reserve lever has been moved fully clockwise, and the hole at the base of the vertical tube is open, thus causing the reserve petrol-supply in the tank to by-pass the vertical tube and enter the tap body through the open hole near the base of the tube and the tank.

Starting the Engine. Before attempting to start up the engine, first make sure that there is a sufficient quantity of engine oil of the correct type

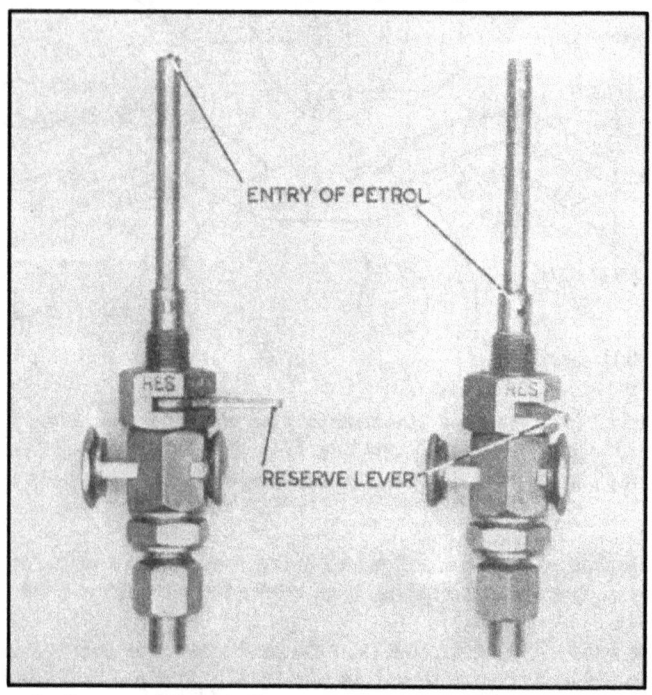

Fig. 6. Showing (Left) Two-level Petrol Tap with Reserve Lever Set for Running on the Main Petrol Supply, and (Right) for Running on the Reserve Supply

and grade in the oil tank (integral with the crankcase), the gearbox, and the oil-bath chain case (*see* Chapter III). Verify also that the various motor-cycle lubrication points (*see* chart on page 48) have been properly attended to and that the tyre pressures are correct (*see* page 156).

The oil tank has a maximum capacity of four pints. See that there is sufficient petrol in the petrol tank, which holds $3\frac{1}{4}$ gal ($2\frac{1}{2}$ gal on Models G, J, J2). On most Royal Enfields the petrol and oil tank filler-caps are opened by turning the cap anti-clockwise until the catch is felt, pushing the cap down, and then turning it anti-clockwise as far as possible and lifting the cap off. To tighten the cap, push it down and then turn clockwise to the maximum extent.

Push your Royal Enfield off its rear or spring-up centre stand, or alternatively keep the machine jacked up. On machines with two-level type petrol taps or twin taps, position the reserve lever correctly (*see* page 7) or turn on the off-side tap respectively. Now adjust the controls correctly for starting up.

1. Verify that the foot gear-change mechanism is in "neutral." It is advisable to check that the rear wheel can spin freely.

2. On 250 c.c. coil-ignition "Clipper" models (with no exhaust-valve lifter or decompressor) switch on the ignition by moving the ignition switch on the headlamp or outside the tool box (*see* page 4).

3. Where manual ignition-control is provided (all models except 250 c.c. "Clippers" and 1956-8 "Bullets"), retard the ignition lever so that it is about three-quarters fully advanced.

4. Open the throttle *very* slightly by turning the twist-grip inwards one-sixteenth to one-eighth of its total movement. If the throttle stop is adjusted to give a moderately fast tick-over with the twist-grip shut right back, this throttle opening is usually sufficient for starting.

5. Close the air lever completely, unless the engine is warm (in which case open it one-third to one-half).

6. If the engine is quite cold, momentarily depress the tickler on the carburettor float-chamber, but do not flood the carburettor so that petrol begins to drip from it. If the engine is warm, leave the tickler alone, or the mixture will become excessively rich.

7. Start up the engine. On a 250 c.c. "Clipper" model give the kick-starter a vigorous kick downward, when the engine should respond immediately. On other models depress the kick-starter until engine compression is felt, raise the valve lifter or decompressor ("Bullets") momentarily to overcome compression, and kick the engine over smartly. If the engine fails to fire immediately, repeat with a slightly varied throttle (and perhaps ignition lever) setting. The best setting of the controls for starting is soon obtained from practical experience, and varies slightly for different engines of the same capacity.

8. As soon as the engine fires, advance the ignition lever (where fitted) fully, and progressively open the air lever fully. Set the throttle opening to provide a moderately fast tick-over. Do not permit the engine to race or run too slowly, and do not continue to run the engine for more than a few minutes with the machine stationary.

Moving Off. It is assumed you have attended to preliminaries and have read and understand the Highway Code. Ease the machine off its stand (if the machine is jacked up) with the engine running and the gear-change lever in "neutral." Then while astride the saddle, fully disengage the clutch and engage first gear. Raise the foot gear-change pedal to its full extent with the toe and then release the pedal. If first gear does not readily engage, move the machine slightly backwards or forwards while operating the gear control, until proper engagement is felt.

To move off, gradually open the throttle by turning the twist-grip *inwards* and simultaneously engage the clutch by releasing the handlebar lever. As the clutch plates "bite," the machine will begin to move forward and gather momentum. On taking up the load the engine speed tends to fall and this tendency must be countered by progressively opening the throttle so as to accelerate the engine and further increase the speed of the machine. A smooth take-off without jerk or transmission-snatch is soon mastered and the correct co-ordination of the controls required to ensure this quickly becomes an instinctive procedure.

Changing Up. When a sufficient road speed has been attained (approximately 12 m.p.h.), disengage the clutch and simultaneously close the throttle slightly; pause a second, and then engage second gear by *depressing* the foot gear-change pedal with the toe *to its full extent* and then releasing it. A firm and decisive movement is required, but force must *not* be used on the pedal, or the selector mechanism may be damaged. As soon as second gear has been engaged, gradually re-engage the clutch and again throttle up the engine so as to take the load and increase the speed of the machine.

To engage in turn third and fourth gears, repeat the gear changing procedure in the manner just described for second gear when the machine has gathered plenty of momentum. Somewhat higher speeds are advised for gear changing on the "Bullet" models. The optimum road speeds at which gear changes should be made depend, of course, on whether the road is level or not. Excessive speeds should be avoided, otherwise wear is accelerated, and dangerous valve float may occur.

Gear changing on an upward gradient calls for the changes to be made at somewhat higher road speeds. A commendable feature of all Royal Enfield (4-speed) gearboxes is that all gears are actuated by a *single* striking fork. This renders impossible the simultaneous engagement of two gears, irrespective of how much wear has occurred inside the gearbox.

Endeavour to make all gear changes smoothly and silently, and avoid fierce acceleration, which is unkind both to the tyres and transmission. Once you are cruising comfortably in top gear, always keep the air lever wide open and the ignition lever (where fitted) fully advanced, retarding it only momentarily in the event of a tendency for pinking to occur.

Changing Down. To change down into a lower gear, simultaneously disengage the clutch, and open the throttle slightly; pause a second, and then *raise* the foot gear-change pedal *fully* to obtain the next lower gear. As soon as the lower gear is felt to engage, gradually re-engage the clutch, release the gear-change pedal, and adjust the throttle opening to suit the prevailing conditions of road and load.

Note that when changing down quickly from fourth or third gear into first gear you need not bother about disengaging the clutch, throttling up the engine and re-engaging the clutch during each individual gear change. It is sufficient to slow down to a slow speed, disengage the clutch, and make two or three full upward movements of the foot gear-change pedal in quick succession, according to whether third or fourth gear respectively was previously engaged. "Blip" the engine (i.e. throttle up slightly) each time you raise the gear-change pedal with the toe.

As in the case of changing up, practice soon enables smooth, silent, and

FIG. 7. NEUTRAL FINDER, KICK-STARTER, AND GEAR-CHANGE LEVER ON 1946–54 350 C.C., 500 C.C. MODELS
Applies also to the 1956–7 350 c.c. "Clipper."

precise changes to be made. Practise gear changing on a quiet road where there is little risk of sudden emergencies occurring.

Hill Climbing. This demands good power output and therefore the engine revolutions (rev./min.) must be kept reasonably high. Always make full use of the four-speed gearbox and *change down in good time*. On no account permit the engine to labour on a hill and never try to force an unwilling mount up a steep hill in top gear.

Just prior to negotiating a hill it is desirable to increase the speed and momentum of the machine by giving it plenty of throttle. Increase the throttle opening as the gradient increases and very slightly retard the ignition control (where fitted) as soon as pinking occurs. Retarding the ignition, however, reduces the power output, and a change down to a lower gear should always be made while the machine still has plenty of momentum.

If a change down is made in good time, a fast climb is possible, and further changes down higher up on the gradient may be rendered unnecessary. After a change down has been made, advance the ignition lever (where manual control is provided) if this has been previously retarded. All normal undulating roads and many main road hills can be tackled in

FIG. 8. NEUTRAL FINDER, KICK-STARTER, AND GEAR-CHANGE LEVER ON 1955–8 350 C.C., 500 C.C. MODELS

Not applicable (*see* Fig. 7) to 1956–7 350 c.c. "Clippers." Note the co-axial shafts for the kick-starter and gear-change lever. At 1 and 3 are the oil fillers for the gearbox and engine respectively, and at 4 the gearbox oil-level plug.

top gear if judicious use is made of the throttle. After climbing a stiff gradient in a lower gear it is advisable to allow the engine to cool down by descending on the other side with the throttle closed and the air lever wide open.

To Obtain "Neutral." A neutralizing lever (Figs. 7 and 8) is fitted on 1946 and later four-stroke models. To obtain "neutral," the following simple procedure is necessary. Disengage the clutch with the machine in motion and then depress the neutralizing lever with the right foot to its *full extent*. The above is applicable to obtaining "neutral" from all gears except first (bottom) gear. To obtain "neutral" from bottom gear, engage second gear; then disengage the clutch and fully depress the neutralizing lever.

Stopping the Machine. To bring a Royal Enfield to a normal stop on the road, close back the throttle twist-grip completely, progressively and simultaneously apply *both* brakes, and before coming to a standstill disengage the clutch and obtain "neutral" (*see* previous paragraph).

When slowing up before coming to a standstill, always make a habit of applying the front and rear brakes together, as this reduces the tendency for skidding and also minimizes and equalizes the wear of the brake shoe linings. Never indulge in the truly damaging habit of using the clutch or exhaust-valve lifter or decompressor for slowing up!

For controlling speed, learn to "drive on the throttle" and use the brakes as infrequently and lightly as possible. Reserve their full use for steep hills and "jaywalking" dogs and pedestrians. In connexion with hills, it should be noted that closing the throttle and opening the air lever wide acts as a powerful brake which can be supplemented by the internal expanding brakes.

Controlling speed by "driving on the throttle" saves both tyres and transmission. Only poor quality riders keep "jumping on the brakes."

Stopping the Engine. Amal carburettors provided on Royal Enfields have a throttle stop designed and (usually) adjusted to enable the engine to idle when the throttle twist-grip is turned right back. To stop the engine after stopping the machine it is necessary (unless the throttle stop is adjusted to close the throttle completely) to raise the exhaust-valve lifter or decompressor (where fitted). However, on 250 c.c. "Clipper" models there is no exhaust-valve lifter or decompressor.

To stop a 250 c.c. four-stroke engine (minus exhaust-valve lifter or decompressor), switch off the ignition, or alternatively close the throttle completely (if the throttle stop is set to give complete closing).

The Steering Damper. Intelligent use should be made of this fitment (provided on some earlier models), and it is quite surprising to those not accustomed to the steering damper how effective it is in steadying the machine at fast speeds. Generally speaking, slacken off at low speeds and tighten at high speeds. The exception to the rule is a sidecar outfit; to obtain comfortable steering it is best always to have the damper tightened down to some extent.

Parking the Machine. To prevent loss by theft, park the machine in an authorized car park, or else place it in a position where an eye can be kept on it, or padlock it. If the machine is left by the kerbside after dark, turn the lighting switch (on all except 250 c.c. Miller coil-ignition "Clipper" models) to the "L" position, as the pilot bulb consumes less current than the double-filament main bulb. With a 250 c.c. Miller coil-ignition

"Clipper" model, turn the switch to the "PARK" position. This switches on the parking lights and switches off the ignition.

When parking a four-stroke coil-ignition machine, be sure to switch off the ignition by means of the ignition switch in the centre of the lighting switch (on the outside of the toolbox, 1955–8 250 c.c. "Clippers"), otherwise the battery will discharge through the contact-breaker if the contacts happen to be closed. The warning lamp will show *red* if the ignition has accidentally been left on after stopping the engine other than by means of the ignition switch. Remove the ignition key.

Running-in (All Four-stroke Engines). If you are the lucky owner of a brand-new shining Royal Enfield or have a second-hand machine with reconditioned engine, go very steady for about the first 500 miles. By doing so you will obtain the maximum life from your engine, plus a performance which will increase with the mileage. Neglect to run-in your engine carefully during the first 500 miles may *permanently* spoil its efficiency.

When new, bearing surfaces appear dead smooth, but actually they are covered with fine tool-marks which are invisible to the naked eye. Until these marks disappear, and a mirror-like gloss and hardness spread all over, local friction is liable to occur and the oil film may break down at one or more vital places.

The essence of proper running-in is *progressively* to increase the work imposed on the engine, and to keep the engine as cool as possible by avoiding excessive throttle openings and piston speed.

To reduce the risk of piston seizure during the vital running-in period and to enable close limits to be used (to prevent piston "slap"), the piston on Royal Enfield machines is formed slightly oval. But this ovality in no way absolves you from the onus of careful running-in. During running-in, observe the following points—

1. Pay due regard to correct lubrication of the engine and machine (*see* Chapter III). After covering 500 miles drain the oil from the oil tank, the timing-case, and the felt oil-filter (*see* pages 41–3).

2. Never permit the engine to tick-over for more than a few minutes with the engine stationary.

3. By making full use of the excellent four-speed gear-box, aim at making the engine run "light" as much as possible, but do not allow the engine to "rev" up too fast in the lower gears; this tends to make the engine hot, and there is insufficient air cooling to dissipate the heat.

4. See that the engine does not labour by running too slowly in top gear or through neglecting to change down to a lower gear in good time when hill climbing. After climbing a steep hill, allow the engine to cool down on the other side (*see* page 11).

5. After covering several hundred miles* (when some bedding-down

---

* A free service scheme is now available for owners of new machines bought in the U.K.

occurs), check the adjustments of the tappets, contact-breaker, and the brakes, and clutch (*see* appropriate paragraphs of Chapter V).

6. Do not exceed 35 m.p.h. (30 m.p.h. on 250 c.c. machines) during the first 200 miles.
7. Avoid using more than *half* throttle (except for very short periods) until 500 miles have been covered.
8. After covering 500 miles it is advisable to facilitate the bedding-down of the piston thrust faces by undertaking *short* speed bursts. Increase their duration *progressively* until the engine begins to thrive on larger throttle openings, but use discretion throughout.
9. After running-in is completed it is permissible to step up the throttle openings gradually, but avoid using full throttle on the level or uphill until you have ridden for about 1,000 miles.

Colloidal Graphite for Running-in. During the running-in of a four-stroke engine it is beneficial to mix Acheson's colloidal graphite with the *engine oil* in the proportions of *one pint* to one gallon of oil. This makes for cooler running and protects the bearing surfaces from metal pick-up. It is also beneficial to the valves. It is possible to obtain the compound from most large garages.

Upper-cylinder Lubricant. It is also beneficial when running-in the engine (and subsequently) to get your garage pump-attendant to add one "shot" of upper-cylinder lubricant (e.g., "Redex") to each gallon of *petrol* inserted in the tank.

If the Piston Seizes. Should there be the slightest tendency for the piston to seize during the running-in period or subsequently, it is important to take *immediate* action. If too much throttle has been given for too long and the engine begins to slow up due to incipient seizure, declutch instantly, close the throttle, and allow the engine to cool down for several minutes. If this action is taken, it is unlikely that damage will occur, and the piston should free itself automatically.

If an actual seizure does occur, remove the piston and have it closely inspected by a competent mechanic. It may be necessary for him to ease down some "high spots" and to eradicate any slight smearing of the piston surface in the vicinity of the piston-ring lands. Do not attempt this work yourself unless highly skilled, otherwise the last state of the piston may be worse than the first.

General Driving Hints. Always drive with due consideration for all other road users and conform with the law both in letter and spirit. Avoid excessive noise, and ride in a state of constantly expecting the unexpected. Selfishness, carelessness, or lack of road sense by one or more of the parties concerned are the causes of most accidents. The great majority of accidents *could* be avoided by the use of ordinary common sense and by observance of the advice given in the Highway Code. Considerations of space do not permit the author delving into legal matters or driving tactics. He would, however, emphasize the importance of *correct hand signals given in sufficient time*. Beware of lady "L" drivers in cars, some of whom are not mechanically minded, acquire road sense very slowly, and are liable to panic in an emergency.

Long Term Driving Licences. Note that substantive driving licences lasting *three years* and costing 15s. are now obtainable by all riders who hold a "provisional" licence and satisfactorily complete their driving test. For other riders, with surnames beginning A–F, a three-year driving licence has been available since 1st September, 1957, subject to the satisfactory completion of Form D.L.I. (*see* page 2, paragraph 4). Those with surnames beginning G–O can obtain a three-year licence from 1st September, 1958. The remaining riders, with surnames starting P–Z, will have to wait until 1st September, 1959, until they can obtain a three-year licence instead of an annual licence.

CHAPTER II

THE AMAL CARBURETTOR

AN AMAL STANDARD-TYPE two-lever needle-jet carburettor is fitted to all 1946–54 250 c.c., 350 c.c., 500 c.c. models, to the 1955 500 c.c. Model J2, and to the 1956–7 350 c.c. "Clipper."
On all 1955–8 models except the 500 c.c. J2 and 350 c.c. "Clipper" models just referred to, an Amal "monobloc" type two-lever needle-jet carburettor is specified. The standard and "monobloc" type carburettors differ somewhat in design, but tuning instructions are similar.

HOW IT WORKS (STANDARD CARBURETTOR)

Referring to Fig. 9, showing a sectional view of the instrument, A is the carburettor body or mixing chamber, the upper part of which has a throttle slide or valve B, with tapered jet-needle C attached by a needle clip. The throttle valve regulates the quantity of mixture supplied to the engine. Passing through the throttle valve is the air valve D, independently operated and serving the purpose of obstructing the main air-passage for starting and mixture regulation. Fixed to the underside of the mixing chamber by the union nut E is the jet block F, and interposed between them is a fibre washer to ensure a petrol-tight joint. On the upper part of the jet block is the adapter body H, forming a clean through-way. Integral with the jet block is the pilot jet J, supplied through the passage K. The adjustable pilot air-intake L communicates with a chamber, from which issues the pilot outlet M and the by-pass N. A throttle-stop screw (Fig. 10, left-hand illustration) is fitted on the mixing chamber, by which the position of the throttle valve for tick-over is regulated independently of the control-cable adjustment. The needle-jet O is screwed in the underside of the jet block, and carries at its bottom end the main jet P. Both these jets are removable when the jet plug Q (which firmly secures the float chamber to union nut E) is removed. The float chamber, which has bottom feed, consists of a chamber R, supplied with petrol through union S. It contains the float T and the float-needle valve U held by the clip V. The float-chamber cover W has a lock screw X for security. Lock-ring Z (held by locking spring $Z1$) holds the mixing-chamber cap Y.

The petrol tap having been turned on, petrol will flow past the float-needle valve U until the quantity of petrol in the chamber R is sufficient to raise the float T, when the needle valve U will prevent a further supply entering the float chamber until some in the chamber has already been used up by the engine. The float chamber having filled to its correct level, the

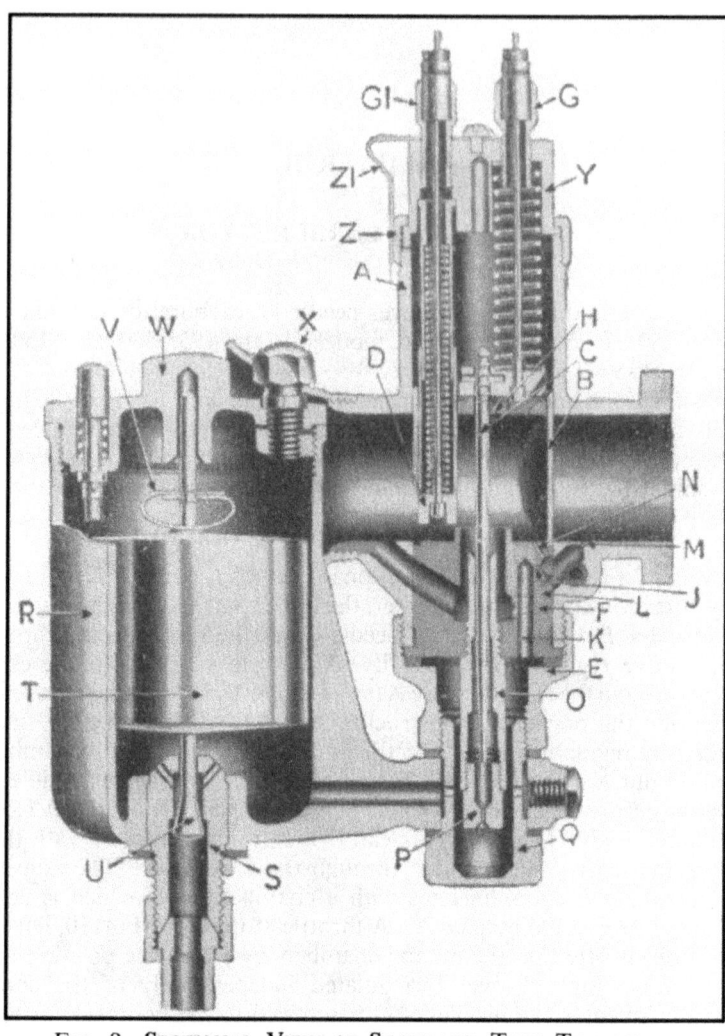

FIG. 9. SECTIONAL VIEW OF STANDARD TYPE TWO-LEVER NEEDLE-JET AMAL CARBURETTOR

KEY TO FIG. 9

A = Mixing chamber
B = Throttle valve
C = Jet needle and clip
D = Air valve
E = Mixing-chamber union nut
F = Jet block
G = Cable adjuster for throttle valve
G1 = Cable adjuster for air valve
H = Adapter body
J = Pilot jet (integral)
K = Pilot feed-hole
L = Pilot air-intake
M = Pilot outlet
N = Pilot by-pass
O = Needle-jet
P = Main jet
Q = Jet plug
R = Float chamber
S = Union for float chamber
T = Float
U = Float-needle valve
V = Float-needle clip
W = Float-chamber cover
X = Float-chamber lock screw
Y = Mixing-chamber cap
Z = Lock-ring for Y
Z1 = Locking spring

fuel passes along the passages through the diagonal holes in the jet plug Q, when it will be in communication with the main jet P and the pilot feed-hole K; the level in the needle and pilot jets is, obviously, the same as that maintained in the float chamber.

Imagine the throttle valve B very slightly open. As the piston descends, a partial vacuum is created in the carburettor, causing a rush of air through the pilot air-intake L, and drawing fuel from the pilot jet J. The mixture of

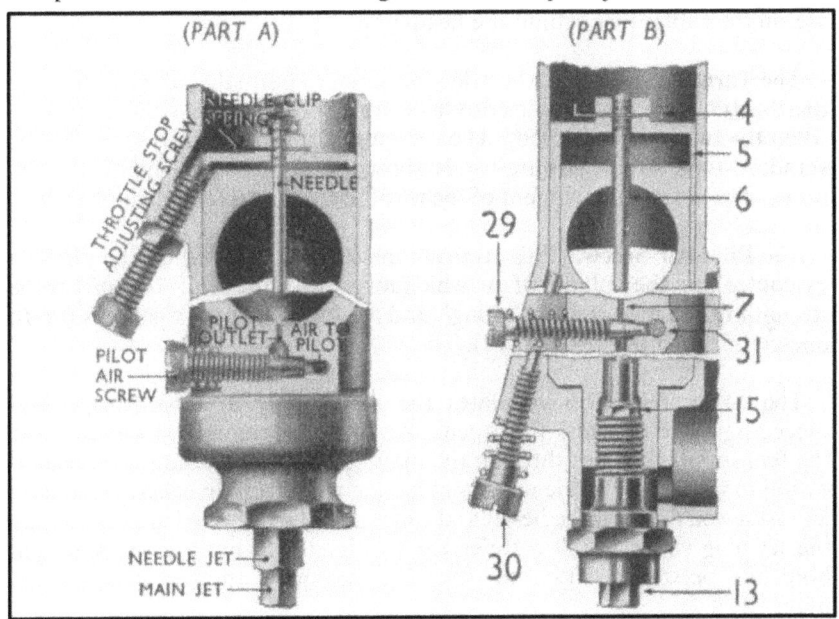

FIG. 10. ARRANGEMENT OF THROTTLE-STOP AND PILOT-AIR ADJUSTING SCREWS

On the left is shown the arrangement on the standard carburettor, and on the right the arrangement of the "monobloc" instrument. For key to numbered parts, *see* page 21.

air and fuel is admitted to the engine through the pilot outlet M. The quantity of mixture capable of being passed by the pilot outlet M is insufficient to run the engine. This mixture also carries excess of fuel. Consequently, before a combustible mixture is admitted, the throttle valve. B must be slightly raised, admitting a further supply of air from the main air-intake. The farther the throttle valve is opened, the less will be the depression on the outlet, M, but, in turn, a higher depression will be created on the by-pass N, and the pilot mixture will flow from this passage as well as from the outlet M.

The mixture supplied by the pilot and by-pass system is supplemented at about one-eighth throttle by fuel from the main jet P, the throttle valve cut-away determining the mixture strength from here to one-quarter throttle. Proceeding up the throttle range, mixture control by the needle position occurs from one-quarter to three-quarters throttle, and from this point the main jet is the only regulation.

The air valve D, which is cable-operated, has the effect of obstructing the main through-way and, in consequence, increasing the depression on the main jet, enriching the mixture. Two cable adjusters G, $G1$ are provided to take up cable stretch. On recent "Bullets," however, the cable adjusters are on the cables just behind the headlamp.

The Throttle Stop. The throttle-stop screw is normally adjusted to prop the throttle slide open sufficiently to enable the engine to tick-over nicely when the twist-grip is closed. The design of the throttle-stop screw on the standard-type Amal carburettor is shown in Fig. 10 (left-hand illustration). The correct adjustment of the throttle stop is explained on page 26.

The Pilot-Air Screw. This controls the suction imposed on the pilot jet by controlling the volume of air which mixes with the fuel. It controls the strength of the mixture for "idling" and for initial throttle openings (up to one-eighth throttle, *see* Fig. 14).

The Main Jet. This regulates the fuel supply at throttle openings exceeding three-quarters full open. At smaller openings of the throttle, the fuel supplied passes through the main jet, but the amount is decreased owing to the needle in the needle-jet having a controlling effect. The main jet is screwed into the needle-jet and can readily be detached after removing the jet plug (Q in Fig. 9). Referring to Fig. 10, to remove the main jet, hold the needle-jet with one spanner, and with another unscrew the main jet.

Each Amal main jet is numbered and calibrated so that its precise discharge is known. It thus follows that any two main jets having the same number are identical in all respects. The larger the jet, the higher is its number. If a larger size jet is needed, on no account attempt to ream the existing jet, but obtain a new one of larger size. Recommended jet sizes are given in the Table on page 25.

The Needle and Needle-jet. The jet needle is attached to, and moves with, the throttle slide. Being tapered, it permits more or less fuel to pass through the needle-jet as the throttle is opened, or closed, respectively. This applies throughout the range of throttle openings, except at nearly full throttle and when "idling." The needle-jet is of a specified size, and normally it should not be changed.

As may be seen in Fig. 10, the position of the taper needle, relative to the throttle opening, can be adjusted according to the mixture required, by securing the needle to the throttle with the needle spring-clip in a particular groove, *five* of which are provided. Position No. 3, for example, means the

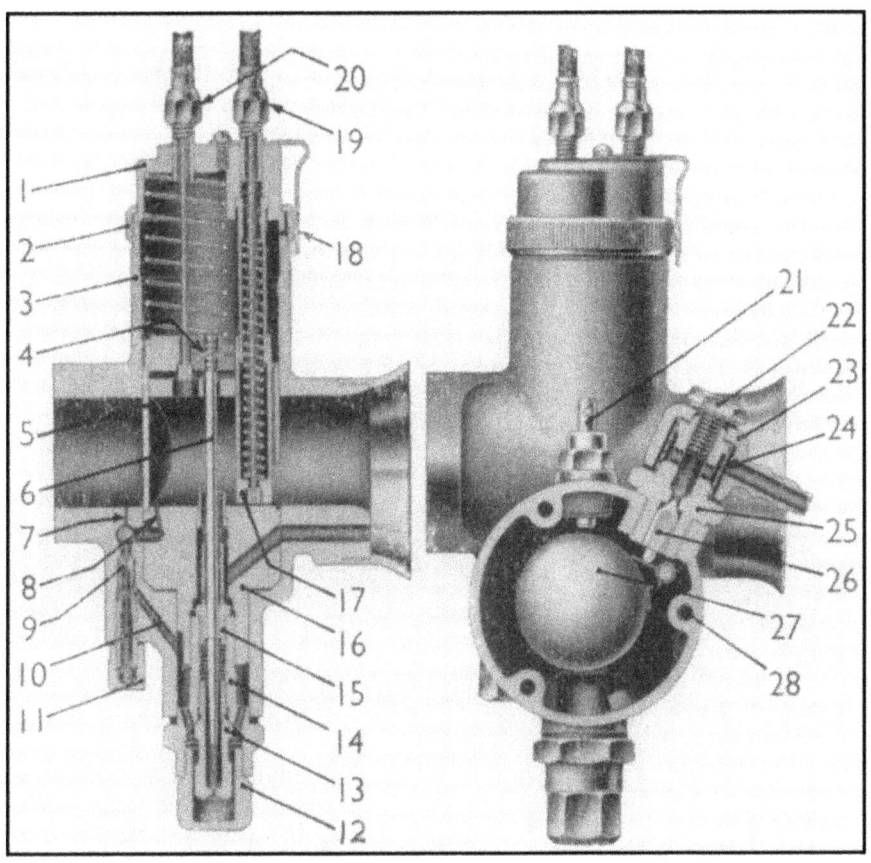

FIGS. 11, 12. SECTIONS THROUGH (LEFT) CARBURETTOR BODY AND (RIGHT) FLOAT CHAMBER OF AMAL "MONOBLOC" CARBURETTOR

KEY TO FIGS. 10 to 13, AND 15

1. Mixing-chamber cap
2. Mixing-chamber lock-ring
3. Body of carburettor
4. Jet-needle clip
5. Throttle valve
6. Jet needle
7. Pilot outlet
8. Pilot by-pass
9. Pilot jet (detachable)
10. Feed to pilot jet
11. Pilot-jet cover nut
12. Main-jet cover
13. Main jet
14. Main-jet holder
15. Needle-jet
16. Jet block
17. Air valve
18. Locking spring for 2
19. Cable adjuster (air)
20. Cable adjuster (throttle)
21. Tickler
22. Banjo bolt
23. Banjo
24. Filter gauze
25. Needle seating
26. Float-chamber needle
27. Float (hinged)
28. Float-chamber cover screws
29. Pilot-air adjusting screw
30. Throttle-stop screw
31. Air passage to pilot jet
32. Feed holes in 9
33. "Bleed" holes in 15
34. Primary air-choke
35. Primary air-passage
36. Throttle-valve cut-away
37. Float chamber
38. Float-chamber cover
39. Locating screw for 16
40. Fibre seal

middle groove or the third groove *from the top*. At throttle openings from one-quarter to three-quarters open, raising the needle enriches the mixture, while lowering the needle weakens it. The needle itself is made in *one size only*.

The Throttle-valve Cut-away. The throttle valve on the atmospheric side is cut away, and this affects the depression on the main fuel supply. The cut-away provides a means of tuning between the pilot and needle-jet range of throttle opening. The actual amount of cut-away is denoted by a number marked on the throttle slide. Thus 6/4 means a throttle type 6 with a No. 4 cut-away. A throttle with a larger cut-away (say, 6/5) *weakens* the mixture. A smaller cut-away, on the other hand, makes the mixture *richer*.

HOW IT WORKS ("MONOBLOC" CARBURETTOR)

Details of the Amal "monobloc" carburettor are shown in Figs. 10 to 13 and 15, and the key to these five illustrations (given on page 21) indicates all the essential parts. Basically, the carburettor works on the same general principles as the earlier type with a vertical and separate float-chamber, non-detachable pilot jet, and needle-jet of the non-compensating type.

Referring to Figs. 10, 11, 13 and 15, the float 27 maintains a constant level of petrol in the needle-jet 15 and the pilot jet 9, and it cuts off the petrol supply when the engine stops.

The selection of the appropriate jet sizes and main-choke bore ensures the proper atomizing and proportioning of the petrol and air sucked into the engine. The air valve 17 is normally kept fully raised and the throttle valve 5 (controlled by the handlebar twist-grip) controls the volume of mixture and therefore the power; at all throttle openings a correct mixture is automatically obtained. The carburettor operates in four stages.

When opening the throttle from the fully closed position to about one-eighth open (for idling) the mixture is supplied by the detachable pilot-jet 9, and mixture strength is determined by the setting of the knurled pilot-air adjusting screw (*see* 29 in Fig. 10). To facilitate adjustment of this screw a coil spring is used instead of a lock-nut. As the throttle is farther opened the main-jet system comes into action, the mixture being augmented from the main jet 13 via the pilot by-pass 8.

The amount of cut-away 36 on the atmospheric side of the throttle valve 5 regulates the petrol-air ratio between one-eighth and one-quarter throttle. The needle-jet 15 and the jet needle 6 take over mixture regulation between one-quarter and three-quarter throttle, and mixture strength is determined by the vertical position of the needle in the jet-needle clip 4 attached to the throttle valve 5. When the throttle is opened beyond three-quarters, the mixture strength is decided only by the size of the main jet 13.

Note that the main jet does not spray petrol direct into the carburettor mixing-chamber but petrol discharges through the needle-jet into the primary air-chamber. From there it enters the main air-choke through the primary air-choke 34 which has a compensating action in conjunction with "bleed" holes 33 in the needle-jet 15. These serve the double purpose of air compensating the mixture from the needle-jet and allowing the fuel to form a well outside and around the needle-jet. This is always available

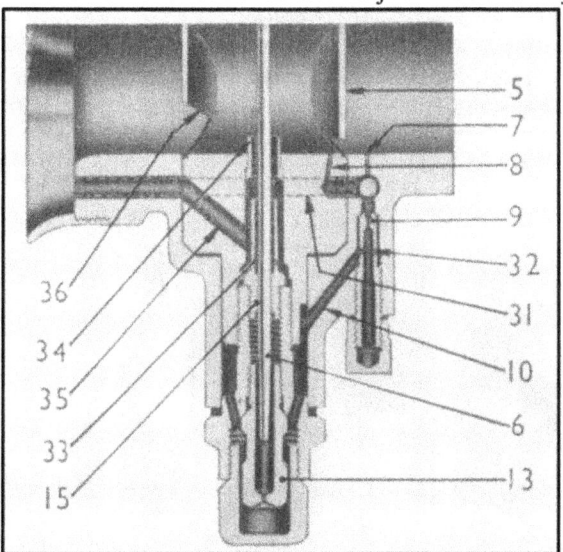

Fig. 13. Diagrammatic Section through Amal "Monobloc" Carburettor

Illustrating only the lower half of the throttle chamber and the internal primary air passages to the main jet and pilot system. The throttle valve is shown slightly open.

for snap acceleration. Pilot-jet and main-jet behaviour are not affected by this two-way compensation governing only acceleration and normal cruising.

TUNING THE CARBURETTOR 1946 ONWARDS)

The correct Amal carburettor settings for the 1946–58 Royal Enfield single-cylinder O.H.V. models are given on page 25. Do not alter these settings (decided by the makers after careful deliberation) without very good reasons.

Note that it is desirable to obtain a slightly weak mixture consistent with good slow-running; an excessively rich slow-running mixture causes a tendency for the engine to run on the pilot jet under normal running conditions. The effect of this is to increase the fuel consumption. To modify the strength of the running mixture, it is necessary to make an adjustment to the position of the jet needle in the throttle valve, or else to alter the size of the main jet.

The Exhaust Flame. Where the carburettor is correctly tuned, there should be no evidence of black smoke. The combustion of fuel is complete and carbon formation almost non-existent. If the mixture is right, the exhaust flame is of a *whitish-blue* colour.

If the mixture is weak, the colour of the exhaust flame is *light blue.* If, on the other hand, the mixture is excessively rich, the flame is of a characteristic *yellow* colour, and some *black* smoke is generally present. Note

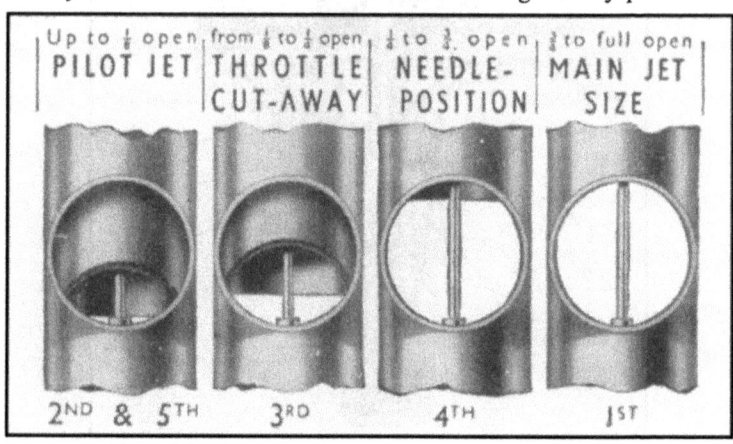

Fig. 14. Range and Sequence of Tuning—
1946 Onwards

that the above references to exhaust flames imply exhaust flames observed at an *open* exhaust port.

Procedure for Tuning. If the carburettor setting (*see* Table 1, page 25) does not give complete satisfaction for particular requirements, there are four separate ways of rectifying matters as given herewith, and the adjustments should be made in this order—

1. Main jet ($\frac{3}{4}$ to full throttle).
2. Pilot-air adjustment (closed to $\frac{1}{8}$ throttle).
3. Throttle-valve cut-away on the air-intake side ($\frac{1}{8}$ to $\frac{1}{4}$ throttle).
4. Jet-needle position ($\frac{1}{4}$ to $\frac{3}{4}$ throttle).

The diagram (Fig. 14) clearly indicates the part of the throttle range over which each adjustment is effective.

The carburettor is, throughout the throttle range, entirely automatic, and the air lever should be kept wide open, except for starting from cold and until the engine has warmed up properly. It is assumed that normal petrol is used for tuning, which should be done in the sequence described below. Throttle openings to be used in the five tuning operations are those indicated in Fig. 14. By following these tuning instructions (which have been recommended by Amal, Ltd.) you will be assured of the most satisfactory performance with maximum economy of fuel. For tuning purposes it is advisable to start up on a quiet road having a slight up-gradient.

1. **To Check Size of Main Jet.** Accelerate up to full throttle and carefully note the response of the engine to twist-grip action. Should power output appear better with the air lever very slightly closed or with the throttle not completely open, this indicates that the main jet is too small, and the next larger size should be tried. Similarly, if there is a tendency for the

TABLE 1

AMAL CARBURETTOR SETTINGS FOR 1946–58 MODELS

Enfield Model	Main Jet†	Pilot Jet*	Slide (Gas)	Needle Groove
G (1946–54)	130	—	6/4	3
J (1946–7)	140	—	6/4	3
J (1948)	150	—	6/4	3
J2 (1946–55)	170	—	6/4	2
"350 Bullet" (1949–54)	140	—	6/4	3
"350 Bullet" (1955–8)	180	30	376/4	3
"500 Bullet" (1953–4)	180	—	29/3	2
"500 Bullet" (1955–8)	200	30	389/3½	2
"250 Clipper" (1954)	75	—	4/4	2
"250 Clipper" (1955–8)	120	25	375/4	3
"350 Clipper" (1956–7)	130	—	6/4	3
(1958)	180	30	376/4	3

* A detachable pilot jet is fitted only to "monobloc" carburettors used on 1955 and later machines.
† If an air cleaner, previously fitted, is removed, fit a main jet two sizes larger.

engine to run "heavily" on full throttle, this denotes that the main jet is too large and the next smaller size should be experimented with.*

If tuning for speed, be careful to choose a main jet of size sufficient to maintain the engine in a cool condition. Make a run at high speed, pull up, and stop the engine immediately. Remove the sparking plug and closely inspect it. If the business end of the plug is sooty, the mixture is too rich. Should the body be dry, grey in colour, the mixture is on the weak side, and a larger size jet is required.

With a properly-proportioned mixture, the plug body should have a bright black appearance. Also, when running, observe the sound of the exhaust; it should be crisp and have no trace of "woolliness." Black smoke at the exhaust shows that the mixture is much too rich.

2. **To Adjust the Pilot Jet (1946 Onwards).** Start up the engine. Allow it to run idle at an excessive speed, with the throttle twist-grip closed and the throttle slide abutting the throttle-stop screw (Fig. 10). Open the air lever wide open and set the ignition lever (where fitted) so that the ignition is about three-quarters fully advanced.

Loosen the nut (1946–54 models) on the throttle-stop screw, and unscrew the latter until the engine slows up and begins to stall. Then screw the pilot-air screw in or out as required to enable the engine to run regularly and faster. To weaken the mixture, screw the pilot-air adjuster screw *outwards*.

Next gently lower the throttle-stop screw until the engine again begins to falter. Now lock the throttle-stop screw with the lock-nut (omitted on "monobloc" carburettor) and begin to readjust the pilot-air adjuster screw to obtain the optimum slow-running. Should this second adjustment cause the engine to tick-over at an excessive speed, repeat the adjustment a third time. When a moderately-fast tick-over† has been obtained, tighten the lock-nut (standard carburettor) on the throttle-stop screw without disturbing the position of the screw.

3. **The Throttle Cut-away.** Should appreciable spitting-back at the carburettor occur on accelerating from rest with the engine idling, stop the machine and slightly enrich the mixture by screwing the pilot-air screw in approximately *half a turn*. If this does not effect the desired result, screw it back to its former position and fit a throttle slide having a smaller cut-away.

* Different size jets are obtainable from Amal spares stockists, or from Amal, Ltd., Holdford Road, Witton, Birmingham, 6.

† Rev the engine up and down sharply several times and note whether the exhaust is nice and crisp, with no "flat spots" as the twist-grip is rotated. It is essential to obtain good acceleration as well as good tick-over. When making this test, the ignition lever (where fitted) must be *fully advanced.* Never run the engine fast with the ignition lever even slightly retarded.

If there is no spitting-back but the engine jerks under load, this shows an over-rich mixture, and the remedy is to fit a throttle slide with larger cut-away, or else to lower the throttle needle one notch.

4. The Jet-needle Position. The tapered jet-needle influences a wide range of throttle openings and affects acceleration. Check performance with the needle in as low a position as possible, i.e. with the clip in the groove nearest the end of the needle. If acceleration declines, and improves by partially closing the air lever, raise the position of the needle by two grooves. If a marked improvement is thereby obtained, try the effect of lowering the needle, by one groove, and leave it in the position where the best performance is obtained.

It should be noted that if the mixture is still excessively rich with the needle clip in groove No. 1 (nearest the end), wear of the needle-jet has probably occurred and renewal of the jet is called for. The needle itself is of stainless steel and wear does not take place, even after a big mileage.

5. Check the Idling Adjustment. Also make any final small adjustment which is required to obtain perfectly smooth tick-over, neither too fast nor too slow.

Causes of Bad Slow-running. If it is found impossible to obtain good slow-running by making the pilot air adjustment as described in paragraph 2 on page 26, it is possible there are air leaks, due to a poor joint at the carburettor attachment to the cylinder and/or a worn inlet-valve guide. Badly seating valves will also weaken the mixture. Defects in the ignition system may also be responsible for poor tick-over. The sparking plug may be oily, or the points set too close (*see* page 93). Possibly the spark is excessively advanced or the contact-breaker needs attention (*see* page 99). See that the h.t. pick-up brush is bedding down and in good condition: also that the slip-ring is clean. Examine the h.t. cable for signs of shorting.

Obstructed Pilot Jet. If the pilot-jet adjustment does not obtain the desired results and the engine will not idle nicely with the throttle almost closed, the air lever wide open, and the ignition (if manual control is provided) three-quarters advanced, it is possible that the pilot jet is obstructed. The jet on the standard carburettor is actually a duct drilled in the jet block, is very small, and can readily become choked.

To obtain access to the pilot jet on the standard carburettor, remove the jet plug and float chamber (*see* Fig. 28), and detach the jet block by pushing or tapping it out of the carburettor body. The pilot jet can then be cleared by blowing. On the "monobloc" carburettor it is only necessary to remove the cover nut 11 below the pilot jet (*see* Fig. 15) and unscrew the pilot jet 9 for inspection and cleaning. The correct size pilot-jet is mentioned on page 25.

Fuel Consumption High. If in spite of a careful check of the carburettor tuning, fuel consumption remains abnormally high, it is likely that one or more of the following causes is responsible: late ignition timing; poor engine compression (caused by badly-fitting piston rings or pitted valves); flooding (caused by a faulty float or needle (see Fig. 16)); air leaks (caused by a distorted carburettor-flange or worn valve-guides); weak valve-springs; leakage at the petrol pipe unions or the float-chamber cover joint ("monobloc" carburettor); or leakage from the base of the carburettor caused (on a standard-type instrument) by a slack mixing-chamber union nut or jet plug, or (on a "monobloc"-type instrument) by a slack main-jet holder or main-jet cover.

MAINTENANCE (1946 ONWARDS)

Dismantling Standard Carburettor. Periodic cleaning is necessary to maintain efficient functioning of the instrument. It is best to disconnect the petrol pipe or push-on fit rubber-sleeve (1956–7 350 c.c. "Clipper"), and remove the carburettor from the face of the inlet port after slackening the carburettor-flange nuts. Referring to Fig. 9, unscrew the mixing-chamber lock ring Z, held by clip $Z1$; detach the mixing-chamber cap Y. Then pull out the air valve D and the throttle valve B, with the jet needle C attached.* To inspect the two valves, or slides, and the jet needle, it is not *necessary* to detach the two slides from the control cables.

Should you desire to detach the air valve D from the control cable, compress the spring and release the nipple from the base of the slide. To remove the throttle valve B from the control cable, compress the spring and permit the cable nipple to vacate the hole in which it seats. Then release the spring and allow the nipple to pass through the larger size hole.

In order to remove the taper jet-needle C from the drum-shaped throttle slide, remove the spring clip which is located at the top of the slide. The normal position for the jet needle is given on page 25. Raising or lowering the needle enriches or weakens the mixture respectively.

Next take the float chamber R off the carburettor. Remove the jet plug Q from the union nut E. Be careful not to lose either of the two fibre washers (one above and one below the chamber lug). Unscrew the lock-screw X and turn the float-chamber cap W until this can be removed from the float chamber. To remove the float itself, compress the spring clip V and withdraw the float T from the float chamber. On removing the float from the float chamber, the needle U will come away from the bottom. Take care not to mislay the two fibre washers (one above and one below the float-chamber lug union).

Now remove the needle-jet O, thereby exposing the main jet P. Afterwards remove the main jet from the needle-jet. Finally unscrew the mixing-

---

* The air and throttle slides can be removed from the mixing chamber either during or after the removal of the carburettor.

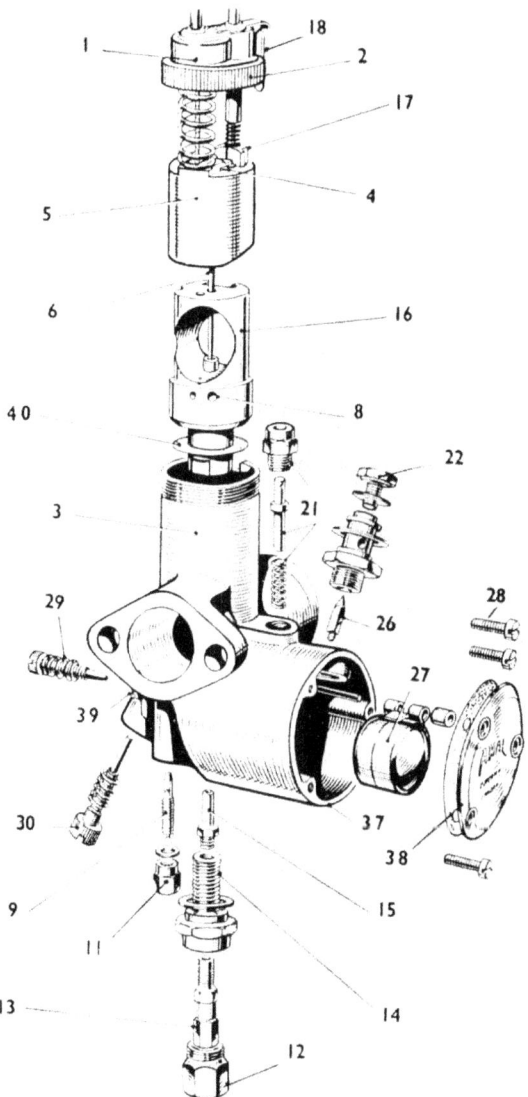

Fig. 15. Exploded View of Amal "Monobloc" Carburettor
A key to the numbered parts of this instrument, fitted to most 1955–8 models is given on page 21.
(*By courtesy of B.S.A. Motor Cycles, Ltd.*)

chamber union nut *E* and detach the jet block *F*. Should this be stiff, tap it out gently, using a wooden stump inside the mixing-chamber.

Dismantling "Monobloc" Carburettor. To remove the "monobloc" carburettor for dismantling and cleaning, first turn off the petrol tap and disconnect the fuel pipe from the float-chamber union (a push-on fit, 1956–8 models). Remove both nuts securing the carburettor flange to the cylinder head and unscrew the knurled cap on top of the mixing chamber. The air and throttle slides can be withdrawn, during or after detaching the carburettor. Do not remove the carburettor slides unless cable or slide renewal is called for.

Referring to Figs. 11 to 13 and 15, dismantling the carburettor is straightforward. To remove the jet needle 6, withdraw the jet-needle clip 4 on top of the throttle valve 5.

To obtain access to the float 27, remove the three screws 28 securing the cover to the float chamber. Lift out the hinged float 27 and withdraw the moulded-nylon needle 26. Lay both aside for cleaning.

The float-chamber vent is incorporated in the tickler 21, and the top-feed union houses a filter element of fine gauze which is readily accessible for cleaning. To remove the filter gauze, unscrew the banjo bolt 22, remove the steel washer, the banjo 23, and then the gauze.

To remove the main jet 13, remove the main-jet cover 12 and unscrew the jet from the jet holder 14. Remove the jet block locating-screw to the left of and slightly below the pilot-air adjusting screw 29. Then push or tap out the jet block 16 through the larger end of the mixing-chamber body. To remove the pilot jet it is only necessary to remove the pilot-jet cover nut 11 and unscrew the detachable pilot-jet 9.

Cleaning Components. Wash all components thoroughly clean with paraffin. Pay due attention to the float chamber, and see that any impurities collected inside are removed completely. Clean the gauze filter occasionally ("monobloc" carburettor), and blow all ducts clear.

Inspecting Carburettor. If the carburettor has been in continuous service for a considerable period, inspect the following—

1. FLOAT CHAMBER. Scrutinize the components closely. Hand-polish the valve part of the float needle (standard carburettor) by rotating the needle in its seat while pulling it vertically upwards. If a distinct shoulder is visible on a needle where it seats, renew the needle immediately. Examine a steel needle for signs of bending.

On the "monobloc" carburettor, check that the joint faces of the float-chamber cover and float chamber are not bruised or damaged, and that the joint washer is sound, otherwise some difficulty will be experienced in obtaining a petrol-tight joint after assembly. See that the gauze filter is undamaged and clean.

2. THROTTLE VALVE. Test in the mixing chamber, and if excessive play is present it is advisable to renew the valve without delay.

3. THROTTLE NEEDLE CLIP. This part must securely grip the needle. Free rotation must *not* take place, otherwise the needle groove will become worn and necessitate a new part being fitted. Be sure to refit the clip in the correct groove (*see* page 25).

4. JET BLOCK. If trouble has been experienced with erratic "idling,"

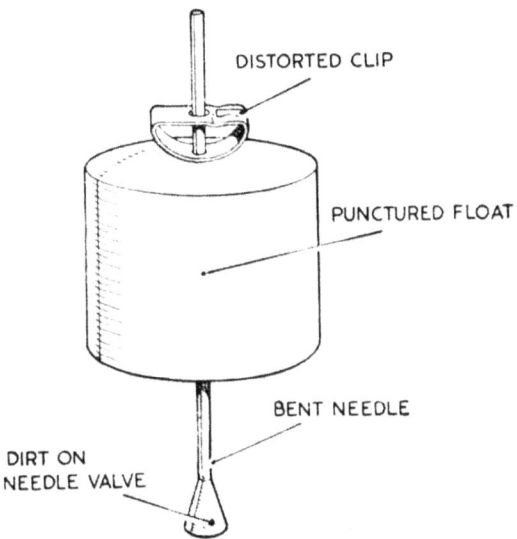

FIG. 16. POSSIBLE CAUSES OF CONTINUOUS "FLOODING"
This type of float is used in the standard carburettor.

ascertain by blowing that the pilot jet is clear, and that the pilot outlet in the mixing chamber is unobstructed.

5. NEEDLE JET. Examine its orifice for wear. The tapered jet-needle (of hard stainless-steel) does *not* wear, but it is often desirable to renew the needle-jet after completing a very considerable mileage (say 15,000–20,000 miles).

6. CARBURETTOR FLANGE. Occasionally check the flange face of the carburettor for truth. Slight distortion sometimes occurs after a considerable mileage. The remedy is to file and then rub the face on emery cloth laid on a surface plate, until a straight-edge shows the face surface to be dead flat. Better still, have the face ground.

To Reassemble Standard Carburettor. Referring to Fig. 9, fit the jet block into the mixing chamber A of the carburettor. It is located by means of a groove and a pin. Screw the needle-jet O into the jet block F.

Now screw the main jet *P* into the end of the needle-jet. Then fit the fibre washer and union nut *E*, and tighten with a fixed spanner.

Position the float *T* in the float chamber *R* and then slip the needle *U* through the bottom of the float chamber and the middle of the float. Compress the spring-clip *V* above the float and pass the needle through the clip also. Then release the spring-clip and allow the clip to engage the needle groove. Screw on the float-chamber cover *W* and secure it by tightening the lock-screw *X*.

Next attach the float chamber to the mixing chamber of the carburettor. Be sure that you replace the *two* fibre washers, one above and one below the float-chamber lug. Then secure the float chamber by screwing the jet plug *Q* into union nut *E*. Also (if previously removed) fit the plug which secures the petrol pipe union to the base of the float chamber. Here again do not forget the *two* fibre washers.

Attach the taper jet-needle *C* to the throttle valve *B* so that the needle is in the correct position. Then (if cable removal was required) thread the two valve-control cables through the mixing chamber. The throttle cable must be nearest to the engine. It can be readily identified, as it has a shorter length of cable protruding from the casing than is the case with the air-control cable.

Slip the two return springs over the control cables. See that the larger spring is placed over the throttle cable. Now fit the air valve *D* to its cable and throttle valve *B* to its cable. Afterwards fit the air slide to the throttle slide. Then allow both slides to enter the mixing-chamber *A*. Be very careful to see that the jet needle *C* enters the needle-jet *O* without any force being used. The jet needle can readily be bent. Now secure the mixing-chamber cap *Y* to the mixing-chamber by means of the lock-ring *Z* which is held after tightening, by the locking spring *Z*1. Finally secure the carburettor to the inlet flange by tightening the two securing nuts and then reconnect the petrol pipe(s) to the float chamber.

To Reassemble "Monobloc" Carburettor. Assemble the instrument in the reverse order of dismantling. The following call for special attention. Referring to Fig. 15, verify that the washer fitted to the bottom of the jet block 16 is in sound condition. Check the condition also of the washer fitted to the main-jet holder 14, and renew the washer if not perfect. When replacing the throttle valve 5, make sure that the tapered jet-needle does actually enter the hole in the centre of the jet block. Check that the throttle slide moves freely when the mixing-chamber lock-ring 2 is screwed down firmly and held by the locking spring 18. Be careful to tighten the pilot jet 9 securely.

When replacing the float 27 in the float chamber, see that the narrower side of the hinge is *uppermost* and contacts the small nylon needle. Do not omit the short distance collar on the spindle. Be sure that the joint faces of the float chamber and cover are clean and undamaged. This is important, otherwise petrol leakage may occur. The gasket is best renewed. See that the petrol-filter gauze is sound and quite clean (*see* page 30). Before replacing the banjo 23 over the gauze, turn on the petrol tap for a second and observe that petrol flows freely. After checking that the small steel-washer is quite clean, secure the banjo by fitting and tightening

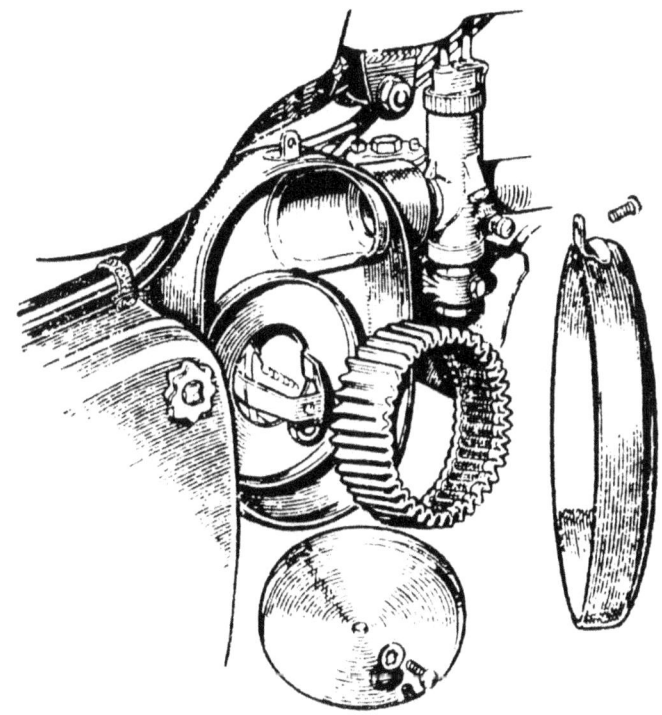

FIG. 17. THE "DRY" TYPE AIR FILTER ON MANY 1955-7 MODELS

The filter element (D-shape on 1957-8 "Bullets") is shown removed. On 1956-7 350 c.c. "Clippers" a three-gauze air-intake is provided instead of an air filter. Before 1955 an "oil-dip" type air filter was specified.

(*By courtesy of "Motor Cycling"*)

securely the banjo bolt 22. Make certain that both the nuts securing the carburettor flange to the cylinder head are tightened *evenly* and not excessively. Avoid using a large spanner for final tightening. The washer at this joint must be perfectly sound. Use a *thin* washer only.

THE AIR FILTER

An air filter is fitted as standard equipment on most 1946 and later Royal Enfield models. Its purpose is to prevent dust and grit entering the cylinder, thereby reducing wear of the bore and piston. Note that, provided the correct carburettor main-jet is used (*see* page 25), the use of an air filter incurs no loss of speed.

Filter on 1946–54 Models. The air filter specified comprises a large rectangular box secured to the off-side of the machine and connected to the air-intake of the carburettor by a rubber connexion. Steel wool (oil-wetted) is packed inside the lower part of the filter box and retained between two wire screens. About every 2000 miles remove the air filter, swill the lower portion out with clean petrol, and then dip it in suitable engine oil (*see* page 36).

Filter on 1955–8 Models. The air filter comprises a metal box or compartment ("Bullets") on the off-side (*see* Fig. 17), containing a felt filter element. This is designed to run dry and should *not* be oiled. Occasionally remove the element and clean it by brushing, and blowing with compressed air. Note that dust and grit collects on the *inside* surface of the element. When the engine is running air is sucked through the element from the inside to the outside.

CHAPTER III

ALL ABOUT LUBRICATION

THIS CHAPTER CONTAINS all the information you need concerning the correct lubrication of your Royal Enfield motor-cycle, including the electrical equipment. Not much attention is required, but this attention is *vital* and on it depend continuous good performance and trouble-free running.

Five Points to Remember. Whatever model you have, there are five essential points to observe. They are—
1. A new or rebored engine must be run-in with great care.
2. Sufficient oil must be kept in circulation.
3. The oil must be of good quality and of the current grade.
4. The oil must be kept clean.
5. Oil dilution must not occur.

Running-in. General advice on running-in the engine during the first 500 miles is given on page 14, and the author would again emphasize the importance of these instructions. With regard to lubrication during the running-in period, the makers recommend the use of some colloidal graphite, and the addition of some upper-cylinder lubricant is beneficial (*see* page 15). It is important to keep the level of oil in the tank high and to change the oil regularly (*see* page 41) while running-in.

Replenish Oil Tank Regularly. Check level *weekly*. If a tank becomes completely empty, the engine is with the dry-sump lubrication system entirely starved of oil and it is only a question of a short time before it "goes west." To be on the safe side, remove the filler cap (at the front of the crankcase, or as indicated at 3 in Fig. 8, on "Bullet" models); with the dipstick attached to its underside ascertain the oil level and replenish with suitable engine oil (*see* page 36) if necessary.

The oil level must always be kept well above the end of the dipstick and the tank should not be replenished beyond *two inches* from the top of the tank, otherwise oil may escape from the vent in the filler cap. On Models G, J, J2 and the "Clippers," over-filling the oil tank will result in the seepage of oil through a breather hole just below the top of the timing chest, on the off-side of the crankcase. Note that the above-mentioned models have oil compartments fore and aft of the crankcase proper, the two compartments being connected by a small passage. Therefore do not hurry when taking dipstick readings after replenishment.

On some Royal Enfield engines there is a mark near the centre of the dipstick (3, Fig. 18) and it is a good plan to keep the oil level up to this mark; this gives highly satisfactory results. Always remember that the more oil there is in circulation, the cooler will the oil and engine be.

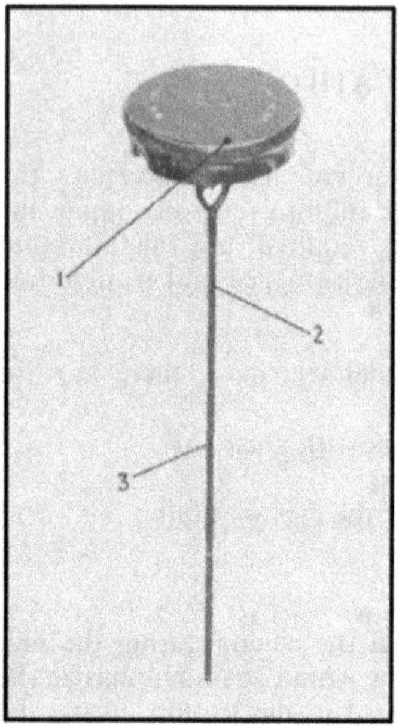

Suitable Engine Oils. Always replenish the oil tank with a reputable brand of engine oil of the correct grade. The importance of this cannot be over-emphasized. Also make a point of buying only from sealed cans or branded cabinets. Suitable engine oils for all four-stroke single-cylinder Royal Enfields are as follows—

1. Castrol Grand Prix (XXL during winter).
2. Shell X-100 50 (40 during winter).
3. Mobiloil D (BB during winter).
4. Esso Extra 40/50 (summer and winter).
5. B.P. Energol SAE 50 (SAE 40 during winter).

FIG. 18. THE DIPSTICK
1. Filler cap; 2. Dipstick; 3. Level mark (if provided).

Detergent Additives. Some of the makers of the engine oils just referred to market oils (SAE 10W/30 or 10W/40) containing detergent additives intended to reduce the tendency for piston-ring gumminess and the formation of sludge. The additive content varies not only with different brands of oils but also with grade variations. Note that if the engine oil has not been drained off and changed at regular intervals (*see* page 41), or if a change over is made from a normal oil minus detergent additives to a highly detergent oil,* the special procedure (*re* draining, cleaning filters, etc.) referred to on page 43 is advised to avoid the risk of any loosened sludge deposits choking ducts or filters, and thereby precipitating an engine seizure or other serious trouble.

Warm Up Engine Gradually. Some riders as soon as they have started the engine proceed to race it, presumably with the idea of impressing bystanders with the powerful mount they are about to ride. This, apart

---

* Your local Royal Enfield dealer will give advice as to which makes and grades of engine oils have sufficient detergency to warrant special precautions being taken.

from the question of ethics, is thoroughly bad practice and is proof of ignorance, for until the engine oil reaches a certain temperature it will not be circulating with maximum efficiency. On the other hand, do not let the engine tick-over too slowly when warming up because this reduces the speed of oil circulation, possibly to a dangerous extent when the oil is in

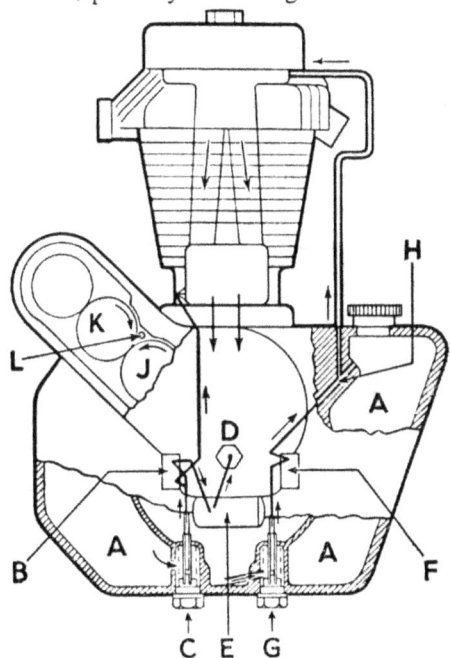

Fig. 19. Diagram Showing Oil Circulation on O.H.V. Singles

On the 350, 500 c.c. "Bullets" a T-shaped external pipe feeds the two separate rocker-boxes, and the oil tank filler-cap is located at the rear.
(*The Enfield Cycle Co., Ltd.*)

a very viscous state. It also tends to cause low-temperature condensation of fuel, which is liable to corrode the cylinder bore.

To Verify Oil Circulation. Remove the tank filler-cap and peer inside when if all is well the oil can be seen issuing from the oil-return pipe in a uniform series of drops. It is advisable to check the circulation occasionally.

DRY-SUMP LUBRICATION SYSTEM

With this type of lubrication system the *whole* of the oil in the oil tank and engine is kept in *constant circulation* by means of delivery and return pump plungers (*see* Fig. 20) housed at the foot of the timing case. A proper understanding of how the oil is circulated is desirable.

The Oil Circulation. On all 1946–58 engines oil is pressure-fed to the rear of the cylinder, the big-end bearing and the overhead valve-gear. The manner in which the oil circulates throughout the engine is shown diagrammatically in Fig. 19. Referring to this diagram, the engine oil is sucked from the oil tank *A*, which is integral with the crankcase (ensuring quick warming-up of oil in cold weather), by means of the double-acting feed pump *B* after passing through the gauze filter *C*.

The primary side of the double-acting feed pump *B* delivers oil through

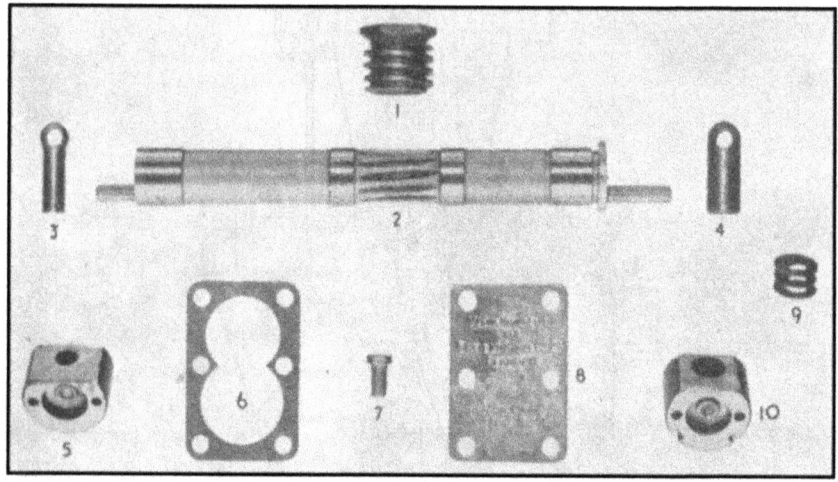

FIG. 20. COMPONENT PARTS OF OIL PUMP

1. Oil-pump worm
2. Pump spindle
3. Delivery plunger
4. Return plunger
5. Disc (feed)
6. Cover-plate washer (2)
7. Cover-plate screw (12)
8. Cover plate (2)
9. Disc spring-washer (2)
10. Disc (return)

the filter *E*, which has a felt element (*see* Fig. 24), to the feed plug *D*. The oil is then pressure-fed through the timing-side main shaft to the big-end bearing of the connecting-rod. Surplus oil from this bearing splash-lubricates the piston, cylinder, and main bearings. A spring-loaded ball valve at the inner end of the timing-side main shaft opens under excessive pressure and permits surplus oil to escape into the sump. The secondary side of the double-acting feed pump *B* pressure-feeds additional engine oil to the rear of the cylinder as indicated. Surplus oil drains to the bottom of the crankcase.

Two wells are provided at the bottom of the crankcase for collecting surplus oil which is sucked up by the double-acting return pump *F* through the gauze filter *G* and returned to the oil tank *A* as indicated in Fig. 19.

A spring-loaded ball valve on all engines is incorporated at position *H* at the outlet end of the return passsage to the oil tank (*see* Fig. 21). The resistance of the ball valve causes some of the returning oil to be forced up into the rocker-box, at a pre-determined pressure, through the external pipe shown diagrammatically in Fig. 21. Surplus oil from the rocker-box (two rocker-boxes on "Bullets") finds its way by gravity down the two push-rod enclosure tubes to the timing gears through grooves cut in the

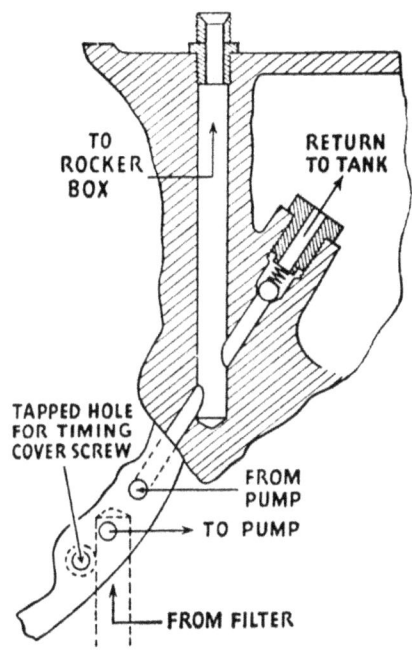

FIG. 21. SECTIONAL VIEW SHOWING SPRING-LOADED BALL VALVE IN OIL RETURN PASSAGE TO TANK
Fitted to engine at H (see Fig. 19).

tappet guides. The intermediate gears J and K pick up the oil and return it to the oil tank A via the channel indicated at L.

Action of Double-acting Feed Pump. Referring to Fig. 22 (left-hand diagram), the pump plunger A is driven by the crank pin B on the end of the worm-driven cross shaft. The plunger is able to reciprocate in a cylinder formed in the disc C which can oscillate in its housing. The disc C is lapped on its seating and is held down by a compression spring located beneath the cover of the pump.

The port T on the lower face of the disc communicates with the pump cylinder. Four ports, W, X, Y, Z are provided on the face at the bottom of the pump housing. Two of these, namely ports Y and Z, are in communication with the delivery pipe from the tank. As regards the remaining two ports, W communicates with the passage connected to the rear of the cylinder, and X communicates with the felt filter shown at E in Fig. 19 and with the oil-feed plug D.

In Fig. 22 (left-hand diagram) the pump plunger A is shown being withdrawn from its cylinder by the anti-clockwise movement of the crank pin B. Ports T and Y register, and consequently engine oil is sucked in from the

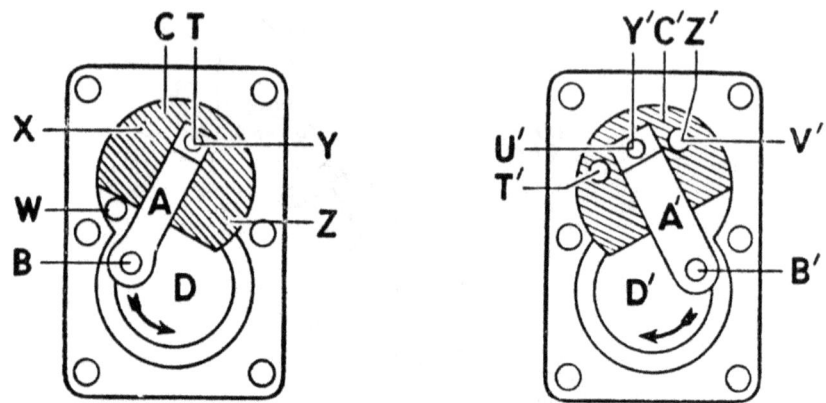

FIG. 22. DIAGRAMS SHOWING ARRANGEMENT OF (LEFT) DOUBLE-ACTING OIL FEED PUMP AND (RIGHT) RETURN PUMP (1946 ONWARDS)

The component parts of the pump are shown in Fig. 20.

(*The Enfield Cycle Co., Ltd.*)

oil tank. The withdrawal of the pump plunger A decreases the clearance space in the housing D and oil is therefore displaced through port W to the rear of the cylinder.

When the pump plunger reaches the end of its outward stroke the disc C partially rotates and during the following inward movement of the plunger, the port W is masked by the disc. Simultaneously port Z remains open and ports T and X register, with the result that oil is pressure-fed through port X to the big-end bearing, and is sucked in from the oil tank through port Z.

Action of Oil Return Pump. The general design of the double-acting return pump is similar to that of the feed pump just described, but the ports are somewhat differently arranged. Referring to Fig. 22 (right-hand diagram), the face at the bottom of the pump housing has two ports Y' and Z'. Port Y' is in communication with the suction passage leading from the oil wells at the bottom of the crankcase. Port Z' communicates with the delivery passage to the oil tank.

Three ports T', U', V' are provided on the lower face of the disc. Port

U' communicates with the cylinder in which the pump plunger A' reciprocates. Ports T' and V' are drilled right through to the upper face. Fig. 22 (right-hand diagram) shows ports U' and V' registering with ports Y' and Z' respectively, on the outward stroke. Engine oil is being sucked in through ports V' and Z'. During the following inward stroke of the pump plunger ports T' and U' register with ports Y' and Z' respectively. This causes oil to be sucked in through ports T' and Y' and displaced through ports U' and Z'.

The Crankcase Breather. On most 1946-55 models this is situated on the top of the near-side half of the crankcase and comprises a small housing (see Fig. 26) containing two pen-steel diaphragms covering two holes drilled in the crankcase. Accurate seating of the diaphragms is ensured by a pen-steel plate held between the breather body and the crankcase. On some 1952-5 "Bullets," however, the crankcase breather is of the "flap valve" type; it comprises a fibre diaphragm in a small housing mounted on the crankcase immediately behind the "Magdyno." The 1956-8 design consists of a piece of Neoprene tube which is flattened at one end so as to convey air pressure in one direction only.

The crankcase breather functions as a non-return valve between the outside atmosphere and the crankcase; it creates a partial vacuum inside the crankcase and the rocker-box(es), thus preventing the entry of excessive oil into the cylinder, and consequent "smoking," and oiling-up of the sparking plug.

MAINTENANCE OF D.S. SYSTEM

The following hints apply to all 1946 and later four-stroke Royal Enfields except where otherwise stated.

Engine Oils to Use. See page 36.

Lubrication of Overhead Valve Gear. All 1946 and later-type models have a positive feed to the rocker-box (two rocker-boxes, on "Bullet" models) by means of an external pipe. The oil fed to the rocker-box provides adequate lubrication for the overhead rockers, push-rods ends and valve guides. No adjustment of the supply is necessary or provided. But see that the pipe unions are kept securely tightened.

Drain Oil Tank and Sump Every 2,000 Miles. After the first 500 miles and thereafter about every 2,000 miles the oil should be drained from the tank and integral sump by removing the two filter plugs shown at C and G in Fig. 19. The rear plug drains the tank, and the front one the sump, except on 1954-8 "Bullets" which have two similarly-placed gauze filters (Fig. 23, left-hand illustration), and a *separate* drain plug for the oil tank at the base of the crankcase below the oil filler. Both gauze filters (see Fig. 23) should be brushed with paraffin to clean them, and the tank and sump swilled through with some clean engine oil, allowed to drain, and refilled with fresh oil. This procedure is conveniently carried out when the machine is being decarbonized.

The oil will flow more readily if the plugs are removed at the conclusion of a ride, or the tank and sump may be allowed to drain over-night. Waste of oil is reduced by allowing the oil level in the tank to become *reasonably* low before draining.

Also Drain Timing Case. As you drain the oil tank (at 2,000 miles) and integral sump, you should also drain the old oil accumulated in the timing

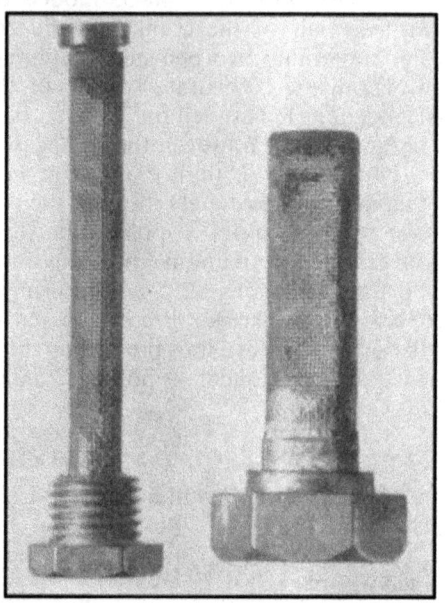

FIG. 23. CRANKCASE GAUZE FILTERS
On the left is shown the filter (two used) on the 1954–8 350, 500 c.c. "Bullets."
On the right is shown the filter (two used) on most other 1946–58 models.

case. To do this, remove the feed plug, indicated at *D* in Fig. 19, and then tilt the machine over on its off-side.

Note that the main oil-feed plug (screwed into the timing-case cover) abuts against a cork oil-seal which is located in a recess in the oil pump worm-nut. The oil seal must be in perfect condition because oil leakage at this point is likely to result in the engine bearings being starved of oil. Fit a new oil seal at once if the condition of the existing seal is at all doubtful.

It should be noted that subsequently to the timing case being drained in the above manner, no oil can be returned from it to the tank until the predetermined level in the timing case has again been built up. Consequently there will be an apparent loss in the oil tank of approximately half a pint. But do not worry; this is only a temporary loss. After changing the oil, allow the engine to tick-over gently for a few minutes.

Clean Felt Filter Every 2,000 Miles. A felt-type oil filter (*see* Fig. 24) is specified on all 1946 and later models. A special feature of the filter design is that in the event of the element becoming clogged through neglect, the oil pressure will raise the spring and cap off its seating and allow the oil to be by-passed. Thus the big-end bearing will not be starved of oil even if the oil is dirty. But for obvious reasons do not neglect the filter.

Every 2,000 miles (i.e. when draining the oil tank, sump, and timing case), remove and clean the felt element by washing it in petrol. The capacity of the element to filter and pass oil quickly enough deteriorates at about 5,000 miles and after this mileage it is advisable to renew the element.

When the felt element is removed for cleaning or renewal, some engine oil escapes from the filter housing. Consequently it is important before running the engine at normal speeds to allow it to tick-over very slowly for about five minutes to enable the oil in the housing to be replaced. It is possible to check this by unscrewing the oil-feed plug in the timing cover half a turn; if oil seeps past the washer, this indicates adequate refilling of the filter housing.

Draining Oil Tank After Changing to Detergent Oil. In the special circumstances referred to on page 36, the following procedure is recommended—

1. Thoroughly drain the oil tank and crankcase when the engine is warmed up, and replenish with the detergent oil.
2. Run the motor-cycle at a reasonable speed for a distance of approximately 50 miles.
3. Drain the oil tank and crankcase again, with the engine warmed up.
4. Flush out the oil tank with detergent oil, remove, clean, and replace the filters (instructions: page 41). It is desirable to renew the felt element in the main filter, shown in Fig. 24.
5. Replenish the oil tank to the correct level with detergent oil.
6. Run the machine for approximately 100 miles and again remove and examine the filters. If clogged up, repeat operations 3–5.

Faulty Crankcase Breather. Unsatisfactory breather action is likely to cause general oil leakage from the engine, possibly a smoky exhaust, and perhaps a tendency for the oil level to rise in the oil-bath chain case. On all 1946–55 models except the 1952–5 "Bullets" the breather can be readily dismantled for cleaning and inspection of the single fibre or twin metal-diaphragms, and the back plate. When reassembling the breather, apply some jointing compound *very sparingly* to the back of the steel plate. See that none of it gets on the diaphragm(s).

On the 1952–5 "Bullets" the breather unit is sealed, and no maintenance is possible other than to dip the complete breather unit in petrol for cleaning. Note that should the crankcase surface be damaged by a breather diaphragm, the best course is to replace the existing breather unit by the latest 1956–8 design referred to on page 41.

Sudden Increase in Oil Consumption. Apart from the possibility of oil leakage at some point (e.g., the external pipe to the rocker-box), a likely

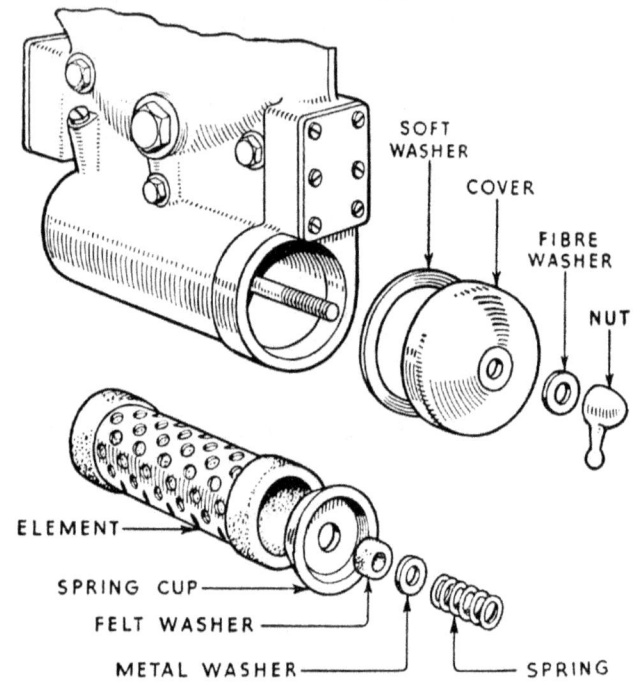

Fig. 24. Exploded View Showing Details of Felt Filter below Timing Case
This filter is incorporated in the position indicated at *E* in Fig. 19.
(*The Enfield Cycle Co., Ltd.*)

cause is the presence of a piece of dirt lodged between the back of the oil-pump return disc (10, Fig. 20) and the disc housing at the front end of the timing cover. Note that it is essential to have perfect contact between the housing and the rear face of the disc. Lapping-in with some very fine abrasive and oil is called for if there is scoring of the disc and/or housing faces.

Dismantling the Oil Pump. Should the oil pump be dismantled (*see* Fig. 20) it is essential when reassembling the pump to make sure that the return plunger (the *larger* one) is fitted to the scavenge end of the pump, at the *front* end of the timing case. Do not omit the disc spring-washers (shown at 9 in Fig. 20), each of which must be fitted between the pump disc and the respective cover plate. The faces of the cover plates and their washers must be absolutely clean.

The Auxiliary Oil Pump. As has been mentioned on page 39, the two idler gears (shown at J and K in Fig. 19) serve as an auxiliary oil-return pump. Correct end-float of these two gears is therefore very important. A genuine Hallite gasket with Royal Enfield Part No. must be used for the timing-cover joint, as its thickness limits the end-float of the above-mentioned idler gears.

Replacing the Timing Cover. If this has been removed, be careful on assembly not to force it home. Very carefully offer up the cover (with Hallite washer in position) until you feel resistance as the helical teeth of the pump spindle contact the oil-pump worm (*see* Fig. 20). Slowly rotate the engine in its normal direction of rotation, while maintaining slight pressure on the timing cover. The pump worm will then screw into engagement with the pump-spindle teeth, and the timing cover can be pressed right home on the timing case.

Lubrication of Lucas "Magdyno" (All Models Except 250 c.c. "Clippers," 1956-8 "Bullets"). The bearings of the machine are packed with grease before a new model leaves the works, and this is quite sufficient until a complete overhaul is necessary when the "Magdyno" unit should be stripped down by a Lucas service agent, the bearings repacked with grease, and the instrument given any other attention that is necessary.

About every 3,000 miles insert a few drops of thin machine-oil on the wick in the contact-breaker base. The wick is carried by a small screw and to remove this screw it is first necessary to remove the spring arm carrying the contact (*see* Fig. 57), when the wick screw can be withdrawn.

When replacing the spring arm carrying the fixed contact, see that the small backing spring is correctly located on the *outside* of the spring arm, with the curved portion facing *outwards*. Replace the spring washer and securing screw, and tighten the latter firmly.

If at any time it is necessary to remove the complete contact-breaker, it is a good plan to push out the tappet from the contact-breaker body and smear the tappet with a little thin machine-oil. Extract the spring circlip and remove the face cam. Where manual ignition-control is provided, the removal and replacement of the cam is facilitated by half retarding the ignition lever; this takes the cam away from its stop-pin. Remove any dirt from the surface of the cam and lightly smear both sides with a little Mobilgrease No. 2. When replacing the contact-breaker see that the stop-pin in the housing, and the plunger of the timing control, engage with their respective slots. A recess is provided for the "eye" of the circlip.

On 1946–9 models equipped with dynamos of the Lucas E3HM type, a lubricator will be observed on the commutator driving-end bracket (*see* Fig. 29). Add a few drops of *thin* oil about every 3,000 miles. All the "Magdynos" fitted to 1950–7 models (including the 1956-7 c.c. "Clipper") embody the Lucas type E3LM dynamo, and this has no lubricator (*see* Fig. 30).

The Contact-breaker (250 c.c. "Clippers"). The 1954 and early 1955 "Clippers" have Miller alternator and rectifier lighting, and coil-ignition equipment, but late 1955–8 models have Lucas alternator and rectifier lighting, and a coil-ignition system. It is advisable in either case to remove the contact-breaker cover about every 3,000 miles and smear the surface of the contact-breaker cam with a little Ragosine Molybdenised non-creep oil (or if not available, a little Mobilgrease No. 2). Be very careful not to permit any oil or grease to get on or near the contacts. It is also desirable at about the same period to apply a little Ragosine non-creep oil to the automatic timing-control mechanism situated behind the contact-breaker. Also apply the grease gun to the nipple on top of the driving-shaft housing; use a light grease.

The Rotating-magnet Magneto (1956–8 "Bullets"). About every 2 years, or when a complete engine overhaul is undertaken, it is advisable to have the Lucas type SR-1 rotating-magnet magneto dismantled at a Lucas service depot or agent, so that the rotor bearings can be repacked with grease and the weights, springs, and toggles of the automatic timing-control mechanism examined and lubricated with medium-viscosity engine oil.

After the first 400 miles and subsequently at 3,000 mile intervals, remove the moulded cover and apply a spot of clean engine oil to the visible end of the contact-breaker pivot post. It is recommended also that some Mobilgrease No. 2 be smeared on the pivot post about every 6,000 miles. To do this, it is first necessary to slacken the nut securing the end of the contact-breaker spring (*see* Fig. 58) and lift off the spring and contact-breaker lever.

Air Filters. For instructions, *see* page 33.

THE MOTOR-CYCLE PARTS

Although correct engine lubrication is of vital importance, proper lubrication of the motor-cycle parts, especially the gearbox and transmission, should never be neglected. Neglect will spoil the efficiency of a well-lubricated and tuned engine, increase fuel consumption, and accelerate wear and tear. A lubrication chart is provided on page 48 for the guidance of Royal Enfield owners.

Four-speed Gearbox Lubrication. On all Royal Enfield (Albion) four-speed gearboxes the correct lubricant to use is engine oil (*see* page 36). The level of oil in the gearbox should be checked every 500–700 miles (preferably when the gearbox is warm) and topped-up, where necessary, on all models except the 1954–8 "Bullets," to the *level of the filler orifice.* Always maintain the oil supply at this level. If any difficulty is experienced in determining the existing level, it is not a bad plan to insert the dip-stick attached to the oil-tank filler cap. See that the machine is on level ground and quite upright.

There is a combined filler and level plug on all models except the 1954–8 "Bullets" low down at the rear side of the gearbox as shown in Fig. 7, but on late 1954–8 "Bullets" the filler plug is located on top of the gearbox as shown at 1 in Fig. 8, and on all 1955–8 "Bullets" a separate level plug is situated as shown at 4 in Fig. 8 on the front vertical-face of the gearbox.

On early 1954 "Bullets" having a filler plug on top of the gearbox, but no separate level plug, replenish the gearbox with engine oil to the level of the flats at the lower end of the dipstick attached to the filler plug or in some instances the loose dipstick included in the tool-box.

On all 1955–8 "Bullets," to replenish the gearbox place the motor-cycle on an even keel, remove the filler plug and the separate level plug, and then with a small funnel pour engine oil through the filler-plug orifice until it begins to exude from the level-plug orifice. Then replace and firmly tighten both plugs. Do not forget to replace or if necessary renew the plug washers.

Do not under *any* circumstances replenish the gearbox with heavy yellow-type grease, or serious under-lubrication may occur, with most disastrous results to the highly-stressed gears. If occasion is had to strip down the gearbox, it is advisable to pack the box with some *soft* grease on assembly and thereafter to top-up with suitable engine oil. The foot gear-change requires no separate lubrication.

Draining the Gearbox. On a brand new machine, after the first 1,000 miles place an oil tray beneath the gearbox, remove the drain plug and allow all the oil to drain off. After replacing the drain plug replenish with fresh engine oil as described above. See that the drain plug is very firmly retightened. Subsequent draining is not necessary.

Oil Leakage from Gearbox. It is sometimes found after a big mileage that some oil leakage occurs from the driving side of the gearbox, or from the bearing for the kick-starter shaft. A simple and permissible method of preventing such leakage, or reducing it, is to substitute a mixture of equal parts of SAE 50 engine oil and medium-grade grease for pure engine oil.

Lubrication of the Primary Chain. On all 1946 and later Royal Enfields the primary chain is completely enclosed in an oil-bath chain case (*see* Fig. 26). About every 1,000 miles remove the oil-filler plug or inspection cover (Models G, J, J2), and also unscrew and remove the oil-level plug (screw) situated low down on the outer half of the chain case. Then, with the motor-cycle on level ground and upright, pour Castrolite or another suitable oil (*see* page 52) through the filler plug orifice or inspection-cover hole until it begins to trickle from the oil-level plug orifice.

About every 10,000 miles drain the oil-bath chain case and, having

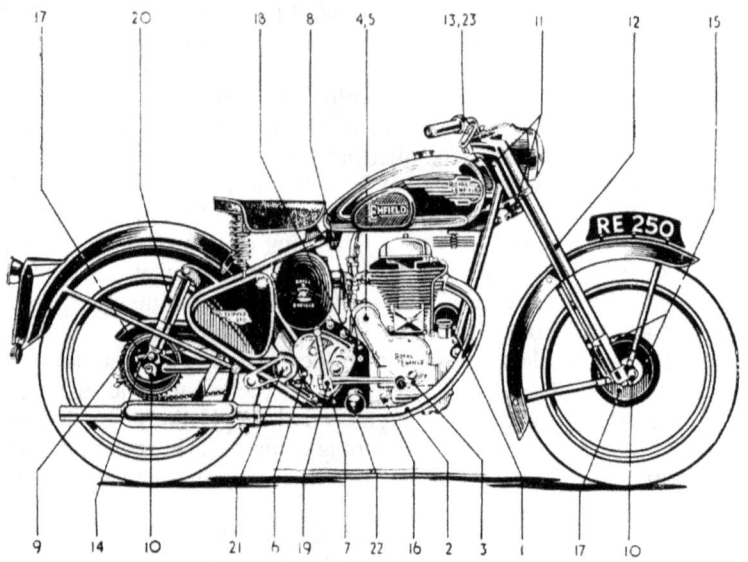

FIG. 25. LUBRICATION CHART FOR 1946–58 ROYAL ENFIELD MOTOR-CYCLES

The above chart (showing a 250 c.c. "Clipper") is generally applicable to all four-stroke singles, except for a few slight differences. The 1946–55 Models G, J, J2 have no rear springing; on all "Bullet" models the oil-tank filler cap is at the rear (*see* Fig. 8), and on 1955–8 "Bullets" the gearbox (*see* text) has separate level and filler plugs. For oil-dip air filters, *see* notes on page 34.

removed the oil-level plug, replenish with new engine oil to the level of the level-plug orifice. See that the level plug is afterwards firmly retightened. Note that excessive filling of the oil-bath is undesirable and may cause the clutch to slip.

Lubrication of the Secondary Chain. The crankcase-breather pipe shown at 1 in Fig. 26 directs oil mist towards the secondary chain, but the amount of lubrication the chain receives from this source is usually quite insufficient. It is desirable to smear some graphite grease with a brush on to the chain about every 500 miles, or whenever the chain seems dry. Alternatively engine oil can be used for the rear chain, and the best method of oiling is to rotate the chain with the wheel and apply an oil can

KEY TO FIG. 25

Item No.	Description	Lubrication, etc., required	See Page
1	Oil tank . .	Weekly check oil level and top-up as required. Every 2,000 miles change oil and clean gauze filter.	35, 41
2	Engine sump . .	Every 2,000 miles drain, and clean gauze filter.	41
3	Timing case . .	Every 2,000 miles drain case, and clean the felt filter. At 5,000 miles renew the element.	42–3
4	Lucas "Magdyno" .	Every 3,000 miles add a few drops of thin oil to the contact-breaker wick, tappet, and dynamo lubricator (if fitted).	45
5	Contact breaker { 250 c.c. "Clipper" 1956–8 "Bullets"	Every 3,000 miles oil cam slightly and apply a little non-creep oil to automatic-timing control mechanism. Every 3,000 miles apply a spot of engine oil to pivot post. Grease post every 6,000 miles.	46
6	Gearbox filler-cap .	Every 500–700 miles remove, inspect oil level; top-up as required.	47
7	Gearbox drain-plug	After the first 1,000 miles drain gearbox, and replenish.	47
8	Primary chain .	Every 1,000 miles top-up oil-bath (if necessary) to correct level. Every 10,000 miles change the oil.	47
9	Secondary chain .	Every 500 miles smear with grease or oil. Every 2,500 miles remove, clean, and grease.	48
10	Wheel hubs . .	Every 1,000 miles grease the nipples sparingly, or every 10,000 miles dismantle and repack bearings with grease.	51
11	Steering head .	At each complete overhaul repack bearings with grease.	51
12	Front forks . .	If "bottoming" occurs on forks (with drain plugs), top-up to correct level.	51
13	Handlebar controls	Weekly oil control levers, exposed cables, and nipples.	53
14	Speedometer drive .	Every 500 miles grease gearbox nipple.	53
15	Front-brake cable .	Weekly oil exposed ends.	53
16	Rear-brake pedal .	Weekly grease the nipple.	53
17	Brake-cam spindles	Every 5,000 miles, remove and grease.	54
18	Clutch operation .	Weekly grease nipple (if fitted).	54
19	Foot gear-change .	Weekly grease nipple (if fitted).	54
20	Rear suspension .	If oil loss occurs (1949–53 units), top-up to correct level.	54
21	"Swinging arm" .	Every 500 miles grease pivot nipples.	54
22	Centre-stand pivot .	Every 500 miles grease the nipple.	55
23	Dipper switch .	Every 5,000 miles oil lightly.	55

to the top of the lower chain-run. See that the oil is falling upon the links, not on the ground, and make a practice of oiling regularly.

If the chain is neglected, undue wear of the chain and sprockets will ensue, and the transmission will be harsh. From time to time (say once every 2,500 miles) disconnect or take off the chain and give it a bath in

Fig. 26. The Oil-bath Chain Case on the 1949–55 "Bullet" Models

On "Clipper" models and 1956–8 "Bullets" the oil-filler plug is on top of the inner half of the chain case, and on Models G, J, J2 a detachable inspection-cover gives access to the chain for replenishment of oil and checking tension.

1. Crankcase-breather pipe
2. Nut securing outer half of chain case
3. Oil-level plug (screw
4. Oil-filler plug

paraffin. If allowed to soak well, the whole of the dirt will be extracted; dry the chain before refitting.

Before refitting the chain the wisest course (if time permits) is to immerse it in a receptable containing a mixture of warm graphite and grease, such as Mobilgrease No. 2, which will then permeate all the roller bearings. There is no better treatment for a main driving chain, although plain engine oil or regular greasing with a brush will answer satisfactorily. After it has cooled, wipe off the excess lubricant. As the lubricant will be gradually squeezed out under load, the process should therefore be repeated about every 2,500 miles. Clean the sprockets and, on replacing the chain, see that the split end of the spring link faces opposite to the direction of the chain travel.

Suitable Greases for Motor-cycle Parts. Grease nipples are provided for the motor-cycle parts which need regular greasing, and a Tecalemit grease

gun is included in the tool kit (*see* Fig. 54) or is available as an extra. Certain parts require to be lubricated with engine oil (*see* page 36) and a transparent oil-can is a useful asset. Always use a good quality grease. Suitable greases, recommended by The Enfield Cycle Company, Ltd., are as under—
1. Mobilgrease MP.
2. Castrolease LM.
3. Shell Retinax A.
4. B.P. Energrease L2.
5. Esso Multipurpose Grease H.

Grease canisters intended for filling the grease gun quickly are available and obviate the somewhat messy job of filling the gun by hand. For winter use, Castrolease Medium is suitable as an alternative to Castrolease Heavy (except for wheel hubs), and the author finds that it can be more readily injected.

Grease Wheel Hubs about Every 1,000 Miles. Inject sparingly some grease such as "Castrolease Heavy" into the nipples on the front and rear hubs about every 1,000 miles. Be careful not to inject excessive grease, otherwise some of it may gradually penetrate to the brake-shoe linings and spoil braking efficiency (*see* page 155).

Note. A better alternative to greasing the hub nipples is to dismantle the bearings about every 10,000 miles and repack them with grease. To dismantle the bearings the shouldered wheel-spindle can conveniently be used as a drift. Unless the hubs are nearly full, the addition of further grease through the nipples may not take effect; if the hubs *are* full, the injection of further grease may tend to cause brake trouble.

The Steering Head Bearings. The ball bearings in the steering head are packed with grease by the makers during their initial assembly. No extra greasing is needed, and therefore no grease nipples are provided. During a complete overhaul it is desirable to repack the bearings with grease if necessary.

Lubrication of Telescopic Front Forks (With Drain Plugs). On the 1946–55 Models G, J, J2, the 1949–52 "Bullets," the 1953 350 c.c. "Bullet," and the 1954–8 250 c.c. "Clippers" a drain plug (serving primarily as an oil-level plug) is fitted to the foot of each fork leg as shown in Fig. 27.

All Royal Enfield telescopic-type front forks are lubricated internally by the damping oil contained in each leg. No external lubrication is required, but it may be necessary very occasionally to top-up both fork legs; leakage past the oil seals does sometimes occur, especially if the machine is often ridden over rough roads. The onset of sudden damping giving the effect of "bottoming" indicates that topping-up is desirable.

Top-up the fork legs with one of the following oils—
Wakefield's Castrolite.
Mobiloil Arctic.
Shell X-100 20.
B.P. Energol SAE 20.
Esso Extra 20W/30.

Before topping-up the telescopic-type front forks, jack up the machine (on level ground) on its rear or centre stand. Check that the forks are in their normal unladen position by pulling upwards on the handlebars and then releasing them. Remove the small screwed plugs (shown at 4 in Figs. 90 and 92) from the tops of the fork legs or the facia, also the washers

FIG. 27. FRONT-FORK LEG BOTTOMS WITH AND WITHOUT OIL DRAIN PLUGS

beneath the screwed plugs. This exposes the gauze filters. Now pour in through each gauze filter one of the above-mentioned oils. Allow the machine to stand for five minutes. Then remove the small drain plugs (*see* Fig. 27) and allow all surplus oil to drain away into suitable receptacles placed beneath the fork legs. When oil ceases to flow from the drain-plug orifices, the correct oil level exists in each fork leg; the oil content is approximately one fluid ounce. Replace the drain plugs, and the screwed plugs and washers at the top ends of the fork legs. See that all four plugs are firmly retightened.

Lubrication of Telescopic Front Forks (Without Drain Plugs). On the 1953 500 c.c. "Bullet," the 1954–8 350 c.c., 500 c.c. "Bullets," and the 1956–7 350 c.c. "Clippers" the telescopic front-forks are slightly different internally from the type just referred to. The foot of each fork leg has a nut, but no drain or level plug is provided (*see* Fig. 27).

Each of the telescopic-fork legs is filled on assembly with $7\frac{1}{2}$ *fluid ounces* of one of the previously-mentioned topping-up oils, and it is normally unnecessary to top-up with any further lubricant. For this reason no level indicators or drain plugs are provided. No attention is necessary except in the event of oil seepage being observed on the aluminium sliding members, caused through worn oil seals or badly worn bearings. The remedy in this case is to dismantle the forks, renew the worn parts, and refill each fork leg with five fluid ounces of oil.

ALL ABOUT LUBRICATION 53

The Handlebar Controls. Apply the oil-can weekly to the cables where they are apt to bind on the control mechanism on the handlebars; tilt the bars so that oil runs into the cable casings. Oil all control levers and the nipples. When fitting new cables and casings, charge the latter with grease. A length of rubber tube can be used in conjunction with the grease-gun to inject grease.

The Speedometer Drive. About every 500 miles (slightly more often if hard driving is undertaken) apply the grease gun to the nipple 2 on the

FIG. 28. THE REAR-HUB SPEEDOMETER DRIVE
1. Speedometer-drive gearbox (see Fig. 89) 3. Union nut
2. Grease nipple 4. Driving cable

speedometer-drive gearbox on the off-side of the rear hub (see Fig. 28). Give only a few strokes of the grease gun.

It is advisable occasionally to unscrew the knurled ring-nut connecting the driving cable to the underside of the speedometer; pull the drive clear and then squirt some oil down between the drive and the outer casing. When reconnecting the drive, make sure that the squared projection on the end of the drive goes properly home before retightening the ring nut.

The Front Brake Cable. Besides oiling the handlebar control weekly (not forgetting the compensating device on 1955-8 "Bullets" with dual front brakes), lightly oil both ends of the exposed portion of the cable (or cables) connected to the brake-cam levers.

The Rear Brake Pedal. Grease the brake-pedal shaft weekly or about every 250 miles by applying the grease gun to the nipple (11, Fig. 88) provided.

The Brake Cam Spindles. Grease nipples are not provided on the ends of the cam spindles of 1946 and later models, as riders often tend to lubricate these shafts excessively and thereby cause deterioration in braking efficiency. The spindle ends on all models are plugged with $\frac{1}{4}$ in. B.S.F. screws, and it is advisable about every 5,000 miles to remove the spindles and smear some grease on them. Alternatively you can remove the plugs, fit grease nipples instead, and apply the grease gun *very sparingly* about every 2,000 miles.

The Clutch Operation. On the 1946-54 models with external clutch operating-lever of the type shown in Fig. 80 there is a grease nipple 7 on the end of the horizontal worm-spindle. On 1955 and later models (except 250 c.c. "Clippers") with internal clutch-operating lever there is a grease nipple on top of the gearbox as shown at 2 in Fig. 8. On the 250 c.c. "Clippers" the grease nipple is on top of the vertical fulcrum-pin as shown at 7 in Fig. 82. Apply the grease gun weekly, or about every 250 miles to the appropriate nipple.

The Foot Gear-change. Where a grease nipple is provided, (e.g. 1956-7 350 c.c. "Clipper"), apply the grease gun weekly, or about every 250 miles.

Rear Suspension Units. Modern "swinging arm" rear suspension is provided on all 1949-58 "Bullets" and 250 c.c. "Clippers," and two quite different types of rear-suspension units have been fitted. Up to 1953 Royal Enfield Mark 1 suspension units were specified, but since late 1954 these units have been superseded by proprietary-type units.

The proprietary-type suspension unit fitted to late 1954 and subsequent models differs from the earlier type in that it has no drain or level plug at its base, and each unit is sealed completely. Unless appreciable wear occurs, there is no risk of oil leakage. When leakage does eventually occur, it is time to fit a replacement rear-suspension unit.

In the pre-1954 Royal Enfield Mark 1 rear-suspension unit the replenishment of each unit with fresh oil to the correct level is advised if loss of oil has occurred for some reason and the suspension has become too "soft." Each Mark 1 unit must be replenished when necessary with one of the special oils recommended on page 52 for topping-up the telescopic front-forks. The following procedure is recommended.

With the machine on its centre stand, remove the filler plugs and washers from the tops of the units and pour in oil. Remove the drain plugs (which act as oil-level plugs) from the bottoms of the units, adjacent to their frame anchorages, and allow all surplus oil to drain off into suitable receptacles. When no more oil flows out, the level of oil in each fork leg is correct. Afterwards replace the filler plugs and drain plugs, with associated washers.

The "Swinging Arm" Pivot. Grease-gun lubrication is advised about every 500 miles. On most "swinging arm" models grease nipples (12,

Fig. 88) are provided at *both* ends of the pivot spindle. On some earlier S.A. models, however, there is a single nipple (rather inaccessible and often dirty) located underneath and in the centre of the sleeve for the pivot spindle.

The Centre Stand Pivot. Apply the grease gun to the nipple about every 500 miles.

Sidecar Chassis (Where Fitted). If greasing the hubs (about every 1,000 miles) of the motor-cycle, remember at the same time to grease the hub of the sidecar chassis. Also about every 250 miles apply the grease gun to the rear spring and shackle-link bolts. Follow closely any special instructions given by the makers of the particular type of sidecar attached.

The Dipper Switch. It is permissible about every 5,000 miles to apply a little *thin* oil to the moving parts of the dipper switch, but apply only a few drops of oil, or you may cause a short-circuit in the lighting system.

CHAPTER IV

CARE OF LIGHTING EQUIPMENT

THIS CHAPTER DEALS SOLELY with the maintenance of the electrical equipment (generators, batteries, lamps) used specifically for lighting purposes, though on 250 c.c. coil-ignition "Clippers" the battery is used for both ignition and lighting. Refer to Chapter III for all lubrication instructions, and to Chapter V for the general maintenance of those items concerned directly with ignition (magneto, contact-breaker coil, etc.). For advice on the use of the ignition switch, *see* Chapter I, page 4.

The Generators on 1946-58 Models. On all 1946-58 Royal Enfields, except the 1954-8 250 c.c. "Clippers," the 1956-8 350 c.c., 500 c.c. "Bullets," and the 1958 350 c.c. "Clipper," a Lucas gear-driven "Magdyno" is used. It has, on 1946-9 models, a Lucas E3HM dynamo, but on 1950 and subsequent models a Lucas E3LM dynamo is fitted; this is similar to the E3HM generator, but has no lubricator (*see* Fig. 30) on the commutator end-bracket. The dynamo of the "Magdyno" feeds current to the battery for lighting purposes only.

The 1954 and early 1955 250 c.c. "Clippers" have a Miller A.C. 60 alternator (mounted on an extension of the drive-side engine main-shaft) which supplies current to a Miller battery via a full-wave rectifier which converts a.c. to d.c. current. Current from the battery is used for the lamps and also to energize the ignition coil. The generator coils and the switch (*see* page 4) provide for an "emergency start."

Late 1955-8 250 c.c. "Clippers" and the 1956-8 350 c.c., 500 c.c. "Bullets" have on the crankshaft extension a Lucas RM13 or RM14 alternator respectively, supplying current to a Lucas battery, via a full-wave rectifier, the current then being drawn upon for the lamps, and for the ignition coil (250 c.c. "Clippers," 1958 350 c.c. "Clipper"). As with the Miller alternator, "emergency starting" (*see* page 4) is provided for.

DYNAMO MAINTENANCE (E3HM, E3LM)

Before interfering with the wiring, always disconnect the battery positive lead* from the switch lead, to avoid the danger of short circuits which might cause serious damage. On 1946-53 models to disconnect, move the rubber shield and unscrew the cable connector; do not touch the frame

---

* On 1953 and later Royal Enfields a "positive earth" system is used, and the battery *negative* lead should be disconnected.

with the connector and cause a short circuit. When reconnecting, pull the rubber shield well over the connector. To disconnect the battery lead from a battery with detachable cable-connexions, unscrew the knurled nut and withdraw the collet or cone-shaped insert. Note that the two terminal collets are not interchangeable, so it is impossible to reconnect the wrong lead.

If at any time the motor-cycle must be ridden with the battery disconnected,

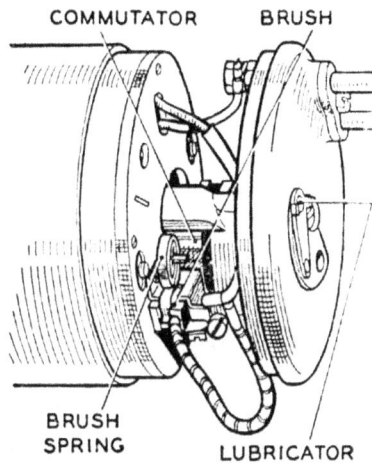

FIG. 29. COMMUTATOR END OF LUCAS E3HM DYNAMO (1946-9)

Some thin machine-oil should be put in the lubricator about every 3,000 miles 1950-7 "Magdynos" have the E3LM dynamo (Fig. 30).

or in any way out of service, it is possible to run with the switch in any position without damaging the electrical equipment.

Brushgear Inspection. It is advisable about every six months to remove the metal cover-band from the dynamo and inspect the brushgear and commutator. When removing the cover-band it is not necessary to disconnect either lead from the battery.

See that the dynamo brushes work freely in their holders. This can be easily ascertained by holding back each retaining spring and gently pulling each flexible lead; the brush should move without the slightest sluggishness. It should also return to its original position directly the lead is let go. When testing a brush in this way, release it gently, otherwise it may get chipped. The brushes should be clean and "bed" over the whole surface; that is, the face in contact with the commutator should appear uniformly polished. Dirty or sticking brushes may be cleaned, after removal, with a cloth moistened with petrol. Always replace carbon brushes in their original positions and see that they make firm contact with the commutator segments.

If the brushes become badly worn, remove them as follows. Release the eyelet on the brush lead by unscrewing the hexagonal nut or screw at the terminal. Then, holding back the spring lever out of the way, withdraw the brush from its holder. Replace with genuine Lucas brushes.

The brush springs should be inspected occasionally to see that they have sufficient tension to keep the brushes firmly pressed against the commutator when the dynamo is running; keep this in mind when the brushes have

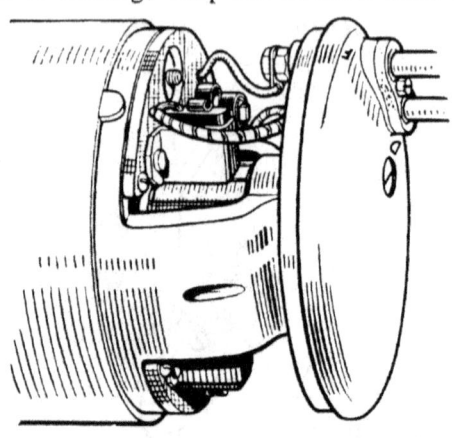

FIG. 30 COMMUTATOR END OF LUCAS E3LM DYNAMO (1950-7)
No lubricator is fitted.

been in use a long time and are very much worn down. It is unwise to insert brushes of a grade other than that supplied with the dynamo, or to change the tension springs. When the brushes become so worn that they no longer bed down on the commutator, go to a Lucas service agent.

Cleaning Commutator. The surface of the commutator should be kept clean and free from oil or brush dust, etc. Should any grease or oil work its way on to the commutator through over-lubrication, it will cause sparking, and carbon and copper dust will be collected in the grooves between the commutator segments.

The best way to clean the commutator without disconnecting any leads is to remove from its holder one of the main brushes and, inserting a dry duster in the holder, hold it, with a suitably-shaped piece of wood, against the commutator surface, causing the armature to be rotated at the same time. If the commutator has been neglected for a long period, it may need cleaning with fine glasspaper. The segments should be *dark bronze* and highly polished.

Dynamo Leads and C.V.C. Unit Terminals. On a Lucas "Magdyno" with a separate compensated-voltage-control (C.V.C.) unit the dynamo positive terminal is marked *D* and the shunt-field terminal *F* on the cover. To connect up, first slacken the fixing screw on the terminal block and remove the clamping plate. Then withdraw the metal sleeve from each terminal. The cables should then be passed through the clamping-plate holes and bared at the ends for ⅜ in. Now fit the sleeves over the cables,

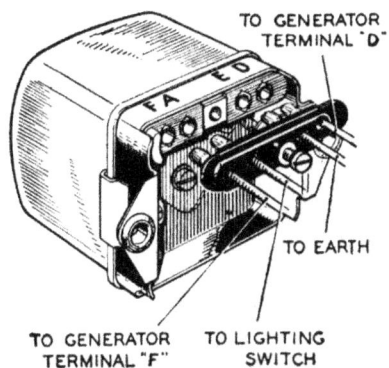

Fig. 31. Lucas C.V.C. Unit (1954-7 "Magdyno" Models)
Showing the Connexions

On earlier models the connexions are in the sequence *F, A, D, E* and two screws are used to hold the connector plate

bend back the wires over them and push the sleeves home into the terminals, finally screwing down the clamping plate (*see* Fig. 31).

Every 10,000 Miles. It is a good plan every 10,000 miles to entrust the dynamo to a Lucas service depot for dismantling, cleaning, servicing, and lubrication.

Compensated Voltage Control. This is used on all 1946 and later "Magdyno" models. Wiring diagrams are given on pages 80-2. The control unit comprises the cut-out and voltage control (working on the trembler principle) neatly housed in a casing mounted on the rear mudguard beneath the saddle. The unit sees to it that the battery is kept properly charged automatically, the dynamo output varying according to the state of charge of the battery and the load.

With C.V.C. equipment the lighting switch is provided with only three positions—*Off, L,* and *H* (*see* page 73). In all three positions the dynamo gives a controlled output, thus relieving the rider of much responsibility. The regulator begins to operate when the dynamo voltage reaches about 7·3 volts. During daylight running when the battery is well charged the ammeter may indicate a charge of only 1 or 2 amp, for the dynamo gives only a trickle charge. The cut-out prevents the battery discharging when the dynamo is not charging.

The regulator provides for an increase of dynamo output as soon as the lamps are switched on. The effect of switching the lamps on after a long run with the battery voltage high is often to cause a temporary discharge reading at the ammeter, but fairly soon the voltage falls and the regulator responds, thereby causing the output of the dynamo to balance the load of the lamps.

When the battery is in a discharged state, the regulator increases the dynamo output and restores the battery to its normal state of charge in the shortest possible time (*see also* page 62).

Note that on "Magdyno" models with C.V.C. unit fitted, it is possible to run with the battery disconnected or removed, and the lamps switched on without incurring any risk of burning out the bulbs. Where the battery is disconnected, the negative lead to it (the positive lead on "negative earth" system) should be taped up, not earthed.

Do not Adjust the C.V.C. Unit. The unit is sealed by the makers, and does not need adjustment once it is correctly set. The only conceivable trouble is from the contacts oxidizing or welding together, owing to accidental crossing of the dynamo field and positive leads. Be careful if making wiring alterations (*see* page 56). Referring to Fig. 31, make sure that the C.V.C. unit connexions are correct, tight, and that the insulation is sound.

To Remove and Replace Dynamo. On 1946 and later "Magdyno" models with compensated-voltage-control, first disconnect the connexions from the dynamo terminals. Unscrew the hexagon nut from the "Magdyno" driving-end cover. Then loosen the two screws which fasten the band clip. The dynamo can then be withdrawn from the rest of the "Magdyno" unit.

On assembling the dynamo, slide it through the band clip so that the fixing screw passes through the hole in the end cover. See that the gears mesh properly. Tighten the end-cover nut and the two band-clip securing screws. Then connect up the connexions to the dynamo terminals. Verify that this is correctly done. Refer to Fig. 31, and it will be noted that the cable from the cut-out and regulator terminal *D* is connected to a similarly marked terminal on the dynamo. The same applies to the cut-out and regulator terminal marked *F*.

No Fuses. In order to simplify the system as far as possible, no fuse is provided. If all the connexions are kept clean and tight, there is no possibility of any excess current causing damage to the equipment.

The Ammeter. This indicates the amount of current flowing into or from the battery and shows whether the battery is being charged or discharged. It is of the centre-zero type and is mounted on a headlamp panel or on a fascia.

THE ALTERNATOR AND RECTIFIER

The Miller A.C. 60 and Lucas RM13, RM14 Alternators. Because, unlike the Lucas E3HM, E3LM dynamos, the alternator (comprising the rotor mounted on the engine-shaft extension, and the stator housed in the primary chain-case) has no rotating windings, commutator, brushgear,

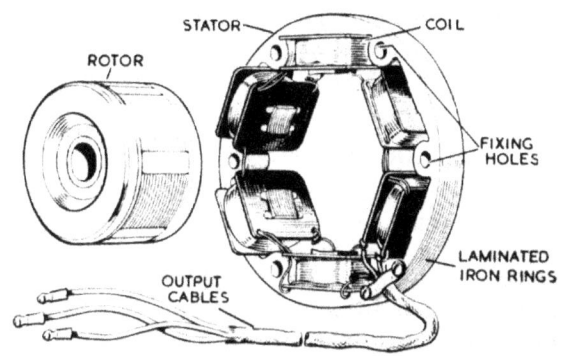

FIG. 32. THE ROTOR AND STATOR OF THE LUCAS RM13 ALTERNATOR

On 1955-8 250 c.c. "Clippers"; 1956-8 350 c.c., 500 c.c. "Bullets" (and 1958 350 c.c. "Clippers") have a Lucas RM14 alternator, similar but of greater output.

bearings, or oil seals, no maintenance whatever is called for other than to see that the three snap-connectors in the output cables (*see* Fig. 32) are tight and clean and the leads unfrayed. Should it be necessary for any reason to withdraw the rotor, there is no necessity to fit keepers to the rotor poles.

The Miller and Lucas Rectifiers. On a machine with a Miller or Lucas a.c. generator (alternator) and modern rectifier lighting equipment, the rotation of the rotor in the six-coil stator induces an alternating voltage in the coils of the stator. Electrical connexion is made between the coils of the stator and a full-wave rectifier clamped by a bracket to the motor-cycle below the front end of the petrol tank.

The rectifier comprises four plates (coated on one side with selenium) and functions like a non-return valve permitting current to pass in one direction only. The alternating current from the alternator is thus converted to uni-directional (d.c.) current for charging the battery. No maintenance is necessary in respect of the rectifier other than to keep the connexions

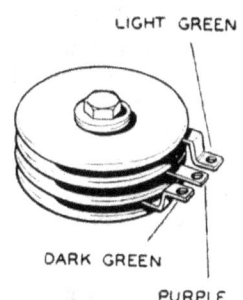

FIG. 33. LUCAS RECTIFIER CONNEXIONS
(*The Enfield Cycle Co., Ltd.*)

tight and clean, and periodically to check that the nut securing the rectifier to the bracket on the motor-cycle is absolutely tight. *Under no circumstances loosen the nut which clamps the rectifier plates together.*

The Rectifier Connexions. If for any reason the leads are disconnected from the rectifier it is essential to see that they are reconnected correctly. Fig. 33 shows the correct connexions for the Lucas rectifier. In the Miller rectifier leads, the cables coloured brown, blue, and red should be connected to the rectifier terminals marked 1, 2, 3 respectively (*see also* wiring diagrams on pages 83–5).

CARE OF THE BATTERY

It is essential to take good care of the battery if this is to continue to maintain its full capacity and enable the lamps to provide maximum trouble-free illumination at all times. On the coil-ignition 250 c.c. "Clippers" this is particularly important. The following are the essential points concerning battery maintenance—

1. Always keep the battery well charged.
2. Top-up the cells monthly with distilled water.
3. Keep the electrolyte level with the tops of the separators.
4. Keep the battery and terminals clean, and the terminals tight.
5. Occasionally check the specific-gravity readings of the electrolyte with a hydrometer.
6. If the battery is not in use, have it charged monthly.

Battery Charging While Riding. On all 1946 and later "Magdyno" models the C.V.C. unit (*see* page 59) automatically controls the dynamo output according to the state of charge of the battery and the load imposed on it. In all three lighting switch positions (*see* page 73) the battery is "on charge" while the engine is running.

On the 1954 and later 250 c.c. "Clippers" and the 1956–8 350, 500 c.c. "Bullets" with alternator and rectifier lighting equipment, no C.V.C. unit is provided, but the position of the combined lighting and ignition switch (Miller equipment) or the lighting switch (Lucas equipment) determines the output of the alternator and the rate of charge of the battery. When no lamps, or only the pilot lights, are switched on, the output of the alternator is sufficient only to trickle-charge the battery and (on 250 c.c. coil-ignition "Clippers") to energize the ignition coil. According to the current demand, i.e. the switch position, so is the alternator output increased accordingly by appropriate alteration in the alternator-coil connexions (*see* page 73).

Battery Discharge While Stationary. To prevent the tendency for slow battery discharge through the contact-breaker (if contacts are closed), it is essential to switch off the ignition (*see* page 13) when leaving a 250 c.c. coil-ignition "Clipper" standing for any appreciable length of time.

CARE OF LIGHTING EQUIPMENT

Note that batteries used on models fitted with rectifier lighting sets (e.g., 1954-8 250 c.c. "Clippers," 1956-8 "Bullets") are prone to lose their charge more quickly than those provided on machines with "Magdyno" lighting; the reason is that a small leakage takes place through the rectifier. If you do not intend to ride for several days, but the rotor of the alternator

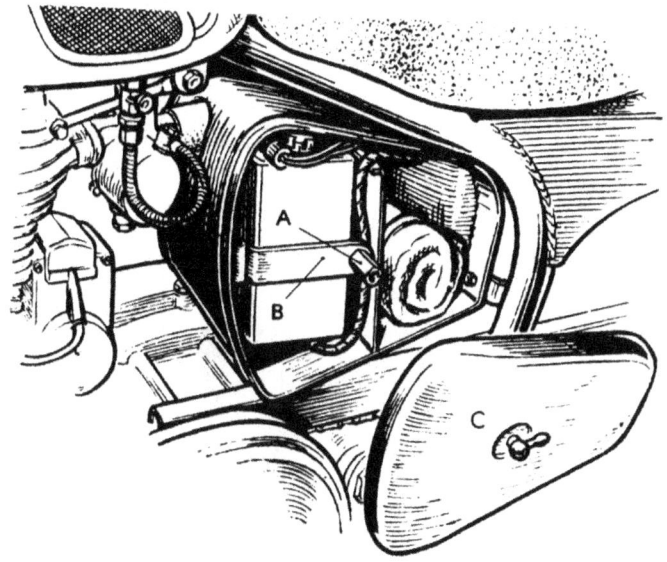

FIG. 34. SHOWING THE NEAT STOWAGE OF THE BATTERY ON THE 1956-8 350 C.C., 500 C.C. "BULLETS"

A single large container, with two detachable covers, houses the battery and tool kit on the near-side, and the air cleaner (see Fig. 17) on the off-side.

(*By courtesy of* "*Motor Cycling*")

is not likely to remain stationary long enough to warrant removal of the complete battery, it is advisable to prevent the risk of leakage through the rectifier by disconnecting the battery earth-lead.

Topping-up the Cells. Inspect the level of the electrolyte about every four weeks, and more frequently in very hot climates. On all models except the 1956-8 "Bullets" unscrew and remove the single slotted-bolt or the two sleeve-nuts which clamp the battery to the battery carrier. On the 1956-8 "Bullets" (*see* Fig. 34) take off the cover *C* and remove the long sleeve-nut *A*. Pull aside the hinged metal-strap *B* and withdraw the battery. Take off the battery lid and remove the three vent plugs. Inspect the hole in each vent plug and make quite sure that it is not obstructed. A choked vent-plug hole causes an increase in pressure within the battery cell when "gassing" occurs, and may create trouble. Check that the rubber sealing-washer for each vent plug is intact, otherwise leakage of the electrolyte may occur.

Wipe the battery top clean with a rag and afterwards wash the rag thoroughly in water or destroy it. See that a supply of clean distilled-water (obtainable from chemists and garages) is available for topping-up the cells. The distilled water, unlike the sulphuric acid, gradually evaporates and must be replenished.

With the vent plugs removed, inspect the level of the electrolyte in each

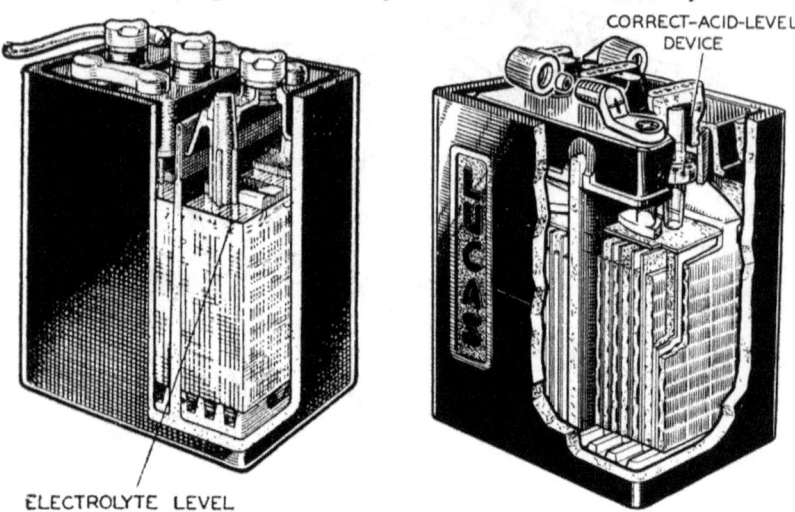

FIGS. 35 and 36. TWO TYPES OF LUCAS BATTERY FITTED TO ROYAL ENFIELD MODELS

The battery shown on the left is fitted to 1946-53 models and differs from the battery shown on the right (fitted to most 1954-8 models) in that no acid-level device is used.

cell. On no account hold a naked light near the vents. If the level of the electrolyte is below the tops of the separators, add distilled water as required to bring the level correct (*see* Fig. 35). Do this *before* a charge run, as the agitation accompanying charging and "gassing" thoroughly mixes the electrolyte solution.

Where no acid-level device (*see* Fig. 36) is provided, insert the nozzle of a Lucas battery-filler into each cell as shown in Fig. 37 until the nozzle rests on the separators. Hold the filler in this position until air bubbles stop rising in the glass container. The cell is then topped up to the correct level (shown in Fig. 35).

To top-up a Lucas battery of later type having an acid-level device, pour distilled water round its flange (not down the tube) until no more drains through into the cell. This occurs when the level of the electrolyte reaches the bottom of the central tube and prevents further escape of air displaced by the topping-up water. Lift the tube slightly to permit the small quantity of water in the flange to drain into the cell; the level of the electrolyte will then be correct. Alternatively use the method just described.

Do not add acid to the electrolyte unless some of the solution has been accidentally spilled. In this case add diluted sulphuric acid of specific gravity equal to that in the cells. Finally replace the vent plugs, fit the

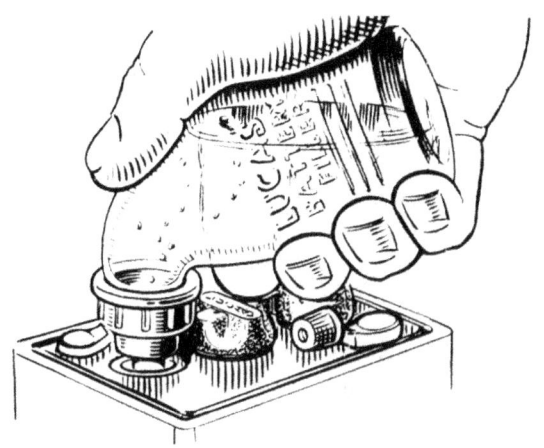

FIG. 37. TOPPING-UP A CELL WITH THE LUCAS BATTERY FILLER

battery, and strap it down securely. See that the battery leads are firmly and correctly reconnected.

Replenishing the Lucas Battery Filler. When replenishing the Lucas battery-filler with distilled water, see that the screw-on nozzle is replaced correctly. Be sure that the rubber washer is fitted over the valve with the small peg in the centre of the valve engaging the hole in the projecting boss of the washer.

Battery Connexions. Always keep the connexions clean, free from corrosion, and tight, otherwise the ammeter readings will *not* indicate the true state of charge of the battery. To prevent corrosion, smear the connexions with petroleum jelly.

Checking Condition of Battery. If any loss of acid has occurred, the battery is misbehaving, or its condition is suspect, it is advisable to check the battery condition by taking specific gravity readings (with a hydrometer) of the electroylte in each cell. Fig. 38 indicates the correct method of doing this. Note that it is not advisable to take S.G. readings immediately after topping-up the battery, as the electrolyte will not then be properly mixed. The Lucas hydrometer shown resembles a syringe containing a graduated float which indicates the specific gravity of the electrolyte in the battery cell from which a sample is taken.

When checking the S.G. of the electrolyte in each cell, note that the spaces between the separators are not wide enough to allow the hydrometer nozzle to be inserted. Therefore, before taking a sample, tilt the battery to bring sufficient electrolyte above the separators. After a sample has been taken and checked, it must, of course, be returned to the appropriate cell. Taking S.G. readings with a hydrometer is the most efficient way of determining the state of charge of the battery and its general condition.

The specific gravity readings (*see* Tables II and III) should be approximately the *same for all three cells*. If the reading for one cell varies substantially from the readings for the other two cells, probably some acid has been spilled, or has leaked from the cell concerned. A short-circuit between the battery plates is also a possibility to be considered. If such a short exists, return the battery immediately to a Lucas service depot for expert attention.

TABLE II

SPECIFIC GRAVITY READINGS FOR LUCAS BATTERIES

(Temperature below 90° F)

Lighting system	Cell Fully Charged	About Half Discharged	Fully Discharged
"Magdyno" Rectifier	1·270–1·290 ,, ,,	1·190–1·210 ,, ,,	1·110–1·130 ,, ,,

TABLE III

SPECIFIC GRAVITY READINGS FOR LUCAS BATTERIES

(Temperature Above 90° F)

Lighting System	Cell Fully Charged	About Half Discharged	Fully Discharged
"Magdyno" Rectifier	1·210–1·230 ,, ,,	1·130–1·150 ,, ,,	1·050–1·070 ,, ,,

Note that a low state of charge of the battery is often caused by parking the machine for long periods with the pilot light or lights switched on, unaccompanied by much daylight running. The remedy is, of course, to undertake more daylight running until the battery regains its normal state of charge. Should over-charging occur, get the compensated-voltage-control unit checked at a Lucas service depot.

First Filling of Batteries. In the United Kingdom the battery on most Royal Enfields will be supplied (and labelled) filled and charged ready for

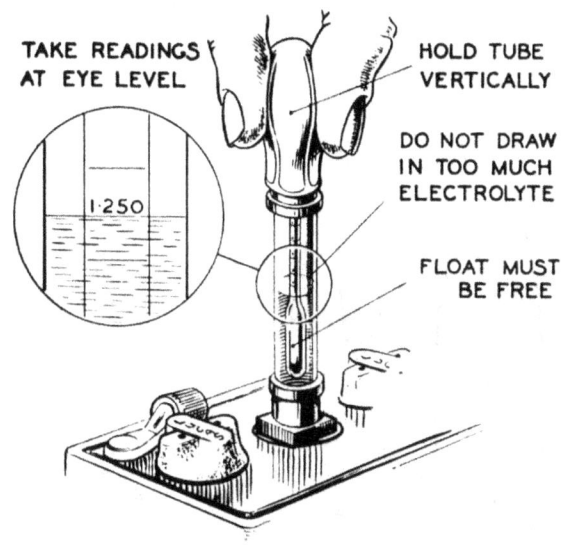

Fig. 38. Checking the Specific Gravity of the Electrolyte with a Lucas Hydrometer
(*The Enfield Cycle Co., Ltd.*)

immediate use. However, on certain models, particularly those sent overseas, the battery is supplied in a "dry charged" condition and requires to be filled with a sulphuric acid solution of the correct S.G. and allowed to stand for one hour before being put into actual service. Note that acid must always be added to water, *never* the reverse. Some times an "unformed" dry battery is supplied and this needs filling with electrolyte of the correct S.G. (each cell to be filled in one operation) and then submitted to a long, slow, continuous charge. For each battery, follow closely the first-filling and other instructions given on the card attached to the battery.

Storage Precautions. If you lay up your motor-cycle for a considerable period, remove the battery, charge it fully, and see that it is given a refresher charge from a garage charger every two to three weeks. All lead-acid batteries slowly discharge when left standing and if a battery is allowed to stand in this condition, the plates will become sulphated and permanently spoiled. In no circumstances remove the electrolyte from a battery placed in storage.

THE LAMPS

Lucas headlamps are fitted to all Royal Enfields except 1954 and early 1955 250 c.c. "Clippers" which embody Miller lighting equipment. Many 1950 and all subsequent headlamps are of the "pre-focus" type having no focusing adjustment. Bulb renewal is dealt with on page 76.

The Lucas DU42 Headlamp (1946-8 Models). This lamp has a double-filament main bulb, one filament providing the normal driving-light, and

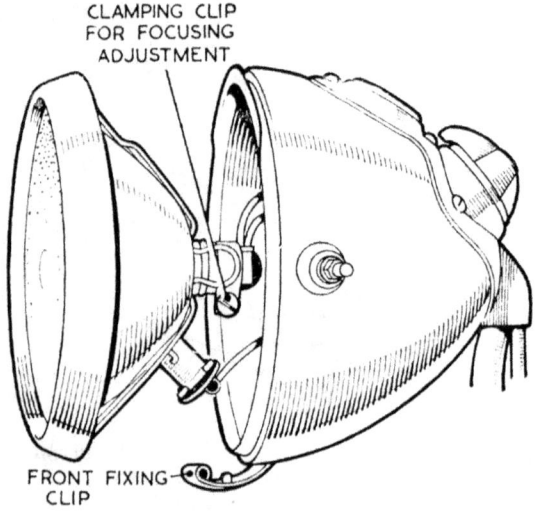

Fig. 39. Lucas Du42 Focusing Headlamp with Front and Reflector Removed
1946-8 models.

the other a dipped beam. The change-over from the normal driving-light to the dipped beam is made by a dipper switch (Fig. 5). A small pilot bulb is provided for parking or when driving in town.

An ammeter is incorporated on top of the lamp. When the lamp is switched on, the ammeter is illuminated by indirect lighting.

To get at the bulbs, release the front fixing-clip (*see* Fig. 39) which secures the base of the lamp front and pull the latter outwards. As the lamp front and reflector come away together, free the top tag of the lamp front from the lamp body by lifting the lamp front slightly upwards. When replacing the lamp front and reflector, first locate the top tag in the slot of the lamp body. Afterwards secure the lamp front by means of the front fixing-clip.

Lucas MU42 Headlamp (1948-50 Models). To gain access to the lamp bulbs, release the spring fixing-catch at the lamp bottom, when the front can be removed. The reflector is secured to the lamp body by means of a rubber bead, and can be withdrawn when the rubber is removed (*see* Fig. 40). When refitting, locate the thinner lip of the rubber bead between the reflector rim and the edge of the lamp body. To replace the front, locate

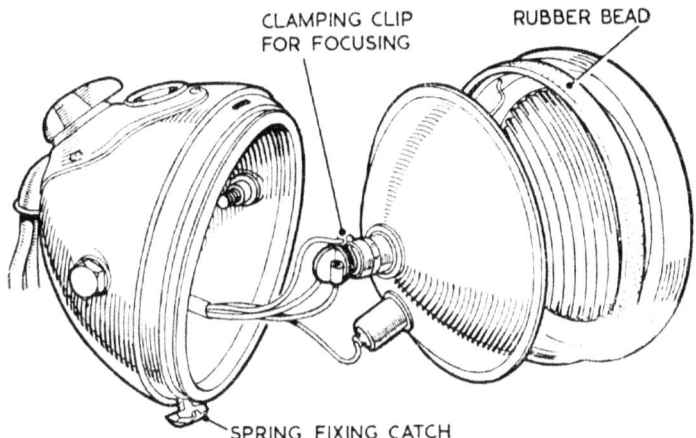

FIG. 40. LUCAS MU42 FOCUSING HEADLAMP WITH FRONT AND REFLECTOR REMOVED
Applies to 1948-50 models.

the metal tongue in the slot at the top of the lamp, press the front on, and secure with the spring fixing-catch.

Lucas SSU700P, SSU700P/1 Headlamps (1950-4 Models). To render the bulbs accessible, first remove the lamp front with Lucas light-unit assembly. Slacken the securing screw at the top of the lamp and then detach the front rim, complete with light-unit assembly (*see* Figs. 41 and 42). When replacing, locate the bottom of the light-unit assembly in the lamp body, press on the front, and secure in position by tightening the top securing-screw.

Some 1951-2 Lucas SSU700P headlamps and the "pre-focus" Lucas SSU700P/1 headlamp with underslung pilot-light (*see* Fig. 42) used on many 1953-4 models have *no focusing adjustment*, and the main bulb cannot be inserted incorrectly. The pilot bulb is carried in a quickly-detachable carrier plate. *See also* page 77.

Lucas MCF700 Headlamp (1954-8 "Bullets," 1956-8 350 c.c. "Clipper"). On this headlamp the Lucas "pre-focus" light-unit assembly and front rim are the same as those used on the SSU700P lamps (*see* Figs. 41 and 42), but the lamp shell itself is built into a "casquette" fork head (*see* Fig. 43) housing twin parking-lamps, the ammeter, lighting switch (and the speedometer).

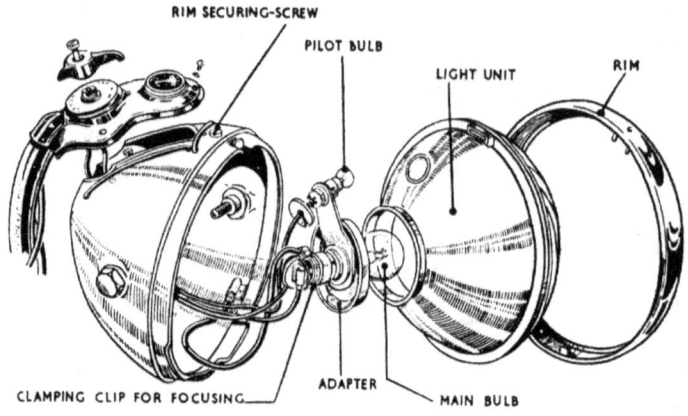

Fig. 41. Exploded View of Lucas SSU700P Focusing Type Headlamp

Applies to 1950-2 models.
(*The Enfield Cycle Co., Ltd.*)

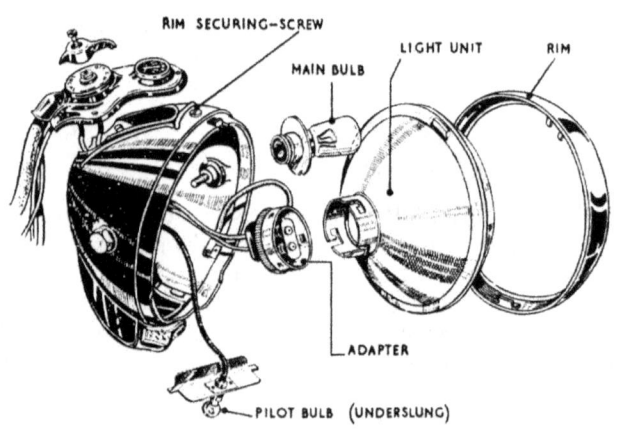

Fig. 42. Exploded View of Lucas SSU700P/1 "Pre-focus" Type Headlamp

Applies to 1953-4 models.
(*The Enfield Cycle Co., Ltd.*)

To obtain access to the "pre-focus" main bulb for renewal, remove the lamp front, with Lucas light-unit assembly attached, as described for the SSU700P headlamp on page 69. To get at each parking-lamp bulb, remove the lamp rim (*see* Fig. 43) by forcing it over the edge of the rubber surround. Note that on the later-type Royal Enfields with "casquette" fork heads, a small security-screw must first be removed. Having removed the parking-lamp rim, pull away the lens, when the bulb itself will be exposed.

Miller Headlamp (1954-5 250 c.c. "Clippers"). On the 1954 and early 1955 coil-ignition 250 c.c. "Clippers" the Miller headlamp is not of the "pre-focus" type and is built into the "casquette" fork head which also

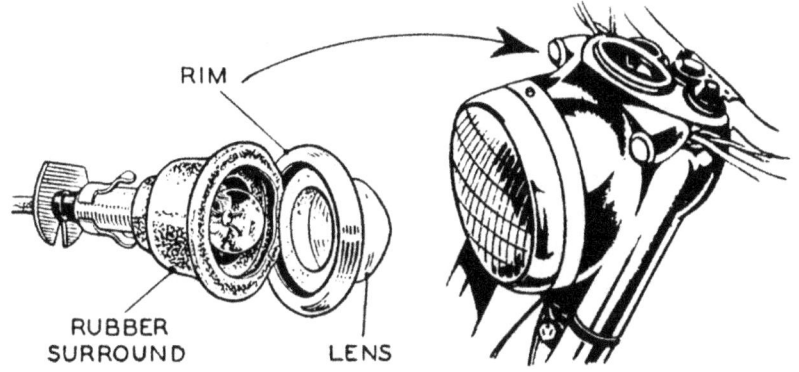

Fig. 43. Lucas MCF700 "Pre-focus Headlamp Built into "Casquette" Fork Head
1954-7 "Bullets," 1956-8 350 c.c. "Clipper."
(*The Enfield Cycle Co., Ltd.*)

houses the ammeter, the ignition warning-light, and the six-way combined lighting and ignition switch (*see* page 73).

To gain access to the double-filament main bulb and the single pilot-bulb, unscrew the screw at the base of the lamp front and withdraw the rim, complete with lens, reflector, and bulb holder. Free the wire clip which secures the bulb holder, hinge the clip rearwards, and withdraw the bulb holder from the back of the reflector. To get at the ignition warning-light bulb, pull the ammeter out of the rubber sealing-ring housed in the "casquette." To facilitate withdrawal (if stiff), first moisten the rubber ring with petrol.

Lucas MCF575 Headlamp (1955-8 250 c.c. "Clippers"). On late 1955 and subsequent 250 c.c. coil-ignition "Clippers" the lamp shell, as on earlier models with Miller equipment, is built into the "casquette" fork head. This also houses the ammeter, three-way lighting switch (and the speedometer). A single parking-bulb is provided inside the headlamp.

To obtain access to the double-filament "pre-focus" main bulb and the parking-light bulb, loosen the securing screw (*see* Fig. 44) at the base of the lamp front, and withdraw the rim and Lucas light-unit assembly. Turn the adapter anti-clockwise and pull it off. The holder for the "pre-focus" main bulb is then exposed. When replacing the adapter, see that the word "TOP" moulded on its back corresponds to the top of the lens of the light-unit assembly (*see* page 73). To get at the parking bulb, pull the bulb holder out of the reflector after freeing the spring claws securing the

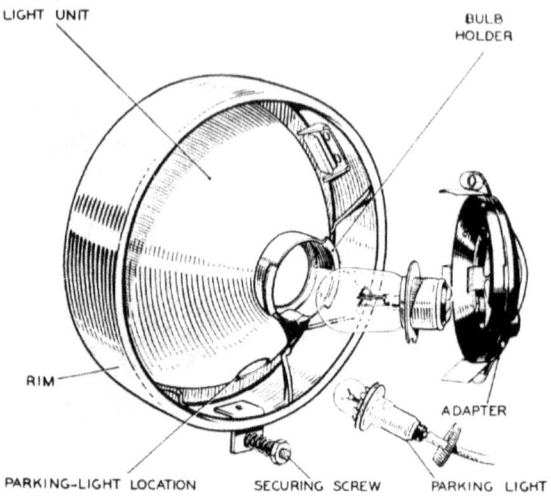

FIG. 44. LUCAS MCF575 "PRE-FOCUS" HEADLAMP
Late 1955 and subsequent 250 c.c. "Clippers."
(*The Enfield Cycle Co., Ltd.*)

holder to the back of the reflector. To get at the ignition-warning bulb, remove the ammeter (*see* previous instructions for Miller headlamp).

To Remove Lens and Reflector from Miller Headlamp. On the 1954-5 Miller headlamp, remove the lamp rim, complete with lens, reflector, and bulb holder (*see* page 71). Next remove the bulb holder and the four spring clips securing the reflector and lens to the lamp rim. Then withdraw the lens and reflector. Renew the washer between the lens and reflector if damaged, otherwise the reflector will become dull. When replacing the reflector, see that the hole for the pilot light and the word "MILLER" on the lens are both at the *top* of the rim. Also see that the four springs securing the lens and reflector to the rim are equally spaced.

The Lucas Light-Unit Assembly. Note that if the lens or the reflector of a Lucas light-unit, fitted to all except the DU42, MU42 head-lamps, sustains damage, it is necessary to fit a complete new light-unit (lens and reflector) after disengaging the four springs which secure the light-unit to the rim. See that the new light-unit is located in the rim so that the word "TOP" on the lens is positioned opposite the tag in the rim, through which the rim securing-screw passes. Also see that the light-unit securing springs (four) are spaced equally around the rim, and that the adapter is positioned properly with the word "TOP" (marked on its back) uppermost.

Lucas Lighting Switch Positions. The lighting switch, mounted on a panel screwed to the top of the headlamp (on all 1946-53 models) or housed on the "casquette" fork head (on late 1955 to 1958 250 c.c., and other 1954-8 machines) has the following positions—

OFF: Headlamp, tail lamp, speedometer light, and sidecar lamps (where fitted) switched off.

L: Headlamp pilot-bulb or twin parking-lamp bulbs (MCF700 headlamp), tail lamp, speedometer light, and sidecar lamps (where fitted) switched on.

H: Headlamp double-filament main bulb, tail lamp, speedometer light, and sidecar lamps (where fitted) switched on.

Note that battery charging while riding (*see* page 62) occurs in all the above three lighting-switch positions; this applies to the "Magdyno" models and also to machines provided with Lucas alternator and rectifier lighting equipment.

Miller Switch Positions. On 1954 and early 1955 250 c.c. coil-ignition "Clippers" the combined lighting and ignition switch is housed (with the ammeter) on the "casquette" fork head and has the following six consecutive positions—

PILOT: Headlamp pilot-bulb, tail lamp, and speedometer light connected by the switch to the battery which is charged (normally at about 2 amp) via the rectifier from four coils of the Miller A.C. 60 alternator. *Ignition switched on.*

HEAD: Headlamp double-filament main bulb, tail lamp, and speedometer light connected by the switch to the battery which is charged (at about 2 amp) via the rectifier from all six coils of the alternator. *Ignition switched on.*

IGN and CH: All lamps switched off, but battery on charge via the rectifier from two coils of the alternator. *Ignition switched on (see* page 4).

OFF: All lamps switched off and battery not on charge. *Ignition switched off* (*see* page 4).

EM IGN: All lamps switched off and battery not on charge. Ignition switched on (*see* page 4), four coils of the alternator being connected *direct* to the ignition coil and contact-breaker.

PARK: Headlamp pilot-bulb, tail lamp, and speedometer light connected by the switch to the battery. *Ignition switched off* (coil not in battery circuit).

Adjusting the Headlamp Position (All Models Except 1954-8 "Bullets" and "Clippers"). If the headlamp is incorrectly aligned and/or the main bulb is out of focus, maximum road illumination will not be obtained, and other road users may be inconvenienced by dazzle. It is easy to rectify both faults.

The best method of checking the alignment of the headlamp is to stand your Royal Enfield facing a light-coloured wall at a distance of 25-30 feet. Switch on the main driving light and note if the beam is projected straight ahead and parallel with the ground (which should be level).

Take vertical measurements from the centre of the headlamp, and from the centre of the illuminated circle on the wall, to the ground. Both measurements should be equal. If not, loosen the two fixing bolts securing the headlamp in the front-fork mounting brackets and tilt the headlamp until the centre of the beam is truly parallel with the ground. Afterwards tighten the two fixing-bolts firmly.

Correct Focusing (Most 1946-52 Models). On all new machines with focusing-type headlamps the double-filament main bulb is carefully focused to give the best illumination. If Lucas bulbs of the correct wattage and number are fitted as replacements, subsequent re-focusing should not be necessary, unless the focusing adjustment has been disturbed. Most 1953-8 models have Lucas SSU700P/1, MCF700, or MCF575 headlamps with a main bulb which is permanently "pre-focused" and fitted to a non-adjustable holder.

Narrowly-converging and widely-diverging beams illuminate the road poorly and are liable to dazzle other road users. Adjust the focus of the headlamp immediately if its *beam* is not uniform, is too wide, is of short range, or has a dark centre. To focus the headlamp (where a focusing adjustment is provided), remove the lamp front (already described) and then slacken the screw on the bulb-holder clamping clip, illustrated in Fig. 40. The bulb holder can then be moved backwards or forwards on the reflector axis until the headlamp is focused correctly. It is desirable to focus the headlamp against a wall 25-30 feet away from the headlamp. See that the bulb holder clamping-screw is firmly retightened after making a final adjustment. For correct bulb renewals, *see* page 76.

Lucas Sidecar Lamp. By unscrewing the locating screw at the bottom of the lamp front, the front and reflector can be withdrawn, giving access to the bulb. When replacing the lamp front, locate the top of the rim first.

Lucas MT110 Tail Lamp (All 1946-50 Models). To remove the back of the lamp carrying the rubber-mounted bulb holder, turni t anti-clockwise to release its bayonet fixing. To replace, engage the bayonet fixing and then turn the back portion of the lamp clockwise until it clips into position.

CARE OF LIGHTING EQUIPMENT

Lucas 480 Tail Lamp (All 1951-3 Models). To obtain access to the bulb, remove the front portion of the lamp by turning it anti-clockwise; this frees the bayonet fixing. To replace the lamp front, engage the bayonet fixing and then turn the front clockwise.

Miller 36E Tail Lamp (1954 250 c.c. "Clippers"). To obtain access to the bulb on the Miller 36E tail lamp (*see* Fig. 45), fitted to 1954 coil-ignition "Clippers," remove in this order: the retaining wire (1), the lens mount (2), and the ruby lens (3). Make sure that components 1, 2, 3 (Fig. 45) are

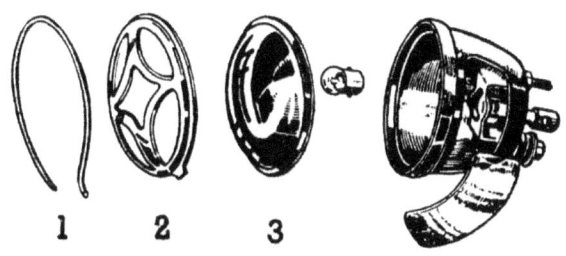

FIG. 45. MILLER 36E TAIL LAMP
1954 250 c.c. "Clippers."

all replaced snugly and securely. It is important to note that the Miller 36E tail lamp is mounted on rubber blocks; consequently an earth wire *must* always be attached to one of the lamp securing-studs.

Miller 37ET Tail Lamp (Early 1955 250 c.c. "Clippers"). To get at the bulb, remove the two screws securing the plastic cover.

Lucas 529 Tail Lamp (Late 1955-8 250 c.c., 350 c.c. "Clippers," 1954-5 Models G, J2). The Lucas 529 tail lamp, (similar to many later types) is shown in Fig. 46. To obtain access to the single-filament bulb, remove the plastic cover after unscrewing its two retaining-screws.

Lucas 525 Stop-Tail Lamp (1954 "Bullets"). To get at the double-filament bulb, remove the two screws securing the plastic cover. The bulb has off-set pins to ensure correct fitting. The 6-watt filament provides the normal rear light, and depressing the rear-brake pedal illuminates the 18-watt filament. Be careful to connect the leads to the lamp correctly. The use of an 18-watt filament for the normal tail-lamp will cause an excessive drain on the battery and perhaps damage the plastic cover through overheating.

Lucas 564 Stop-Tail Lamp (1955-8 "Bullets"). This lamp with double-filament bulb is similar to the 525 stop-tail lamp, but has a reflector formed in the plastic cover. The 525 instructions above apply.

Cleaning Lucas Lamps. The reflector is primarily responsible for good illumination. Therefore never scratch the surface of a detachable reflector during handling, and avoid finger-marking the surface, readily done on the Lucas DU42 and MU42 focusing-type headlamps.

On no account clean the surface of a reflector with metal polish. All Lucas reflectors have a colourless and transparent protective covering.

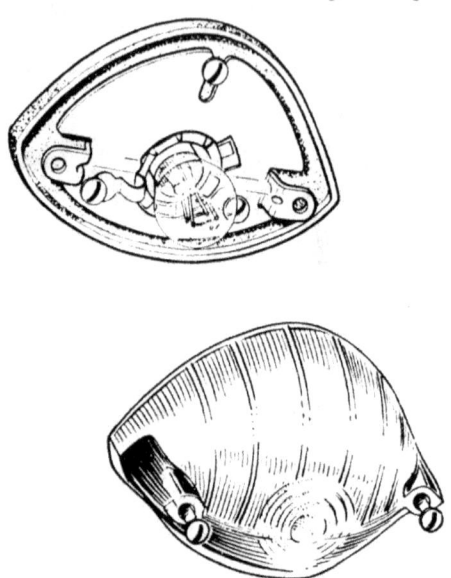

FIG. 46. LUCAS 529 TAIL LAMP
Late 1955-6 "Clippers," 1954–5 Models G, J2.

To remove finger marks from this covering it is quite sufficient to polish the surface gently with a chamois leather or with a clean, *soft*, dry cloth.

Use a good car polish to clean the black surfaces of a lamp shell. Clean all chromium-plated surfaces with a chamois leather or a soft, dry cloth, after first removing any dirt with a cloth moistened with water.

RENEWING BULBS

When fitting a new bulb to a Lucas or Miller headlamp, always see that the renewal bulb is of genuine Lucas or Miller manufacture. These bulbs are specially designed for use in conjunction with reflectors of the same manufacture, and other proprietary bulbs will not necessarily give equally good results. All main double-filament bulbs, except those of the "prefocus" type have a bayonet-type fixing, and the same applies to most pilot and tail-lamp bulbs. Obtaining access to the headlamp and tail-lamp bulbs has already been dealt with in the previous section of this chapter.

CARE OF LIGHTING EQUIPMENT 77

Where a focusing-type double-filament main bulb is concerned it is essential to make quite sure that the bulb is fitted with *the dipped beam filament above the centre filament.* In the focusing-type of headlamp (1946-50 DU42, MU42 and many 1950-2 SSU700P lamps) it is advisable to check the focus of the headlamp (*see* page 74) after fitting a new main bulb. A "pre-focus" main bulb cannot be fitted incorrectly.

Lucas DU42 Headlamp (1946-8). On the DU42 headlamp (Fig. 39) to renew the main or pilot bulb, after removing the lamp front and reflector (*see* page 68), push aside the two securing-clips and remove the bracket which secures the bulb holders to the reflector. The correct renewal bulbs are as follows—
Main bulb: 6-volt, 24/24-watt, double-filament, SBC, Lucas No. 168.
Pilot bulb: 6-volt, 3-watt, single-filament, SCC, Lucas No. 200.

Lucas MU42 Headlamp (1948-50). If a Lucas MU42 headlamp (Fig. 40) is fitted, the correct bulbs for renewal are those stated above for the DU42 headlamp.

Lucas SSU700P, SSU700P/1 Headlamps (1950-4 Models). Where a focusing type SSU700P headlamp without "pre-focus" main bulb (*see* Fig. 41) is fitted, the correct renewal bulbs are—
Main bulb: 6-volt, 30/30-watt, double-filament, SBC, Lucas No. 169.
Pilot bulb: 6-volt, 3-watt, single-filament, SCC, Lucas No. 200.

When renewing the No. 169 main bulb, always replace it correctly in the SSU700P headlamp (*see* page 76). To assist correct replacement, the metal cap is marked "TOP." The bulb holder is secured in position by two spring-loaded pegs and can readily be removed from the rear of the Lucas light-unit after detaching the lamp front and light-unit assembly.

Some 1951 SSU700P and all 1953-4 SSU700P/1 headlamps with underslung pilot light are of the "pre-focus" type (Fig. 42) with no focusing adjustment, and require the following bulbs—
Main bulb: 6-volt, 30/24-watt, double-filament, Lucas No. 312.
Pilot bulb: 6-volt, 3-watt, single-filament, MCC, Lucas No. 988.

The No. 312 "pre-focus" bulb can be readily identified, as it has a broad locating flange on its cap. It can be fitted in its holder in one position only, and cannot be fitted to a focusing type SSU700P headlamp. Referring to Fig. 42, to replace a "pre-focus" bulb, turn the adapter *anti-clockwise*, pull it off, and remove the bulb from the holder in the rear of the reflector. Fit the new bulb (No. 312) in the holder, engage the projections on the inside of the adapter with the slots in the bulb holder, press on the shell, and secure by turning clockwise.

If the underslung pilot-bulb of a Lucas SSU700P/1 "pre-focus" headlamp requires renewing, slide out the metal carrier-plate above the pilot lens, and fit the new bulb (No. 988). See that the plate is pressed firmly home afterwards, or it may work free while riding and cause the pilot light to go out, possibly unnoticed by the rider. Those who dislike underslung pilot-lights are well catered for by various proprietary makes of "dual-lights," which can be readily fitted, one on each side of the headlamp.

Lucas MCF700 Headlamp (1954-8 "Bullets," 1956-8 350 c.c. "Clippers"). To remove the "pre-focus" main bulb, first remove the lamp front, complete with Lucas light-unit assembly (*see* page 69) from the lamp shell in the "casquette" fork head. Then remove the bayonet-fixing adapter as just described for the "pre-focus" SSU700P/1 headlamp, extract the bulb, and fit a new one of the correct type. Instructions for dealing with the twin parking-lamp bulbs in the "casquette" fork head are given on page 69. Suitable bulbs to use are —

Main bulb and twin parking bulbs: as for the SSU700P/1 headlamp (*see* page 77).

Miller Headlamp (1954-5 250 c.c. "Clippers"). After removing the lamp rim, complete with lens and reflector, withdraw the bulb holder (*see* page 71). Note that the bulbs will not light when the bulb holder is removed unless the reflector portion of the holder is first earthed. The correct bulbs for renewal are—

Main bulb: 6-volt, 24/24-watt, double-filament, SBC, (Part No. MI/62/13).

Pilot bulb: 6-volt, 3-watt, single-filament, SBC, (Part No. MI/36/6).

Lucas MCF575 Headlamp (1955-8 250 c.c. "Clippers"). Appropriate instructions for removing the "pre-focus" main bulb, and the parking-light bulb from the MCF575 headlamp (Fig. 44) are given on page 71. The correct renewal bulbs are—

Main bulb and parking-light bulb: as for the SSU700P/1 headlamp (*see* page 77).

Lucas and Miller Tail Lamps (1946-58 Models). Instructions for getting at the bulbs for renewal purposes are given on pages 74-5. It is important to note that the law now requires that on all motor-cycles the minimum wattage of a single-filament tail-lamp bulb, or the tail-lamp filament of a double-filament bulb used on a stop-tail lamp, shall be 6-watt. Hitherto 3-watt bulbs have been extensively used. Suitable tail lamp bulbs are—

LUCAS MT110, 480 TAIL LAMPS: 6-volt, 6-watt, single-filament, SCC, Lucas No. 205 (3-watt equivalent: Lucas No. 200).

MILLER 36E, 37ET TAIL LAMPS: 6-volt, 6-watt, single-filament, SCC.

LUCAS 529 TAIL LAMP: 6-volt, 6-watt, single-filament, MCC, Lucas No. 951.

LUCAS 525, 564 STOP-TAIL LAMPS: 6-volt, 6/18-watt, double-filament, SBC, Lucas No. 383.

Sidecar Wing Lamp. The lamp facing forward on the wing of a sidecar outfit generally requires a 6-volt, 3-watt, single-filament SCC bulb such as the Lucas No. 200.

CARE OF LIGHTING EQUIPMENT

Speedometer Light. The bulb holder is accessible when the knurled ring is unscrewed. Fit a 6-volt, 1·8-watt (0.3 amp) MBC bulb.

Ignition Warning Light (250 c.c. "Clippers"). To effect a bulb replacement on a coil-ignition model, withdraw the ammeter (*see* page 71) and fit a 2·5-volt, 0·3 amp bulb.

THE ELECTRIC HORN

No adjustment is normally desirable to the electric horn (except perhaps very occasionally a tone adjustment) after the initial works adjustment.

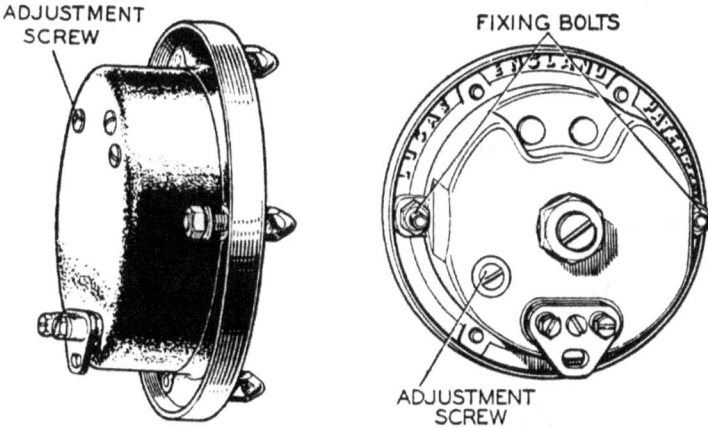

FIG. 47. REAR VIEW OF (LEFT 1946–51 AND (RIGHT) 1952–7 LUCAS TYPE HF1234 ELECTRIC HORNS, SHOWING POSITION OF TONE ADJUSTMENT-SCREWS

A Clear Hooters horn is fitted to the "Clipper" models, and a Lucas HF1234 to most other Royal Enfields. A faulty horn is best returned to a service depot for inspection and overhaul. Note that an uncertain horn action resulting in a choking sound or complete failure to vibrate does not necessarily mean that the horn itself is defective. It is possible that a short-circuit has occurred in the wiring of the horn, a connexion is loose, the horn-push bracket makes poor electrical contact with the handlebars, or the battery is badly discharged. The vibration of some part close to the horn can also upset the action of the horn diaphragm.

Tone Adjustment on Lucas Horns. On a few Lucas type HF1234 horns produced during 1950-1 no tone-adjustment screw was fitted, but on all other Lucas type HF1234 horns an adjustment screw is provided as shown in Fig. 47. If the performance of a horn deteriorates (roughness of tone and loss of power) the following tone adjustment can be effected. Depress the horn-push and turn the adjustment screw *anti-clockwise* until the horn

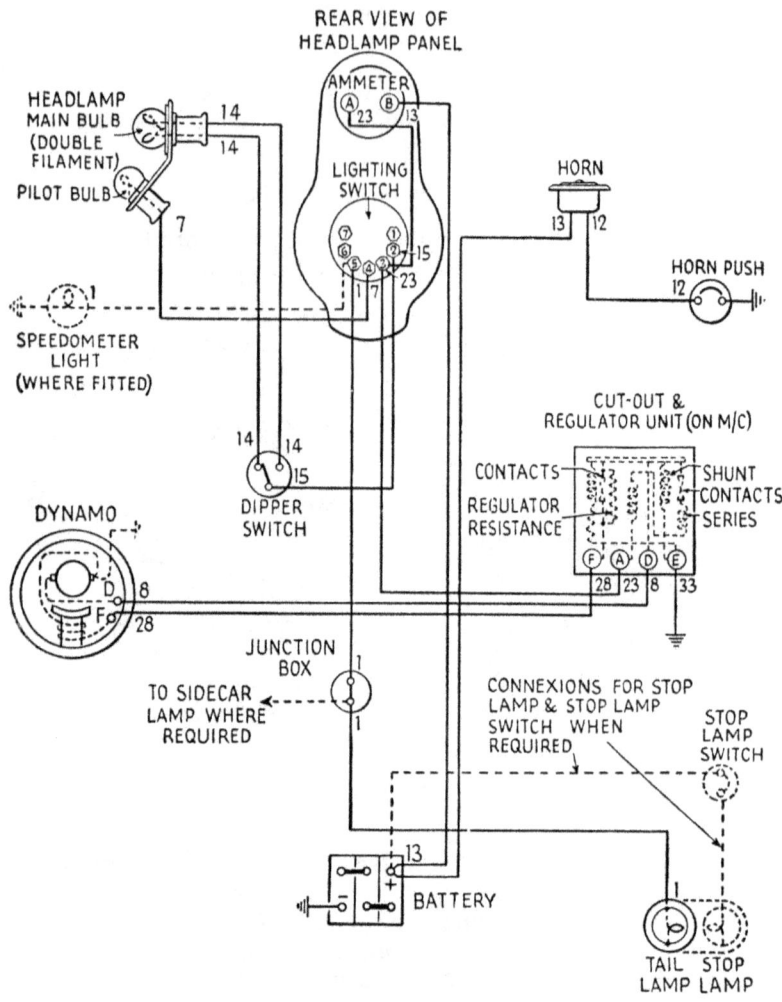

FIG. 48. WIRING DIAGRAM FOR LUCAS "MAGDYNO" LIGHTING EQUIPMENT (1946-52 MODELS)

Applies to machines having a "negative earth" system, and a Lucas DU42, MU42, or SSU700P headlamp.

KEY TO CABLE COLOURS

1. Red. 7. Red and black. 8. Yellow. 12. Yellow and purple. 13. Yellow and black. 14. Blue. 15. Blue and white. 23. White and purple 28. Green and black. 33. Black.

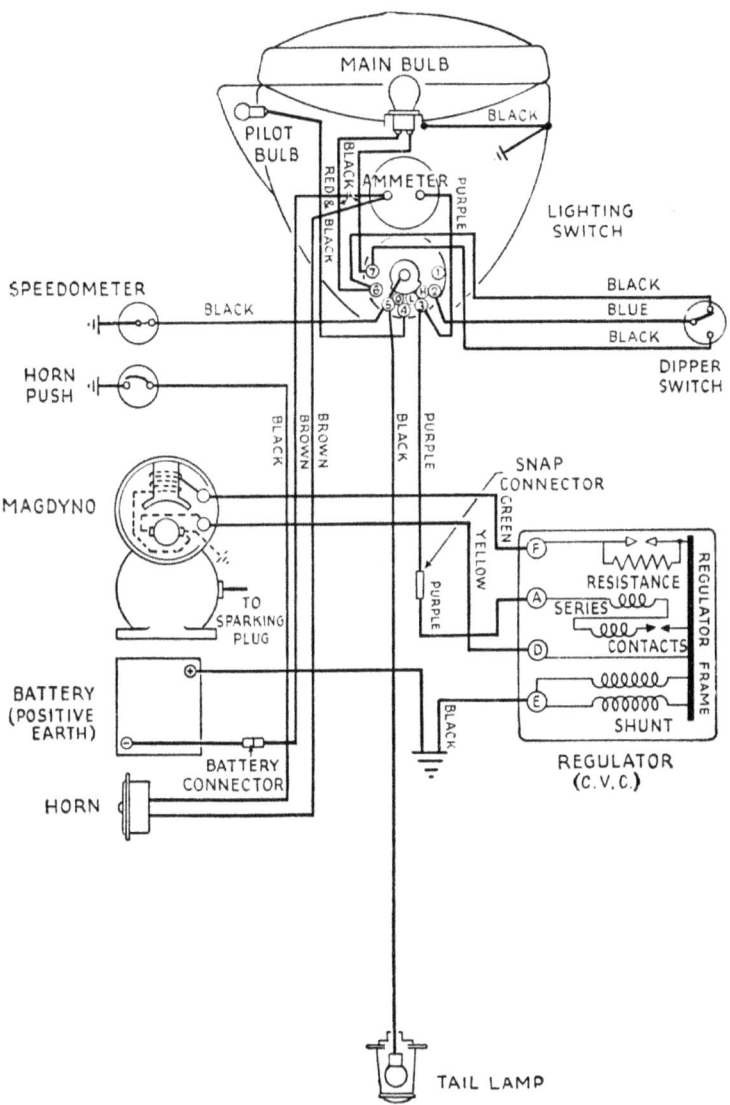

Fig. 49. Wiring Diagram for Lucas "Magdyno" Lighting Equipment (1953-4 Models Except "Bullets," "Clippers")

Applies to 1953-4 machines having a "positive earth" system and a Lucas SSU700P/1 headlamp. Should a stop-tail lamp be fitted, the lead for the stop-light filament should be connected to the battery negative-terminal (with brake switch interposed).

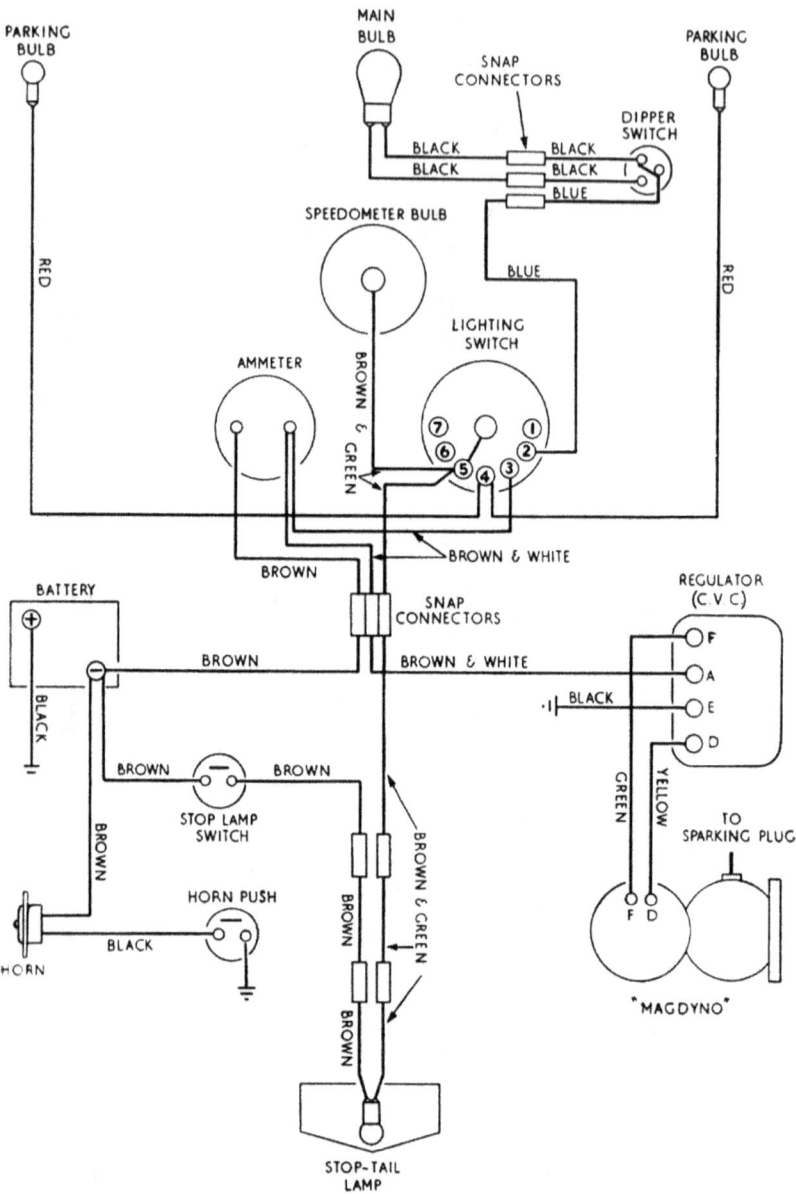

FIG. 50. WIRING DIAGRAM FOR LUCAS "MAGDYNO" LIGHTING EQUIPMENT (1954-5 "BULLETS," 1956-7 350 C.C. "CLIPPERS")

Applies to machines having a "positive earth" system and a Lucas MCF700 headlamp (and twin parking lamps) built into the "casquette" fork head.

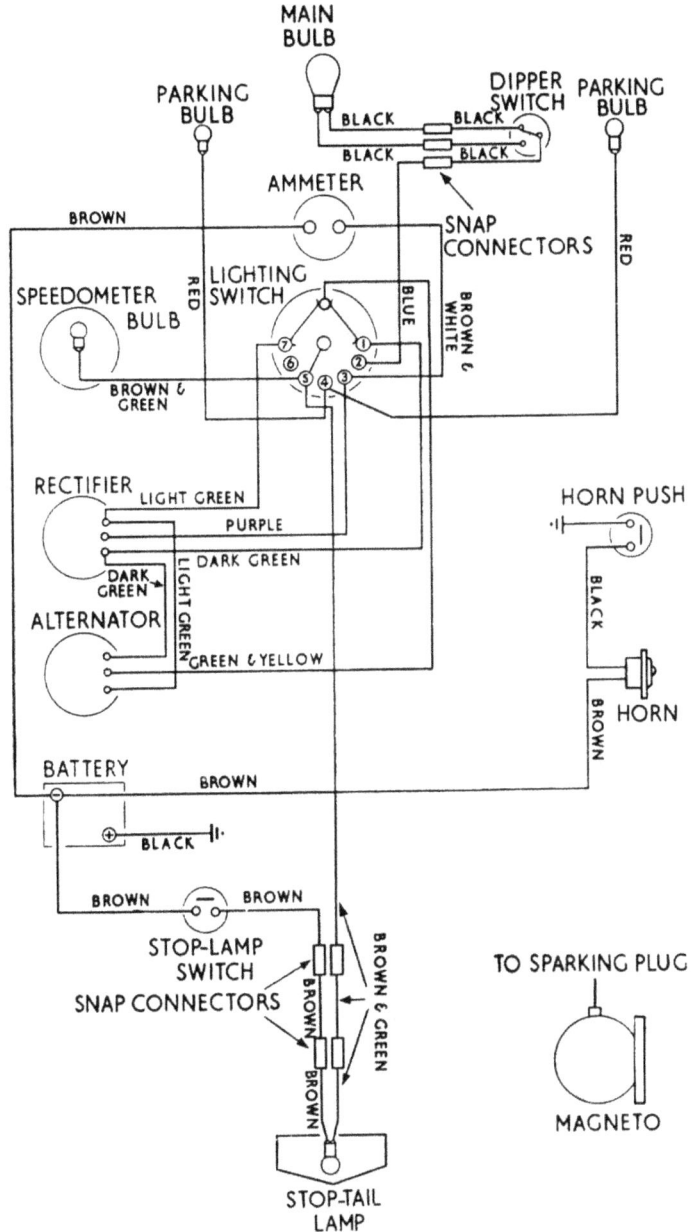

Fig. 51. Wiring Diagram for Lucas Rectifier Lighting and Magneto-ignition Equipment (1956-8 350, 500 c.c. "Bullets")

Applies to "Bullets" having a Lucas (RM14) alternator, separate SR-1 rotating-magnet magneto, MCF700 headlamp, and "positive earth."

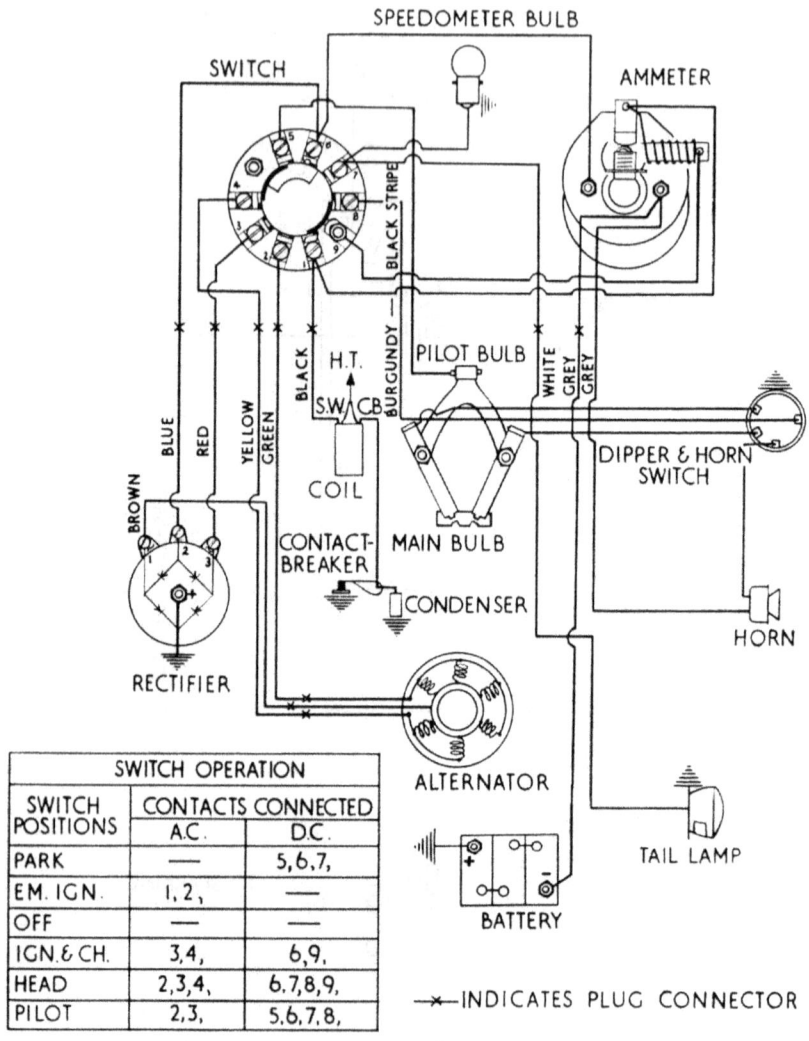

Fig. 52. Wiring Diagram for Miller Rectifier Lighting and Coil-ignition Equipment (1954–5 250 c.c. "Clippers")
Applies to coil-ignition machines having a "positive earth" system and a Miller headlamp built into the "casquette" fork head.

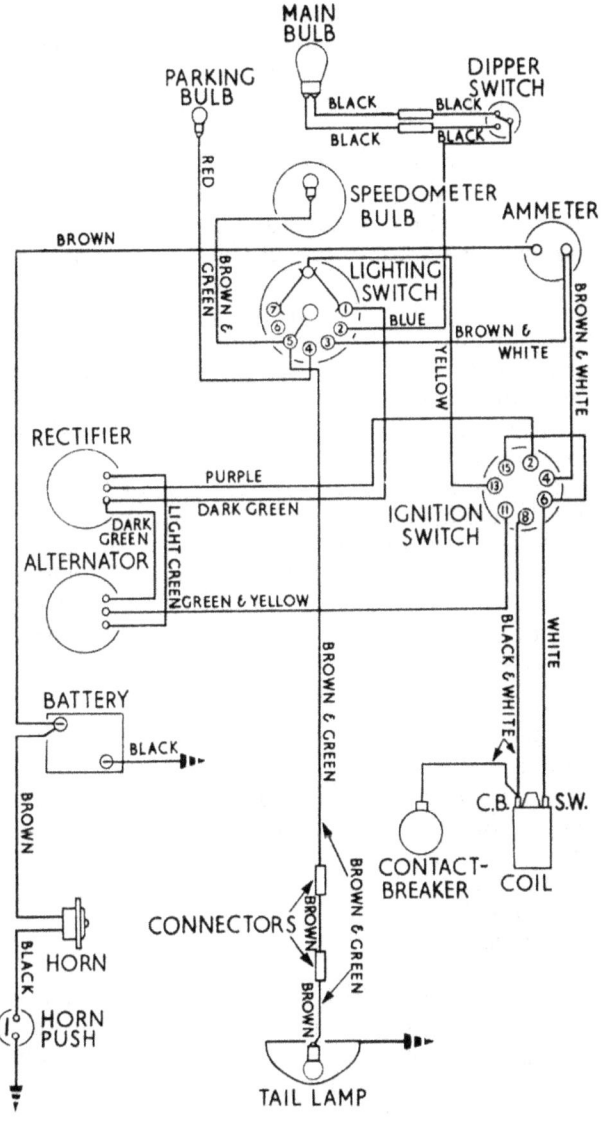

FIG. 53. WIRING DIAGRAM FOR LUCAS RECTIFIER LIGHTING AND COIL-IGNITION EQUIPMENT (1955-8 250 c.c. "CLIPPERS")

Applies to all coil-ignition machines having a "positive earth" system and a Lucas MCF575 headlamp built into the "casquette" fork head.

just fails to sound. Release the horn-push and turn the adjustment screw *clockwise* for six notches (i.e. a quarter of a turn), when the original performance of the horn should be restored, assuming no serious fault exists. If further adjustment is needed, turn the screw *clockwise* one notch at a time.

WIRING OF THE EQUIPMENT

Inspect the braided wiring-harness occasionally and see that no chafing of any of the leads is taking place. Tape up with insulation tape where necessary and make good use of rubber clips (obtainable from accessory firms).

Before you make any alterations to the wiring, or remove the lighting switch, always disconnect the appropriate lead (*see* page 56) from the battery. All cables to the DU42, MU42, SSU700P, SSU700P/1 headlamps are taken direct to the switch which, together with the ammeter, is incorporated in a small panel which can be withdrawn when its three retaining-screws are removed.

The lighting cables can be readily identified by their coloured, braided insulation, by coloured plastic insulation, or by coloured sleevings. The colour schemes used and diagrams of connexions are given in the six wiring diagrams (Figs. 48-53). When making a connexion to the switch, bare about $\frac{3}{8}$ in. of the cable, twist the wire strands together, and turn back about $\frac{1}{8}$ in. Remove the grub-screw from the appropriate terminal and insert the wire in the terminal post. Replace and tighten the grub-screw.

Diagnosing Ignition Trouble ("Magdyno," Magneto, and Coil Models). The symptoms of ignition trouble vary. The engine may be hard to start, run irregularly, or cut right out. To diagnose the exact trouble, use a process of elimination. First check that the h.t. lead to the plug is properly connected at *both* ends and that there is no shorting due to its insulation being damaged or burned. Verify that the external insulation of the plug and h.t. lead are not wet. On coil-ignition models inspect the connexions to the alternator, rectifier, battery, contact-breaker, and coil. See that *all* connexions are sound.

If you find the above-mentioned points are in order, remove the sparking plug and test it by holding the plug body in contact with the cylinder head and kicking over the engine. A good spark should be observed (and a "click" heard). On coil-ignition models do not forget to switch on the ignition before testing the plug. If a good spark is present, the ignition system is in order. If no spark at all, or a poor spark, is obtained, test the h.t. lead (*see* page 96). If a good spark is obtained from the end of the h.t. lead, the sparking plug *must* be at fault. Inspect it carefully. If the electrode points are burned and irregular, fit a new plug of the correct type (page 92). If the plug is dirty or oiled-up, dismantle and clean it thoroughly (page 94). See that the gap is correct (page 93).

CARE OF LIGHTING EQUIPMENT

Where the sparking plug is in sound condition and a poor spark, or no spark at all, is obtained at the plug *and* the end of the h.t. lead, suspect a faulty contact-breaker. See that the points are clean and that their gap is correct (page 93). On "Magdyno" models examine the h.t. pick-up (page 102), and on coil-ignition models switch on the lamps and note the intensity of illumination. A badly discharged battery affects the ignition adversely. In this instance, turn the ignition switch to the "emergency ignition" position (*see* page 4).

CHAPTER V

GENERAL MAINTENANCE

ALL ESSENTIAL INFORMATION concerning the routine maintenance dismantling, and assembling of 1946-58 single-cylinder four-stroke Royal Enfields is included in this chapter. Attend to maintenance regularly, and do not wait until the machine "calls out" for attention! To enable you to turn quickly to the specific instructions you need, this chapter has been subdivided into a number of main sections. All detailed references to carburation, lubrication, and the lighting system have been omitted, as these subjects have already been fully covered in Chapters II to IV.

Spares and Repairs. Should you have occasion to forward or deliver any parts to the Service Dept. of The Enfield Cycle Company, Ltd., or to an appointed dealer, do not forget to attach to each part a label bearing clearly your *full name and address*. To ensure prompt attention it is advisable to keep correspondence concerning technical advice and repairs on *separate* sheets. To facilitate identification of a part or unit, always quote the year of manufacture and the model (e.g., 1955 Model J2), also the engine or frame number (*see* page 2), according to which applies.

Note that useful illustrated spares lists are obtainable from the makers or from appointed spares stockists. Widely distributed throughout the United Kingdom are numerous stockists who maintain a comprehensive stock of Royal Enfield spares; many of them undertake general servicing and repair work. In the London area the largest and best known Royal Enfield specialists are E. S. Motors, Ltd., of 325 High Road, Chiswick, W.4 (Phone: Chiswick 2246); this firm (which undertakes repairs and supplies new and second-hand machines) has a spares per return C.O.D. service. Among other London spares stockists may be mentioned: Marble Arch Motor Supplies, Ltd.; Kays of Ealing, Ltd.; Claude Rye, Ltd.; Gander & Gray; and Young's.

Useful Accessory Firms. Among large accessory firms (some of which have branches throughout the U.K.) handling motor-cycle accessories, equipment, proprietary spares, tools, clothing, etc. may be mentioned: Marble Arch Motor Supplies, Ltd.; E. S. Motors, Ltd.; The Halford Cycle Co., Ltd.; Whitbys of Acton, Ltd.; James Grose, Ltd.; Claude Rye, Ltd.; George Grose, Ltd.; Kays of Ealing, Ltd.; Pride & Clarke, Ltd.; and Turner's Stores.

Items Needed for Maintenance. Some items, in addition to the standard tool kit (*see* Fig. 54), will be needed for maintenance, and they should be kept handy in the lock-up or garage. These include: a can of paraffin for cleaning purposes; a stiff brush for scouring dirt from beneath the crankcase and gearbox; a tin of suitable engine oil for the engine and gearbox (*see* page 36); a small funnel for topping-up the oil tank and gearbox; a canister of grease for replenishing the grease gun (*see* page 50); a large drip-tray for placing beneath the engine (also necessary when draining the oil tank and sump); a medium-size galvanized pail for washing parts with paraffin; some non-fluffy rags; a fairly broad, blunt screwdriver for chipping off carbon deposits; a tin of valve-grinding paste such as Richford's (coarse and fine); a set of engine gaskets. You should also have available: a pair of new gudgeon-pin circlips; a small pair of snipe-nose pliers (for removing and fitting circlips); a pair of medium-size cutting pliers; a good make of adjustable spanner; a six-inch steel rule; a small electrical screwdriver; a valve-spring compressor (*see* page 121) for removing the valves; a suction-type valve grinding tool (*see* page 121). A gudgeon-pin extractor may also prove very useful (*see* page 116), and it is desirable to obtain a wire brush for cleaning the sparking plug, and a set of feeler gauges for checking tappet clearances, plug gap, etc., also a plug regapping tool (*see* page 93).

For the maintenance of the motor-cycle parts you should obtain: a tyre-pressure gauge (such as the Dunlop pencil type No. 6, the Romac, the Schrader No. 7750, or the Holdtite), a box of spare chain-links; a chain-rivet extractor; an extractor for the clutch centre (*see* page 138); a Lucas battery filler (*see* page 64); a hydrometer for occasionally checking the specific gravity of the battery electrolyte (*see* page 65); a chamois leather; a couple of sponges and a pail (if a hose is not available) for washing down; some soft dusters (preferably of the Selvyt type); a tin of good wax or other polish for the enamelled parts; and a tin of really good hand cleanser.

Tools for Repair Work. If you wish to do as much repair work as possible, apart from routine general maintenance, stripping-down and assembly, it is desirable to rig up a suitable bench, complete with vice, and to buy some extra tools.

To begin with, it is a good plan to buy a medium-weight hammer, a mallet, a hand-drill and a few twist-drills, a small hack-saw, a centre-punch, some large and small (smooth and rough) files, a rifler (for ports) and a good soldering outfit for the repair of control cables. Repair work, however, is beyond the scope of this handbook, and you require some appreciable technical knowledge and skill in handling tools.

If rebushing of the engine and other components is undertaken, this will involve the use of suitable extractors, punches, etc. A number of Royal Enfield special service tools are obtainable, and details of these

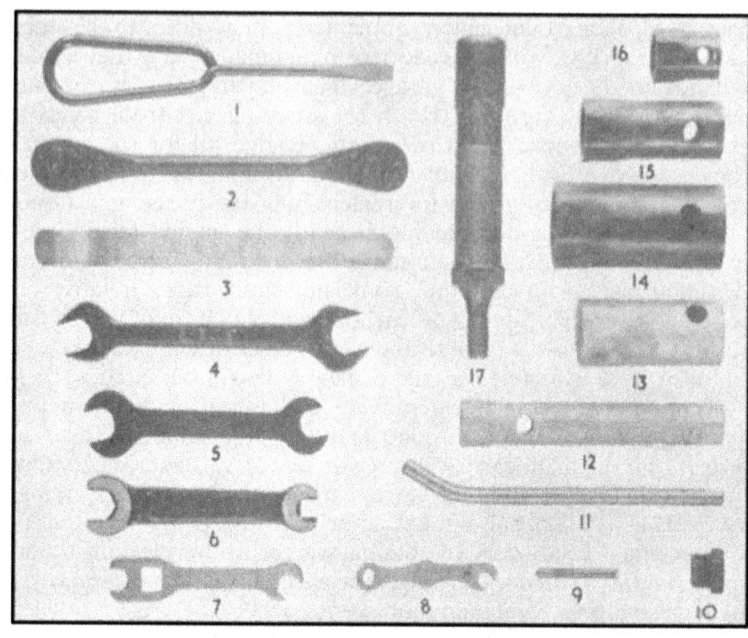

FIG. 54. THE ROYAL ENFIELD TOOL KIT

The kit shown (supplied with each new machine)* applies to the 1949-58 "Bullet" and "Clipper" models; it also applies to the 1946-55 Models G, J, J2, except that box spanners 12 and 16 are replaced by box spanners $0\cdot801$ in. $\times$ $0\cdot709$ in. hex., and $\frac{3}{16}$ in. W. respectively; an additional $\frac{1}{4}$ in. W. box spanner is also included. There is also a key for steering-head wedge bolt (not shown) required on 1954-8 "Bullets" and "Clippers." A valve-spring compressor and a valve grinding tool (see Fig. 73) are obtainable as extras, and the same applies to the useful service-tool shown in Fig. 69.

1. All-metal screwdriver.
2. Tyre lever.
3. Tyre lever.
4. Double-ended spanner ($\frac{1}{4}$ in. $\times$ $\frac{5}{16}$ in. W.) for tappets, etc.
5. Double-ended spanner ($\frac{3}{16}$ in. $\times$ $\frac{1}{4}$ in. W.) for tappets, etc.
6. Combination general-purpose spanner.
7. Double-ended spanner ($0\cdot380$ in. $\times$ $0\cdot343$ in. hex.) for pipe unions, etc.
8. Contact-breaker spanner, with $0\cdot012$ in. feeler gauge.
9. Key for Schrader valve "inside."
10. Extractor for pinion on contact-breaker or magneto shaft.
11. Tommy bar (bent).
12. General-purpose box spanner ($\frac{1}{4}$ in. $\times$ $\frac{5}{16}$ in. W.).
13. Box spanner ($\frac{1}{2}$ in. W.) for rear-wheel spindle nuts, etc.
14. Box spanner ($\frac{1}{16}$ in. W.) for steering-head bearing adjuster-nut.
15. Sparking plug spanner ($\frac{7}{16}$ in. W.).
16. Box spanner ($\frac{3}{8}$ in. W.) for gearbox top and bottom bolts, etc.
17. Tecalemit grease gun.

* The makers reserve the right to delete or add tools to the kit supplied with each new machine, as they think fit.

GENERAL MAINTENANCE 91

tools can be had from the makers or from any large Royal Enfield spares stockist.

Keep Your Machine Clean. Regular cleaning pays good dividends and a clean motor-cycle always delights the eye. If a habit is formed of allowing a machine to go dirty, defects are liable to pass unnoticed, rust will inevitably occur, performance may suffer and depreciation will accelerate rapidly. Never leave your Royal Enfield soaking wet overnight. If you have no time for cleaning in wet weather, grease the machine all over *before* use.

Cleaning the Engine and Gearbox. See that the cylinder barrel and cylinder-head fins are kept clean and black. If the enamel has worn away (cast-iron fins only), paint the fins with some proprietary cylinder black after thorough cleaning with a stiff brush dipped in paraffin. Note that rusted fins, besides looking shabby, cause an appreciable loss in heat dispersion.

Scour off all filth from the lower part of the engine and gearbox with stiff brushes and paraffin. Clean all aluminium-alloy and bright surfaces with a rag damped in paraffin, assisted by brushes where necessary. When dismantling, clean all parts with paraffin and lay on a clean sheet of paper.

Cleaning Enamelled Parts. Never attempt to remove mud from the enamelled parts when dry and caked, as this is likely to damage the surfaces. Soak the mud off with a hose if available. With a very dirty machine it may be advisable to paint the surfaces over with a cleaning compound such as "Gunk" before directing a stream of water on to the dirty surfaces. Be careful not to allow any water to get inside vulnerable parts such as the "Magdyno," contact-breaker, rectifier, or carburettor. If a hose is not available, soak the mud and then disperse it with plenty of clean water, using a sponge and pail.

Having removed all dirt, dry the enamelled surfaces with a chamois leather and afterwards polish them with soft dusters and some good wax polish or a proprietary polish such as "Karpol."

"Dry weather" riders can keep a machine in almost showroom condition merely by rubbing the enamel over with a paraffin-damped rag, followed by a dry, soft duster.

Cleaning Chromium Surfaces. Never employ liquid metal-polish or paste, as this will wear down the thin surface. A good chromium-cleaning compound can, however, safely be used, though too frequent use is not desirable. The normal method of removing tarnish (salt deposits) is to clean the surfaces regularly with a damp chamois-leather and then polish them with soft dusters.

To Reduce Tarnishing. During the winter months it is a good plan to wipe over occasionally all surfaces with a soft cloth soaked in a proprietary anti-tarnish preparation. An example is "Tekall," obtainable in $\frac{1}{2}$ pint and 1 pint tins.

Check Nuts Regularly for Tightness. This is particularly important during running-in (*see* page 14), as some "bedding down" of parts occurs. Regularly apply spanners to the various external nuts to ensure tightness, paying special attention to the engine bolts and nuts, the engine mounting nuts, pipe unions, and oil plugs. After running-in, make a regular check once a month, but after decarbonizing and running for a short mileage, check the cylinder-head nuts for tightness.

Carburettor Maintenance and Tuning. For detailed instructions, *see* Chapter II.

Lubrication. Detailed instructions for the lubrication of 1946 and later models are given in Chapter III, and the lubrication chart on page 25 shows when and where the application of grease or oil is required.

CARE OF THE IGNITION SYSTEM

In this section the alternator and battery (used for lighting and ignition on the 1954-8 coil-ignition "Clippers") are not dealt with, these components having already been covered in Chapter IV which discusses the lighting system. The ignition switch and warning light on coil-ignition models are referred to on pages 4-5.

Recommended Sparking Plugs. To ensure easy starting, a cool-running engine and good all-round performance, it is essential always to run on a type of sparking plug recommended by the engine manufacturers. Three reliable and recommended makes are the Lodge, the K.L.G., and the Champion. Suitable types are as follows—

ALL EXCEPT 500 C.C. "BULLET" ENGINES. On the 1946-55 Models G, J, J2, and on the 1954-8 250 c.c. and 350 c.c. "Clipper" engines, you are recommended to fit a 14 mm. ($\frac{1}{2}$ in. reach) detachable-type Lodge H14 or a K.L.G. F70 or PF70 (platinum-pointed) sparking plug, or alternatively a Champion L7 plug.   350 c.c. "Bullets": as above.

500 C.C. "BULLET" ENGINES. On the 1949-58 500 c.c. "Bullet" engines recommended plugs to fit are a 14 mm. ($\frac{3}{4}$ in. reach) non-detachable type Lodge H-LN or Champion N5 sparking plug, or a detachable-type K.L.G. FE80 plug.

For regular bad-weather riding it is very advisable to fit a weatherproof terminal cover or to fit a watertight plug corresponding to the appropriate non-watertight plug recommended above. If your machine was registered before 2nd July, 1953, it is legally necessary to fit an "ignition-suppression" type plug, or a terminal cover with built-in suppressor, so as not to cause inconvenience to users of wireless and television sets. It is socially desirable to do this anyway. Note that "suppressor" type plugs have longer wearing electrodes.

The Sparking Plug Gap. Difficult starting or occasional misfiring can usually be traced to a dirty or unserviceable sparking plug. The life of a good plug is considerable, but the points of the electrodes gradually burn away and eventually the gap becomes too large and it is necessary to reset the points.

It is advisable to check the plug gap regularly (say every 2,500 miles) and to adjust the gap if burning of the points has caused the gap to exceed

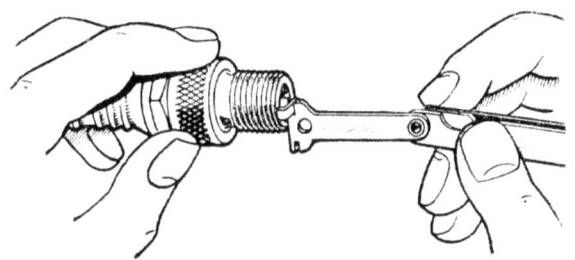

FIG. 55. A SAFE METHOD OF RE-GAPPING A PLUG
The Champion tool shown includes suitable gauges.

0·022 in. The Enfield Cycle Company, Ltd. recommend a gap of 0·018-0·022 in. (0·020 in.-0·030 in.* on coil-ignition models). For obvious reasons, when re-gapping it is advisable to set the gap at or near the *bottom* limit. Check the gap with a suitable feeler gauge. The gauge should just enter without springing the points.

When adjusting the plug gap, never attempt to bend or tap the centre electrode. Use a pair of snipe-nose pliers, or a plug regapping tool (shown in Fig. 55), to bend the outside (earth) electrode(s). Tapping the earth electrode(s) is not a good method. When the plug has to be thoroughly cleaned, this should be done as described below, and the plug re-gapped *afterwards*.

Cleaning the Plug. If carburation is correct and excessive oil is not entering the combustion chamber, it should not be necessary to dismantle and clean the sparking plug thoroughly more often than once about every

* On coil-ignition models the plug gap can often be safely increased to as much as 0·035 in., the limit being set by possible misfiring at high speeds. Where an "ignition-suppression" type plug or terminal cover is fitted, the plug-gap should be not less than 0·025 in. This applies to both coil- and magneto-ignition models.

3,000 miles. When running-in a new or rebored engine, it is advisable to remove and check the plug for cleanliness at intervals of about 500 miles.

Quick cleaning of a plug can be done by brushing the points and slightly rubbing their firing sides with smooth emergy-cloth. Alternatively the plug

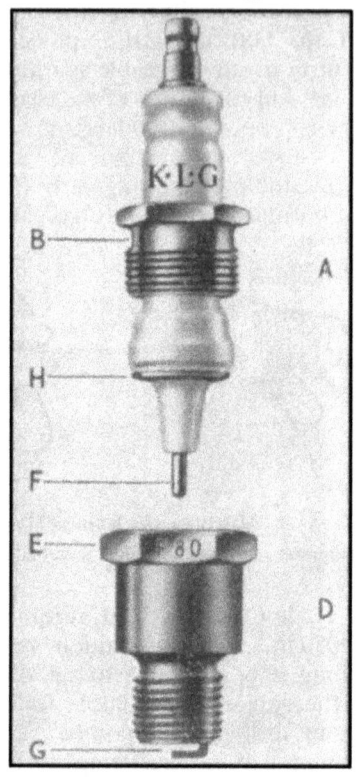

FIG. 56. DETACHABLE-TYPE SPARKING PLUG (K.L.G.) DISMANTLED FOR THOROUGH CLEANING

The gland nut *B* and the internal washer *H* are shown still in position on the insulation.

can be cleaned with a proprietary gadget. Thorough cleaning (internal and external), however, is not possible without dismantling the plug.

To Clean K.L.G. and Lodge Plugs Thoroughly. Fig. 56 shows a typical detachable type (K.L.G.) sparking plug dismantled for thorough cleaning. To dismantle a detachable-type sparking plug, hold the smaller hexagon of the gland nut *B* lightly in a vice or with a suitable spanner. If you use a vice, be most careful not to exert any pressure on the hexagon faces. Then with a suitable box spanner applied to the larger hexagon *E* of the plug body, unscrew the body until it is separated from the gland nut.* The centre electrode F with its insulation (comprising the insulated electrode assembly A) can now be detached from the gland nut. Take care not to lose the internal sealing washer H.

To clean the insulation, wipe it clean with a cloth soaked in petrol or paraffin. If the insulation is coated with hard-carbon deposits, remove these with some fine emery-cloth, but make no attempt to scrape off the deposits. The internal sealing washer H and the surfaces on the insulator, and in the metal body on which this washer rests, are very important as they prevent gas leakage through the plug. Therefore wipe them only with a rag soaked in petrol or paraffin. Any damage caused while dismantling will render the plug unserviceable.

To clean the metal parts (plug body and gland nut) wipe them clean with petrol, or, if necessary, scrape off the deposits with a small knife, or use a wire brush. Afterwards rinse the parts in petrol. The gland nut seldom gets very fouled, but the inside of the plug body may be very dirty, and the same may apply to the external threads of the plug. Clean and polish the points of the centre and outside (earth) electrodes F and G (Fig. 56) with some fine emery-cloth.

See that there is no dirt or grit lodged between the body of the plug and the insulation, and particularly on the internal sealing washer and the contacting faces. Smear a little thin oil on the internal washer and make sure that it seats properly. When assembling the sparking plug, see that the centre electrode and insulation are positioned centrally in the body bore. If they are not, remove, re-position by rotating assembly A a quarter of a turn, and reassemble. Do not attempt to force it into position or bend it.

Avoid excessive tightening of the gland nut B. Finally verify that the plug gap is correct (*see* page 93).

Cleaning Champion Plugs. To clean a non-detachable type Champion plug, take it to the nearest garage equipped with a Champion Service Unit. With this apparatus the plug can be cleaned of all deposits in a few minutes, washed, subjected to a high-pressure air line, and afterwards tested for sparking on the Champion apparatus at an air pressure of over 100 lb per sq in.

Replacing the Plug. Before replacing a plug, renew the copper washer if it is worn or flattened, and clean the plug threads with a wire brush. Screw the plug home by hand as far as possible, and always use the box spanner shown at 15 in Fig. 54 for final tightening.

* Where a detachable-type sparking plug has been in service for a very considerable time, the plug may be found extremely difficult to dismantle, in which case the attempt should be abandoned.

Lubrication of "Magdyno," Magneto, or Contact-breaker. For appropriate instructions, *see* Chapter III, pages 45–6.

Testing The Plug and H.T. Lead. The usual method of testing for h.t. current at the plug terminal is to bridge the terminal and the cylinder head with the steel blade of a *wooden-handled* screwdriver, when a spark should be visible on rotating the engine. To test the plug itself, remove it with the h.t. lead attached, clean it, lay it on the cylinder (with the terminal clear of the head) and ascertain whether it sparks satisfactorily with the

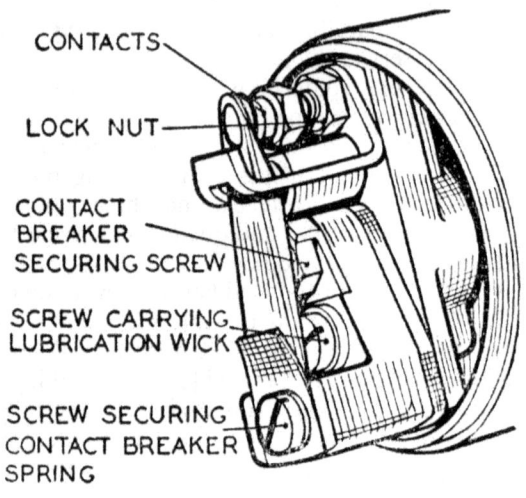

Fig. 57. The Face-cam Type Contact-breaker on the Lucas "Magdyno" (1946 Onwards)

engine rotated with the kick-starter. In daylight the spark is not bright, but it should be distinctly heard.

Lucas "Magdyno" Contact-breaker Gap (1946-55 Models G, J, J2; 1949-55 "Bullets," 1956-7 350 c.c. "Clipper"). Little attention to the ignition portion of the Lucas "Magdyno" is needed, other than occasional lubrication (*see* page 45) and attention to the face-cam type contact-breaker, shown in Fig. 57. Any serious internal trouble should be dealt with by a Lucas service agent.

The contacts of the contact-breaker (Fig. 57) should be examined on a new machine after the first 500 miles, and subsequently about every 3,000 miles. If the "break," with the contacts full open is appreciably more, or less, than will just hold a 0·012 in.–0·015 in. blade of a feeler gauge the contacts should be adjusted (*after* cleaning, if necessary). Too great a gap will advance the timing. The magneto-spanner gauge (shown at 8 in Fig. 54), or the blade of a proprietary set of feelers, can be useful for checking the "break," the procedure for which is as follows—

1. Remove the contact-breaker cover and rotate the engine slowly forwards until the contacts of the contact-breaker are wide open (i.e. near T.D.C. on the compression stroke).
2. Insert the blade of the feeler gauge between the contacts.
3. If the feeler gauge *just* slides in without friction, the gap is correct and no adjustment is needed. If the gauge is a slack fit or the contacts have to be sprung to enable it to enter, adjust the gap as below.
4. With the magneto spanner loosen the lock-nut which secures the

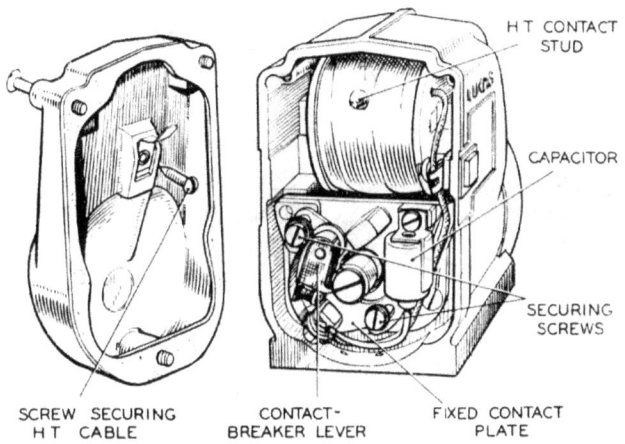

Fig. 58. THE LUCAS SR-1 ROTATING-MAGNET MAGNETO WITH COVER REMOVED TO SHOW CONTACT-BREAKER, ETC.
Applies to all 1956–8 "Bullet" models.

adjustable-contact screw (*see* Fig. 57) and then adjust this screw by means of its hexagon head until the correct gap is obtained between the fixed and movable contacts.

5. Retighten the contact screw lock-nut and again check the gap. If correct, replace the contact-breaker cover.

Lucas SR-1 Magneto Contact-breaker Gap (1956–8 "Bullets"). On 1956–8 350, 500 c.c. "Bullets" (with independent rectifier lighting and magneto ignition) remove every 3,000 miles (also after the first 400 miles) the moulded cover from the Lucas rotating-magnet magneto (*see* Fig. 58) and check the contact-breaker gap with a suitable feeler gauge. The gap between the contacts, with the engine turned so that they are fully open, should be 0·010 in.–0·012 in. (0·25–0·3 mm), and the gauge should be a sliding fit. If the contact-breaker gap varies appreciably from the

correct gap, an adjustment is necessary. Referring to Fig. 58, this should be effected as follows—
1. Turn the engine so that the maximum gap is obtained.
2. Loosen the two securing screws.

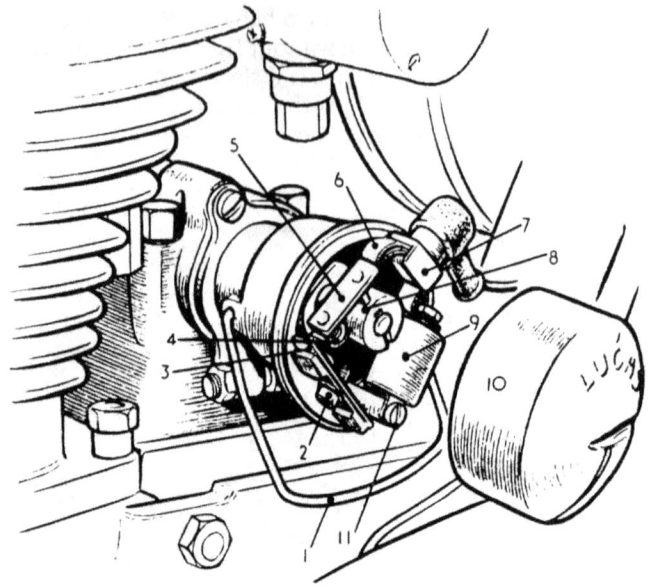

FIG. 59. THE LUCAS 15D1 CONTACT-BREAKER UNIT (1955–8 250 c.c., 1958 350 c.c. COIL-IGNITION "CLIPPERS")

1. Cover retaining-spring
2. Screw securing 3
3. Fixed-contact plate
4. Contacts
5. Spring arm
6. Spring on 5
7. Nylon block
8. Cam
9. Condenser
10. Metal cover
11. Screw securing 9

(*By courtesy of "Motor Cycling"*)

3. Position the fixed contact plate to give the correct gap.
4. Retighten the two securing screws, and again check the gap.

Lucas 15D1 Contact-breaker Gap (1955–8 250 c.c., 1958 350 c.c. "Clippers"). On 1955–8 250, 350 c.c. "Clippers" with rectifier lighting and coil-ignition equipment, check the contact-breaker gap after the first 500 miles and subsequently at intervals of about 3,000 miles. Referring to Fig. 59, prise aside the retaining spring 1 and remove the metal cover 10 from the contact-breaker. Check the gap between the contacts 4 with a suitable gauge. The correct gap is 0·014 in.–0·016 in., and the

gauge should be a sliding fit when the engine is turned so that the gap is at its maximum. If an adjustment is needed, effect this as follows—
1. Slowly rotate the engine until the gap is at its maximum.
2. Loosen the screw 2 at the side of the fixed-contact plate 3.
3. Slide the fixed-contact plate endwise on its (outer) support plate (which has a slotted hole for screw 2) until the correct gap is obtained.
4. Retighten screw 2 and again check the contact gap.

Miller Contact-breaker Gap (1954-5 250 c.c. "Clippers"). On the 1954 and early 1955 250 c.c. "Clipper" models with Miller rectifier-lighting and coil-ignition equipment, check the contact-breaker gap every 3,000 miles. Push aside the spring blade and remove the metal cover from the contact-breaker. Then check the gap between the contacts with a suitable feeler gauge. The gap should be 0·015-0·018 in., and the feeler should be inserted with the engine turned so that the contacts are wide open. If required, an adjustment can be readily made. Referring to Fig. 60, slacken the screw which passes through the elongated hole 3 in the fixed-contact plate, and move the plate radially about the spring arm pivot-post until the correct gap between the fixed and moving contacts (4 and 6) is obtained. Afterwards be sure to retighten the screw securely and again check the gap.

Cleaning the Contact-breaker Contacts. At intervals of about 3,000 miles, when checking the contact-breaker gap, scrutinize the contacts closely. If the contacts are allowed to become dirty or oily, rapid burning, pitting, and consequent ignition-trouble will ensue.

If inspection reveals that the contacts have a *grey, frosted* appearance, with no blackening or pitting, do not interfere with them (assuming that the gap is correct). If the contacts are only slightly discoloured, clean them with a thin cloth moistened with petrol.

On examination after a big mileage the contacts may be found to have irregular and blackened areas due to pitting and burning (especially if the contacts have not been kept clean and correctly adjusted). In this case it is essential to clean them up, otherwise misfiring and rapid deterioration of the contacts will probably follow.

To clean the contacts, use a *fine* carborundum slip or a piece of *fine* emery-cloth or silicon-carbide paper (do not use a nail file), and with the contact-breaker spring arm removed, clean and polish the contacts until all pitting disappears and the contact surfaces are smooth all over. Be careful to keep the contact faces "square" as well as uniform. *This is most important.** If pitting is not appreciable it is permissible to insert the emery cloth between the two contacts, while both are in position. If pitting is very substantial and deep, it may be necessary to remove the complete contact-breaker to restore the contacts to serviceable condition. Always

* Note that some recent type Lucas contacts have slightly convex (not flat) faces, which must be cleaned with fine emery-cloth only.

remove the spring arm (*see* below) first, and remove any traces of rust from it. Note that it is highly inadvisable to remove much metal from the contact faces. Always fit a new pair of contacts (including, of course, a new spring-arm) if a reasonable amount of facing-up fails to renovate the contacts satisfactorily. When fitting a new spring-arm (with moving contact attached), make sure that the spring-arm is properly located (*see* next paragraph). After trueing up the contacts as described above, be careful to remove all metal dust with a petrol-moistened cloth, and do not forget to check the contact-breaker gap which will have increased if much pitting has been eliminated.

To Remove the Spring Arm (Lucas "Magdyno"). To remove the spring arm (carrying the moving contact) on the face-cam type contact-breaker (*see* Fig. 57), it is only necessary to remove its securing screw and spring washer. When replacing the spring arm, make certain that the small backing spring is replaced immediately under the securing screw and spring washer, with the curved portion facing *outwards* as shown in Fig. 57. See that the contacts are perfectly aligned before firmly tightening the securing screw.

It is desirable at long intervals to remove the complete contact-breaker and inspect the small fibre-tappet which operates the spring arm. If its edges are at all worn, renew the tappet immediately. Smear a little thin machine-oil on the tappet before fitting it to the contact-breaker body.

To remove the complete contact-breaker after detaching the spring arm, unlock the tab-washer and remove the contact-breaker securing screw, when the complete contact-breaker can be withdrawn, and dealt with on a bench or table if desired. When replacing the contact-breaker, see that a new tab-washer is fitted and locked over the securing screw.

To Remove the Spring Arm (Lucas SR-1 Magneto). Slacken the nut securing the low-tension terminal assembly, and withdraw the spring and spring arm (*see* Fig. 58).

To Remove the Spring Arm (Lucas 15D1 Contact-breaker). Referring to Fig. 59, first remove the screw 11 which secures the condenser. Next pull off the rubber terminal-cover and remove the terminal and the nylon washer. Then lift from the contact-breaker housing the assembly comprising the condenser 9, the terminal, and the spring arm 5, with integral spring 6. When reassembling the contact-breaker, make quite sure that the nylon block 7 is replaced *with its widest edge at the top.*

To Remove Spring Arm (Miller Contact-breaker). Referring to Fig. 60, loosen both terminal nuts 2 and withdraw the spring arm. As this arm is pulled away, the slot 5 in its spring will disengage the end of the terminal stud 1. When replacing the spring arm, be sure that the slot 5 in its spring engages the terminal stud between the fibre insulating-washer 9 and the rectangular head 10 of the terminal stud 1, otherwise the primary circuit in the coil will be permanently earthed through the fixed-contact plate, and the ignition system will not function and the battery will discharge.

Automatic Timing Control (1956-8 "Bullets," 1954-8 250 c.c. "Clippers"). No attention to the timing-control mechanism (located behind the contact-breaker) is normally needed, but occasional lubrication (*see* page 46)

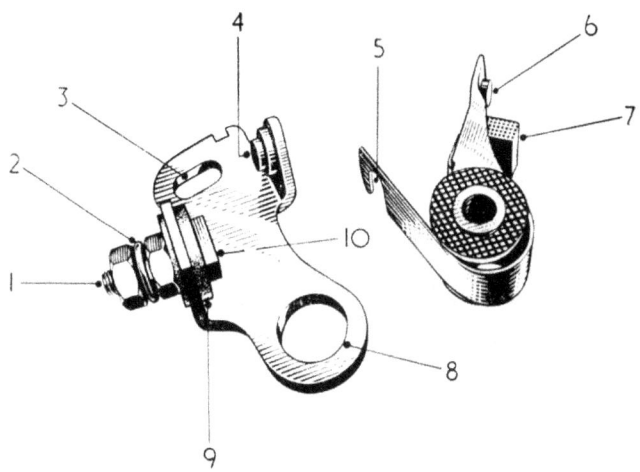

Fig. 60. Showing the Fixed-Contact Plate and the Spring Arm Removed from Miller Contact-breaker

Applies to 1954 and early 1955 250 c.c. "Clippers."

1. Terminal stud
2. Terminal nuts
3. Elongated hole for screw securing fixed-contact plate
4. Fixed contact
5. Slot in spring
6. Moving contact
7. Fibre-heel contacting cam
8. Hole for pivot post
9. Fibre insulating-washer
10. Head of terminal stud 1

is advisable on the 250 c.c. "Clippers". With the Lucas SR-1 rotating-magnet magneto (1956-8 "Bullets") it is advisable about every two years (when a complete engine overhaul is undertaken) to have the magneto stripped down by a Lucas service depot or an agent, so that the springs, toggles, and weights of the automatic timing-control mechanism can be inspected and lubricated with some medium-viscosity engine oil; at the same time the magneto bearings can be repacked with grease.

Ignition Timings. For the correct ignition timings and setting procedure (where manual control is provided), see the appropriate instructions on pages 129-34.

The Slip-ring (Lucas "Magdyno"). Moisture, oil, or dirt accumulating on the "Magdyno" slip-ring is liable to cause difficult starting and misfiring. About every 6,000 miles remove the h.t. pick-up from the "Magdyno" and thoroughly clean the flanges and track of the slip-ring. Do this by holding a soft, dry cloth, wrapped round a pencil, through the pick-up hole, and, with the cloth lightly pressed against the slip-ring, slowly turn the engine. The h.t. pick-up is secured to the body of the "Magdyno" by two small screws which must be removed.

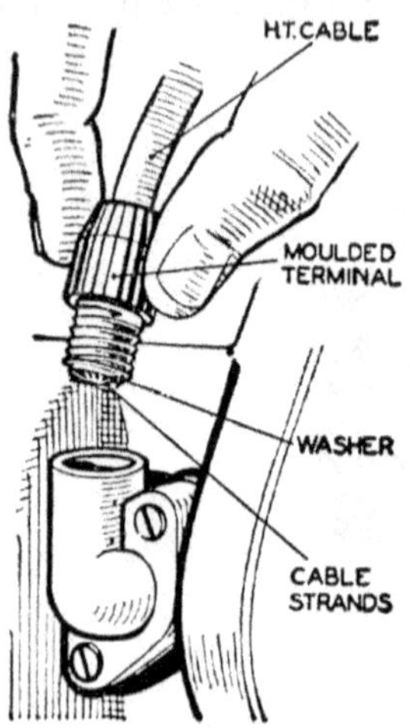

The H.T. Pick-up (Lucas "Magdyno"). When cleaning the slip-ring, also clean the surface of the pick-up moulding with a cloth moistened with petrol, and polish with a fine, dry cloth. Examine the pick-up moulding for cracks, and closely inspect the spring and carbon brush. The brush must move freely in its holder, but be careful not to stretch the spring. Renew the spring at once if it has weakened, and always renew a brush which has worn to within $\frac{1}{8}$ in. of the shoulder. When replacing the h.t. pick-up, do not forget to replace the small gasket between the body of the "Magdyno" and the pick-up moulding.

FIG. 61. FITTING LUCAS H.T. CABLE TO "MAGDYNO"

To Renew the H.T. Cable. When renewing a cracked or perished h.t. cable, always use 7 mm neophrene-covered ignition cable. On "Magdyno" or coil-ignition models (250 c.c. "Clippers") bare the end of the cable (see Fig. 61) for about $\frac{1}{4}$ in. and thread the cable through the moulded terminal nut. Pass the wire through the bronze washer and then bend back the cable strands radially. Finally screw the moulded terminal nut into the "Magdyno" pick-up or coil connexion.

To renew the h.t. cable on a Lucas SR-1 rotating-magnet magneto, remove the moulded end-cover and unscrew the pointed screw securing the h.t. cable (see Fig. 58) from the inside of the end-cover; pull out the old cable. Cut the new 7 mm. cable to the required length and push one end fully home into the terminal. Tighten the cable securing-screw. The pointed end of this screw will pierce the cable insulation and make contact with the cable core.

The Ignition Coil. The coil used on some "Clippers" requires no maintenance whatever other than occasional external inspection to see that it is clean and free from water, particularly between the terminals. At intervals wipe the terminal cap with a cloth moistened with petrol, and check that the terminal connexions are tight and the cables in good condition.

The Alternator (Coil Ignition Models). This requires no maintenance (*see* page 61). Note that if the stator, rotor, crankshaft, or the rear half of the primary chain-case is disturbed, it is desirable to check the radial air gap (0·020 in.) between the stator and rotor.

To Remove the Lucas "Magdyno." To remove the instrument for overhaul or during the course of a thorough engine strip, first remove the timing cover as described on page 134. Next remove the lock-nut securing the "Magdyno" driving gear to the taper on its shaft. When doing this, engage top gear and lock the back wheel. Afterwards extract the driving gear with the extractor (Part No. 14835) provided in the tool kit (shown at 10 in Fig. 54). Unscrew the nut from the bolt on the "Magdyno" securing strap, and pull the strap clear. Then withdraw the complete "Magdyno." When replacing the instrument, make quite sure that the felt washer, retainer, and spring are replaced in their original positions.

To Remove Contact-breaker Housing and Bracket (Coil-ignition Models). First disconnect the lead to the ignition switch. Next remove the contact-breaker driving gear as just described for the Lucas "Magdyno" driving gear. Then on all the 1955-8 coil-ignition "Clippers" with Lucas equipment, remove the contact-breaker housing secured to the bracket by a single round-headed screw, and withdraw the housing. Now remove the bracket from the crankcase by removing the two fixing bolts.

On 1954-5 250 c.c. "Clippers" with Miller equipment, after disconnecting the lead to the switch and removing the contact-breaker driving gear, loosen the nut on the securing-strap bolt and withdraw as a unit the contact-breaker and its housing.

TAPPET ADJUSTMENT

The maintenance of correct tappet adjustment on all Royal Enfield four-stroke engines is extremely important. Upon this adjustment depends the correct lift of the valves and to some extent precision of valve timing. Insufficient valve clearances may cause damage to the valves (particularly the exhaust valve) and will cause loss of compression and power output. Excessive clearances will cause tappet noise, subject the valves to considerable stresses, and lower general efficiency.

On new or reconditioned engines, because of the initial bedding-down of contacting surfaces, it is advisable to check and if necessary adjust the setting of the tappets after about 250 miles' running. Also check tappet adjustment after grinding-in the valves. Subsequently tappet adjustment should be called for only at fairly long intervals. Check the adjustment about every 1,000 miles. The expert and experienced rider can tell by the "feel" and exhaust note of his engine whether the tappets are in need of adjustment. Whenever loss of compression develops or excessive tappet noise occurs, check the tappet adjustment *immediately*, especially if there are signs of overheating. Table IV shows the correct tappet adjustment for all 1946-58 single-cylinder four-stroke engines.

TABLE IV
VALVE CLEARANCES (1946–58 FOUR-STROKE SINGLES)

Royal Enfield Engine (Cold)	Inlet Valve	Exhaust Valve
1946–55 Models G, J, J2	0·002 in.	0·004 in.
1949–58 350, 500 c.c. "Bullets"	nil	nil
1954–8 250 c.c. "Clippers"	0·002 in.	0·004 in.
1956–7 350 c.c. "Clippers"	0·002 in.	0·004 in.
1958 350 c.c. "Clipper"	0·002 in.	0·004 in.

Before Checking Tappet Adjustment. It is essential to turn the engine over slowly so that the piston is at the top of the compression stroke (T.D.C.) with both valves closed, also to check that there is sufficient clearance at the exhaust-valve lifter (where fitted). Unless both valves are fully closed, it is impossible to check tappet adjustment accurately.

Checking Tappet Adjustment. First move the inspection cover (secured by a single thumb-nut) from the tappet chest at the base of the cylinder barrel on the off-side. Appropriate feeler gauges should be used to check the valve clearances except where the clearances (*see* Table) are specified as *nil*. It is not practicable to check the valve clearances with feeler gauges at the bottom of the push-rods on account of the ball and socket joints used, and to make a feeler-gauge check of the tappet adjustment it is necessary to remove the rocker-box cover (Models G, J, J2 and 1956–7 350 c.c. "Clipper") and insert the gauge between the hardened end-cap on each valve stem and the pad on the corresponding overhead rocker. An experienced owner can dispense with a feeler-gauge check and rely on the feel of the push-rods. The inlet push-rod should be just free to spin, with no up-and-down play, and the exhaust push-rod should be able to spin, with just a perceptible degree of up and down play. Where a valve clearance of *nil* is required (1949–58 350 c.c. and 500 c.c. "Bullets"), it should be possible to spin both push-rods freely with the fingers, accompanied by no end movement.

Adjusting the Tappets. Referring to Fig. 62, with two spanners hold the push-rod bottom end (top hexagon) and the lock-nut (middle hexagon). Loosen the lock-nut by turning the nut to the left. Then to make a tappet adjustment, screw the push-rod cup (bottom hexagon) to the left or right to decrease or increase the clearance respectively. When doing this, hold the push-rod bottom end. Having made the required adjustment, lock the lock-nut against the push-rod end. After tightening the lock-nut, again check the tappet adjustment. Finally replace the inspection cover on the tappet chest.

Exhaust Lifter Adjustment (Models G, J, J2, 1956-7 350 c.c. "Clipper"). It is most important before checking the tappet adjustment, and at all

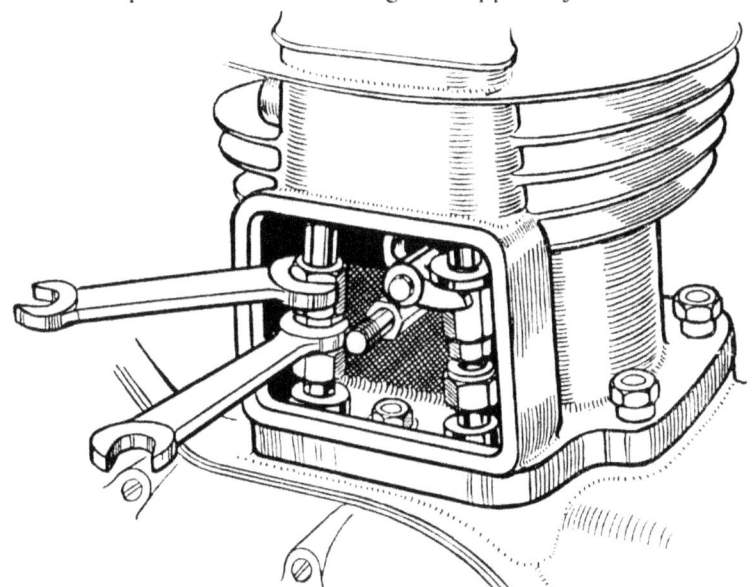

FIG. 62. THE TAPPET ADJUSTMENT ON ALL 1946-58 SINGLE-CYLINDER FOUR-STROKE ENGINES
On the "Bullet" engines the tappet chest is part of the crankcase casting.
(*The Enfield Cycle Co., Ltd.*)

other times, always to maintain a small amount (about $\frac{1}{8}$ in.) of backlash at the exhaust-valve lifter lever with the exhaust valve fully closed, otherwise it is quite impossible for the valve to seat properly and loss of compression, power and burning of the valve will inevitably occur, accompanied probably by a considerable amount of banging in the exhaust system and a very hot exhaust-pipe. The necessary adjustment of the exhaust-valve lifter can readily be made by means of the adjustable cable-stop provided above the tappet chest at the rear. See that the lock-nut is afterwards securely retightened.

The Decompressor (1949-58 "Bullets"). This unit, entirely independent of the exhaust valve, is screwed into the cylinder head on the off-side and the unit has a cable adjusting-screw and lock-nut on top of the cable block (Fig. 63) to enable a little backlash to be maintained at the handlebar operating-lever. See that this backlash (about $\frac{1}{8}$ in.) is always maintained, because should the decompressor valve fail to seat perfectly, loss of compression and power output will inevitably occur.

Failure of the decompressor valve to seat perfectly can also be caused by pitting of the valve face or seat, carbon deposits on the valve, or burning and possibly slight bending of the valve stem, causing it to stick. Leakage resulting from pitting or carbon deposits can generally be cured by grinding the decompressor valve in as one would a poppet-type engine valve. Grinding-in the valve does not necessarily involve completely dismantling the unit, though this is essential if the stem of the valve is bent or the spring requires to be renewed. A tendency for the valve to stick open, unaccompanied by any burning or bending of the valve stem, can usually be corrected by very thoroughly washing the unit in petrol.

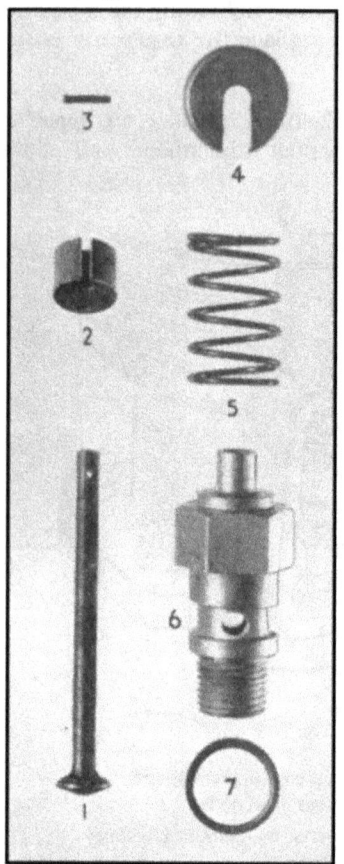

FIG. 63. THE DECOMPRESSOR UNIT DISMANTLED

Applies to 1949-58 "Bullet" models.
1. The valve
2. Cable block
3. Peg
4. Cap
5. Spring
6. Body of unit
7. Copper washer for 6

To Remove Decompressor Unit. First remove the screw and nut which secure the control lever to the bracket of the handlebar clip. With a suitable pair of pliers pull away and disconnect the control cable from the lever. Remove the lever and pull the cable and ferrule out of the bracket slot. Then unscrew the body of the decompressor from the cylinder head. Never attempt this until you have first disconnected the control cable from the handlebar lever. Do not omit to cover up the hole exposed in the cylinder head.

Disconnecting the Cable. Having removed the decompressor unit with control cable attached, as described in the preceding paragraph, use the following procedure. Referring to Fig. 63, compress the spring 5 with the fingers and detach the cap 4. Next unscrew the cable adjusting-screw (complete with lock-nut) from the cable block 2, and pull the cable from the slot in the cable block. Push the spring 5 upwards with the fingers and then pull the large cable-nipple from the hole in the body 6. The nipple is soldered to the cable, but it also has a security screw. Now thread the cable and nipple through the spring. This leaves the decompressor body 6 (with valve, cable block and spring) disconnected entirely from the control cable. Replace the cap 4 and carefully inspect the valve 1 and its seat for pitting and carbon deposits.

Grinding-in the Valve. With the decompressor unit on the bench, apply a thin film of *fine grade* valve grinding paste (*see* page 89) to the bevelled valve face and oscillate the valve by means of the cable block 2 fixed to its upper end. Lift the valve off its seat occasionally so as to re-position the valve, and avoid continuous rotation. Rotate the valve about a third of a turn in one direction and then the same amount in the opposite direction. Continue grinding-in until all pitting is removed and there is a continuous good contact between the valve face and its seat. Avoid excessive grinding-in, and afterwards remove every trace of grinding paste. Wash the whole assembly in clean paraffin while opening and shutting the valve with the fingers. If preferred, you can, of course, dismantle the complete unit and then reattach the cable block to the valve, before grinding-in.

To Dismantle Decompressor Unit Completely. To strip down the unit to renew the spring or valve, remove the small peg 3 from the valve stem and draw off the cable block 2. The entire assembly can now be stripped down. Reassemble the unit in the reverse order of dismantling, and when screwing the unit home in the cylinder head, do not omit to replace the copper washer 7 over the threaded end of the decompressor body. After reconnecting the cable, check that there is sufficient free movement in the control, as described on page 105.

DECARBONIZING AND VALVE GRINDING

The removal of carbon deposits is generally necessary only when the engine displays a tendency to run hot, and when certain characteristic symptoms (*see* below) become manifest. Under normal running conditions decarbonizing should be undertaken only after the first 2,500 miles and thereafter at periods exceeding 5,000 miles, and not till the engine *really needs it*. Valve grinding may be needed when decarbonizing, and the valves and their seats should be inspected. Valve removal facilitates cleaning the ports. Two items required for the complete maintenance operation are illustrated on page 121.

The cylinder barrel should also be removed at every alternate decarbonizing and the piston and rings inspected. The big- and small-end bearings can be checked for wear (*see* page 136) at the same time. Decarbonizing is very simple, and it is not necessary to remove the cylinder barrel during each "top overhaul" because most of the carbon deposits form on the piston crown, which is accessible on removing the cylinder head. The necessity for decarbonizing is indicated by a gradual falling off in power (especially on hills), a tendency for "pinking" (injurious to the engine) under slight provocation, and a "woolly" exhaust. The sparking plug also tends to become dirty very quickly.

Removal of Petrol Tank (All Models). This is a necessary preliminary to decarbonizing. Turn off both petrol taps (there is only one tap on 1954

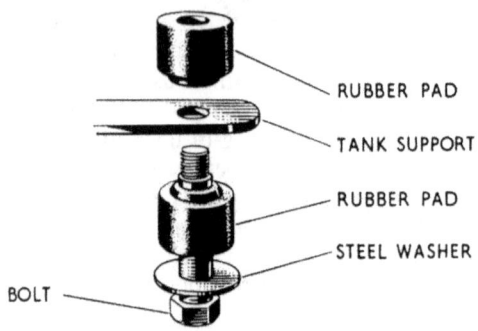

Fig. 64. Mounting of Petrol Tank on Tank Supports

Applies to 1946-55 Models G, J, J2. On the 1949-58 "Clipper" and "Bullet" models two transverse bolts, one at the front and one at the rear, secure the tank. 1957-8 petrol tanks have detachable chromium-plated panels (except on "Clippers").

and later "Bullet" and "Clipper" models), and disconnect the petrol pipe. To facilitate tank removal it is also advisable to remove the saddle front-attachment bolt, or the dualseat (where fitted). Now remove the tank as follows—

1. On the 1946-55 Models G, J, J2, remove each of the four vertical bolts securing the under-side of the petrol tank to the four support brackets on the frame top-tube. Then lift off the tank. Remove, and note the assembly order of the eight rubber pads and four steel washers (*see* Fig. 64). If the rubber pads are damaged or perished, renew them.

2. On the 1949-58 "Clippers" and "Bullet" models, remove the two transverse bolts (actually, studs) securing the petrol tank to the frame lugs at the front and rear, and lift the tank off.* Note that a distance tube and a rubber buffer-sleeve are fitted (in this order) over the *front* securing

* If necessary, remove the saddle front attachment-bolt or the dualseat, with rear mudguard on 1956-8 "Bullets" (*see* page 153).

bolt to counter the effects of hard tightening of the nuts and vibration while riding respectively. The rear bolt usually has a thick plain-washer in addition to the shake-proof washers provided. Observe the precise arrangement of all washers to ensure their correct replacement.

To Remove Cylinder Head (1946-55 Models G, J, J2; 1956-7 350 c.c. "Clippers").

Referring to Fig. 65, the following dismantling procedure is necessary to remove the cylinder head—

1. Disconnect the petrol pipe and remove the petrol tank as described in the appropriate paragraph on page 108.
2. Detach the h.t. lead from the sparking plug and remove the latter, using the spanner shown at 15 in Fig. 54.
3. Remove the Amal carburettor. If an air filter is fitted disconnect the rubber connexion at the carburettor air-intake (roll the end back). Then unscrew the ring nut on top of the mixing-chamber and withdraw the throttle and air slides. Place them, with cables attached, in a safe position out of the way. Now remove the carburettor flange-securing nuts and remove the carburettor as a unit. Examine its flange washer; if damaged, this will have to be renewed. Examine the flange also (see page 31).
4. Remove the exhaust system (duplicated on Model J2) after removing the nuts and washers securing the exhaust pipe and silencer brackets to the frame. The exhaust pipe is a push-in fit in the exhaust port. If the pipe is stiff, tap it out gently from the port, using a mallet or raw-hide hammer; be very careful not to dent the pipe.
5. Disconnect the oil-feed pipe 1 to the rocker-box by unscrewing union nuts 2, 3. It is advisable to remove the pipe from the engine to avoid the risk of damaging it. Also (on the 350 c.c. "Clipper") disconnect the engine steady-stay.
6. Remove the rocker-box cover 4 which is secured by a single centrally-positioned nut and washer 5. Be careful not to damage the oil-sealing gasket 6.
7. Turn the engine over slowly until the piston is at top-dead-centre (T.D.C.) with both valves fully closed. Feel the overhead rockers to ensure complete valve closure.
8. Remove the eight $\frac{1}{4}$ in. nuts and washers 7 securing the rocker-bearing caps 8, 9, and remove the central stud 10 to which the rocker-box cover was secured.*
9. Remove as a unit the overhead-rocker assembly comprising the two upper bearing-caps 8, 9, the overhead rockers (see 9 and 10, Fig. 72), and the lower one-piece bearing caps 11.

* Removal of the central stud 10, followed by removal of the one-piece bearing caps 11, is not essential, but removal of the projecting stud avoids the risk of its being damaged when the cylinder head is laid on the bench for valve removal and decarbonizing.

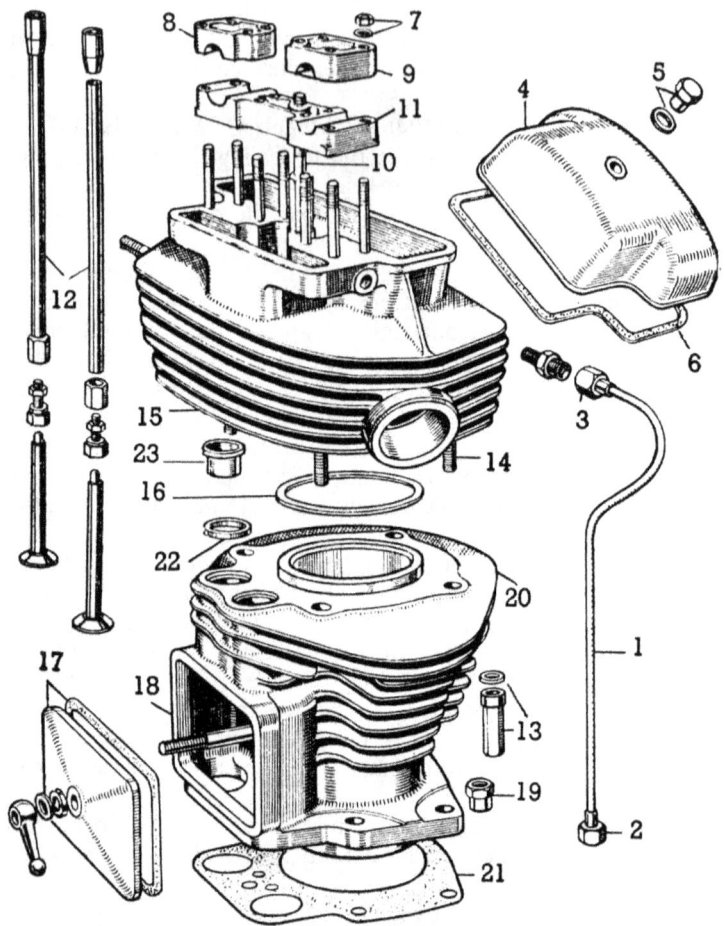

Fig. 65. Exploded View Showing Cylinder Head, Rocker-box, Cylinder Barrel, etc., on the 1954-8 250 c.c. "Clipper" Engine

The overhead rocker and valve assembly is shown in Fig. 72. Pre-1958 350 c.c. "Clippers" and Models G, J, J2 have similar parts, but the exhaust push-rod has a collar (for the exhaust-valve lifter) at its base, and ordinary nuts are used instead of long sleeve-nuts to secure the cylinder head (below the head) to the cylinder barrel. Slacken all nuts in a diagonal order. This 250 c.c. engine was discontinued early in 1955.

(*The Enfield Cycle Co., Ltd.*)

GENERAL MAINTENANCE 111

10. Withdraw from *above* both push-rods 12 from their tubes or cast-in tunnels (1956-7 350 c.c. "Clippers"). Should the collar (for the exhaust-valve lifter) on the exhaust push-rod fail to clear the joint between the cylinder head and the cylinder barrel, leave the exhaust push-rod in position until the cylinder head has been removed.

11. Remove the four $\frac{5}{16}$ in. nuts (sleeve-nuts, 250 c.c. "Clippers") and washers 13 (below the cylinder-head fins) from the inverted cylinder-head studs 14.

12. Lift the cylinder head carefully and vertically from the cylinder barrel 20. If the joint is stiff, tap the head carefully with a wooden mallet or raw-hide hammer applied below the inlet and exhaust ports (not the fins) until the head is freed. Inspect the copper gasket 16 which usually comes away with the head. It may require to be annealed (*see* page 124) before assembly. If there are any blackened areas indicating "blowing," a new gasket will have to be fitted. Do not forget to cover up the exposed cylinder bore and piston with a clean cloth before removing the carbon deposits (*see* page 119) from the piston, or proceeding with cylinder barrel removal (if it is considered desirable to inspect the piston and rings). As mentioned on page 107, too frequent removal of the cylinder barrel is not recommended.

To Remove Cylinder Head (1954-8 250 c.c. "Clippers"). Strip down the engine and remove the cylinder head as just described for the Model G, J, J2 engines, but disregard the previous hint (sub-paragraph 10,) concerning the exhaust push-rod. The 250 c.c. "Clippers" have no exhaust-valve lifter, and therefore the exhaust push-rod has no collar at its base. Mark one push-rod appropriately to ensure the rods not being interchanged during reassembly.

To Remove Cylinder Head (1949-58 350 c.c., 500 c.c. "Bullets"; 1958 350 c.c. "Clipper"). Referring to Figs 66, 67, to remove the cylinder head, strip-down the upper part of the engine thus—

1. Remove the petrol tank 1, the sparking plug 2, the carburettor 3, and the exhaust system 4, as described on page 109 (sub-paragraphs 1-4). Note that on some pre-1956 engines there is no flexible pipe between the carburettor air-intake and the filter (as shown in Fig. 17). In this instance after removing the flange-securing nuts, push the carburettor towards the filter until the flange clears the securing studs, and then pull the carburettor clear of the rubber clamp-ring inside the filter box.

2. Disconnect the engine steady 5 from the lug at the rear of the cylinder head.

3. Remove the two-way oil-feed pipe 6 to the separate rocker-boxes after unscrewing the union nut 7 connecting the pipe to the front of the crankcase, and the two union-screws and washers 8, which secure the banjo ends of the composite pipe to the inlet and exhaust rocker-boxes.

4. Remove the covers, 9, 10 and gaskets 26 from both rocker-boxes. Each cover is secured by three long sleeve nuts 11 and one short sleeve nut 12. The shorter nut is at the front on the exhaust rocker-box, and at the rear on the inlet rocker-box. Note their positions for reassembly.

5. Remove the decompressor unit 13 from the cylinder head after first disconnecting the control cable from the handlebar lever (*see* page 106).

FIG. 66. CLOSE-UP VIEW OF 500 C.C. "BULLET" ENGINE

This high-performance sports engine with magneto ignition ("Magdyno," pre-1956) is similar to the 350 c.c. version except for bore and stroke differences. Both engines have separate inlet and exhaust rocker-boxes, and a valve chest which is integral with the crankcase.

6. Turn the engine over slowly so that the piston is at top-dead-centre with both valves fully closed (feel the overhead rockers).

7. Remove the eight $\frac{1}{4}$ in. nuts and washers 14 securing the rocker-bearing caps.

8. Remove as a unit each overhead-rocker assembly comprising; the upper bearing-cap 15, the inlet or exhaust rocker (*see* Fig. 72), and the lower bearing-cap 16.

9. Withdraw from *above* both push-rods 17. They are not interchangeable, the inlet push-rod being shorter than the exhaust rod.

10. Remove the four long sleeve-nuts, washers 18 (in pairs inside the rocker-boxes) from the long crankcase studs 19 which secure the cylinder head and cylinder barrel to the crankcase. Also remove the nut (located on the near-side of the head adjacent to the sparking plug) from the fifth long crankcase-stud securing the head and barrel.

GENERAL MAINTENANCE

11. Remove the nut and washer 20 from the short head-securing stud 21 screwed into the top of the cylinder barrel on the off-side. It is also advisable to remove the $\frac{1}{4}$ in. nut and washer 22 (located just above the

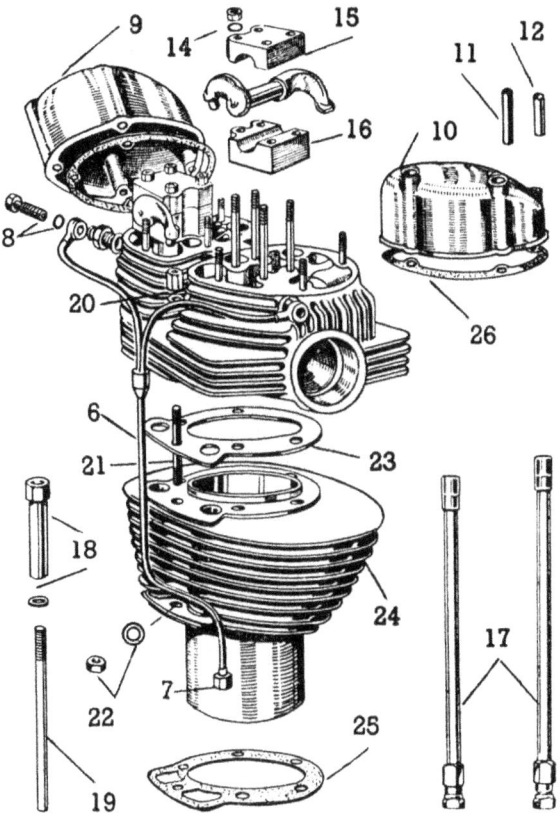

FIG. 67. SHOWING DETAILS OF CYLINDER-HEAD, ROCKER-BOXES, CYLINDER BARREL, ETC., ON THE 1949–58 350 C.C., 500 C.C. "BULLET" ENGINES

For valve spring details, *see* Fig. 72. Note that the reference numbers in Fig. 66 correspond to those in the above sketch.

(*The Enfield Cycle Co., Ltd.*)

tappet chest) from the short crankcase-stud. This will avoid the risk of damaging the stud when all the other vertical crankcase-studs have had their nuts removed as described above.

12. Lift the cylinder head off the barrel vertically and with care until it clears the five long crankcase-studs projecting through the cylinder barrel and head (four of them into the rocker-boxes) and the shorter stud projecting from the barrel on the off-side. If the head joint is stiff, tap it

carefully in the manner suggested on page 111 (sub-paragraph 12). Be careful not to damage the gasket 23, and cover up the cylinder bore and piston pending further dismantling or decarbonizing.

To Remove Cylinder Barrel (1946–55 Models G, J, J2; 1956–7 350 c.c. "Clippers"). As stated on page 107, it is not good practice to disturb the cylinder barrel each time you decarbonize. This applies to all engines. Referring to Fig. 65 remove the cylinder barrel in the following manner—

1. Remove the cylinder head and copper gasket as described on page 109.
2. Turn the engine over slowly until the piston is at or near bottom-dead-centre (B.D.C.).
3. Remove the cover and washer 17 from the tappet chest 18. This exposes one of the five nuts (*see* Fig. 62) securing the cylinder barrel to the crankcase. Remove all five nuts 19 from the crankcase studs. When doing this first loosen all the nuts in a diagonal order.
4. Disconnect the exhaust-valve lifter control cable.
5. Lift the cylinder barrel 20 vertically upwards until its base clears the crankcase studs, and the piston emerges. Steady the piston with the hand and do not permit its skirt to fall sharply against the connecting-rod, or the rod against the edge of the crankcase mouth.
6. Cover up the crankcase hole with a clean cloth to prevent dirt or foreign bodies entering the crankcase. This is a most important precaution. Remove the joint washer 21 from the crankcase face; and renew it. Paper washers are cheap and all such washers are best renewed. Clean the joint faces thoroughly (*see* page 115).

To Remove Cylinder Barrel (1954–7 250 c.c. "Clippers"). Follow the instructions already given in respect of the 350 c.c. "Clipper" but disregard sub-paragraph 4 above concerning the exhaust-valve lifter control cable. On the small capacity coil-ignition models no valve lifter is needed or provided.

To Remove Cylinder Barrel (1949–58 350 c.c., 500 c.c. "Bullets"; 1958 350 c.c. "Clipper"). Removal to inspect the piston and rings is simple. Referring to Fig. 67, remove the barrel as follows—

1. Remove the cylinder head and copper gasket as described on page 111.
2. Turn the engine over slowly until the piston is at or near bottom-dead-centre (B.D.C.).
3. Check that the $\frac{1}{4}$ in. nut and washer 22 (located centrally above the tappet chest) have been removed from the short stud on the off-side of the crankcase.
4. Lift the cylinder barrel 24 vertically upwards until its lower fin clears the crankcase studs and the piston emerges from the bore. Steady the piston with one hand to prevent its skirt falling sharply against the connecting-rod and to prevent the rod striking the edge of the crankcase mouth.

GENERAL MAINTENANCE 115

5. To prevent dirt or foreign matter entering the crankcase, and to protect the piston, wrap a cloth round the connecting-rod and piston so that it effectively blocks the hole in the crankcase. Remove and renew the paper washer 25, and thoroughly clean up the barrel and crankcase joint

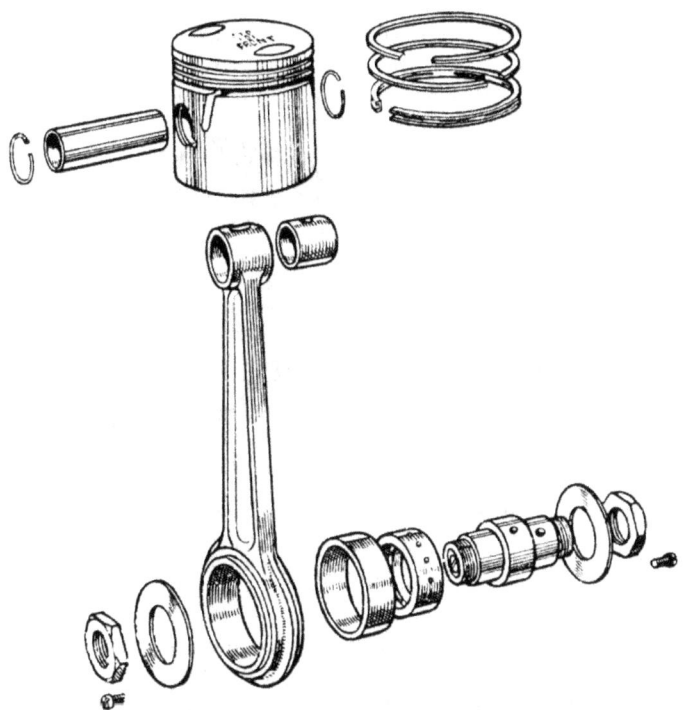

FIG. 68. SHOWING THE PISTON, PISTON RINGS, GUDGEON-PIN, CONNECTING-ROD, AND BIG- AND SMALL-END BEARINGS

On the high-compression 350 c.c., 500 c.c. "Bullet" engines the piston crown is not flat, but dome-shaped (see Fig. 69). On the 1958 350 c.c. "Clipper" the bearings are slightly different from those shown.
(*The Enfield Cycle Co., Ltd.*)

faces. A carpenter's scraper plate is useful for removing jointing compound without scratching or damaging the aluminium crankcase face.

Removing the Piston. The piston fitted to Royal Enfield engines is a split-skirt type (250 c.c. "Clippers" and "Bullets") with two compression rings and one slotted scraper ring (see Fig. 68). It is held to the small-end of the connecting-rod by a fully floating gudgeon-pin, secured to the piston by two circlips. It is advisable to warm the piston before removing the gudgeon-pin. This can be done by wrapping a cloth round the piston after immersing the cloth in hot water and wringing it out.

116   THE BOOK OF THE ROYAL ENFIELD

Where a piston has been in service for a considerable mileage, it is sometimes possible to push out the gudgeon-pin by hand, provided the piston is reasonably warm. But it is generally necessary to press out the gudgeon-pin by means of the special Royal Enfield extractor shown in Fig. 69.

Remove *both* circlips (some owners remove only one circlip) after first checking that the crankcase mouth is completely covered with a cloth. Use a small screwdriver or a pointed instrument such as the tang end of a

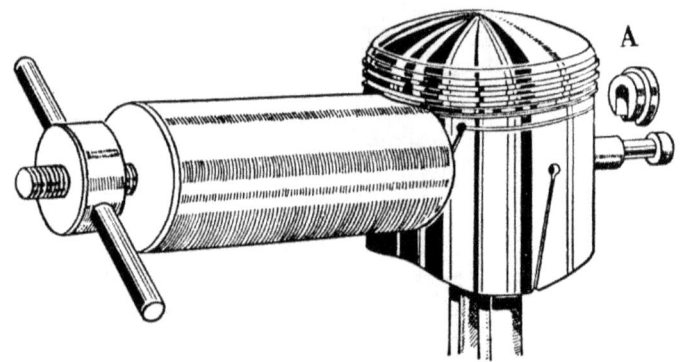

FIG. 69. THE ROYAL ENFIELD GUDGEON-PIN EXTRACTOR
Suitable for piston removal and fitting on all single-cylinder O.H.V. engines
A proprietary extractor such as the Terry is also suitable.
(*The Enfield Cycle Co., Ltd.*)

file to remove each circlip, which must subsequently be renewed. Having removed the circlips, position the extractor tool (Part No. E5477) as shown in Fig. 69 and fit the collar A on the spindle of the extractor. Then turn the tommy bar anti-clockwise until the gudgeon-pin is drawn out, when the piston can be removed. It is not necessary to mark the piston, if it is of the split-skirt type, as the split must be towards the *front*, but if there is no such identification, scribe a suitable mark on the inside of the piston to ensure its being replaced in its original position when engine assembly is undertaken. Before laying aside the gudgeon-pin, file a small nick on one end to ensure that the pin is refitted in its original position. This is important.

Inspecting and Removing Piston Rings. The piston rings are responsible for maintaining good compression. Therefore they must be full of spring, free in their grooves, and set with their slots opposite to each other (i.e. at 120° in the three-ring piston which is fitted on all Royal Enfield engines). If all three rings are bright all the way round, they are obviously being polished against the cylinder walls, and are perfect, and should be left alone. If, on the other hand, they are discoloured at some points, they are not in proper contact with the walls of the cylinder, causing gas to blow past them. Perhaps they are stuck in their grooves with burnt oil, and will function properly if the grooves are cleaned. If the rings are scored, or have lost their tension, or are vertically loose in their grooves, or have brown patches, the rings must be renewed.

Piston rings are of cast-iron and, being of very small section, must be handled very, very carefully. If not, they will certainly be broken. Scraper rings are particularly vulnerable; they cannot safely be opened out wider than will allow them to slip over the crown of the piston. Therefore, to

TABLE V
SOME USEFUL DATA

Model	C.R.	C.C.	Bore (mm)	Stroke (mm)	Fuel (gal)	Oil (pt)
G	6/1	346	70	90	2¾	4
J	5·5/1	499	84	90	2¾	4
J2	5·5/1	499	84	90	2¾	4
"250 Clipper"	6·5/1	248	64	77	3¼	4
"350 Clipper"	6·5/1	346	70	90	3¼	4
"350 Bullet"	6·5/1*	346	70	90	3¼	4
"500 Bullet"	6·5/1	499	84	90	3¼	4

* On 1955-8 350 c.c. "Bullets" the compression ratio is 7·25/1. Other compression ratios are also available. 1958 "350 Clipper": 6·75/1.

put them on or remove them it is advisable to insert small strips of sheet-metal, about ⅜ in. wide by 2 in. long, which are placed in the manner shown by Fig. 70. Be most careful to note the order in which the rings are removed to ensure correct replacement. When fitting piston rings, thoroughly clean the grooves into which they fit, as any deposit left at the back of new rings forces them out and makes them too tight a fit. Paraffin usually loosens stuck piston rings.

When renewing piston rings, always fit rings supplied by The Enfield Cycle Company, Ltd., or one of their approved dealers. Piston rings are made to extremely fine limits and on new engines have a side clearance of 0·003 in. in their grooves. Never attempt to fit oversize rings to compensate for wear unless an oversize piston and a rebore are necessary. Pistons 0·020 in. and 0·040 in. oversize, with similar oversize rings to suit, are available.

The gap for all new piston rings, tested in an unworn part (the top or bottom) of the bore, on Royal Enfield engines should be 0·011 in.-0·015 in. It is advisable when it is necessary to remove the piston to check the gaps of all three piston rings, using suitable feeler gauges. Renew any ring whose gap exceeds $\frac{1}{16}$ in. (0·060 in.). If new standard or oversize rings are fitted, check their gaps before fitting them to the piston. When checking the gaps, insert each piston ring into an unworn part of the cylinder bore and slide up the piston afterwards so that its crown contacts and squares up the ring.

Scrutinize the ends of each ring. If they are bright, the ring gap is too small; if, on the other hand, they are heavily coated with carbon, the

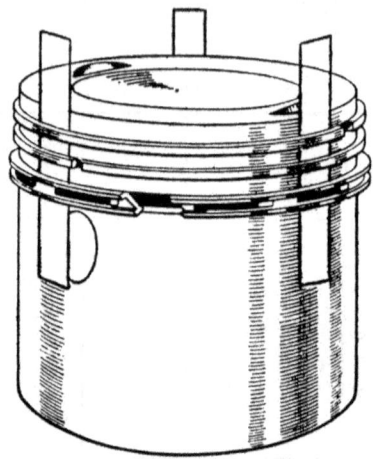

FIG. 70. A SAFE METHOD OF REMOVING PISTON RINGS

This method (*see* text) can also be used for fitting rings. Note the slotted scraper ring below the two compression rings. The top ring is chromium-plated.

gap is probably excessive. Should the gap of a ring be less than 0·008 in., clamp the ring between two wooden blocks in a vice and file one of the diagonal ends *slightly*. If a new ring is found to be rather a tight fit in its groove, rub down one side of the ring on a sheet of carborundum paper laid flat on a piece of plate-glass. The slotted scraper ring (*see* Fig. 70) fitted to Royal Enfield pistons can be fitted either way up. All three rings should be assembled, using the safe method shown in Fig. 70. A final word of good advice: if engine compression is good and the piston is doing its job well, leave the piston rings alone.

Decarbonizing the Cylinder Head. Carbon forms less readily on smooth surfaces; therefore always decarbonize thoroughly. Remove all carbon deposits from the cylinder head with a proprietary scraper, a blunt knife, or a blunt screwdriver. Be careful not to scratch deeply the combustion chamber, especially where the light-alloy head of a "Bullet" engine is concerned. The author finds that a small electrical screwdriver is excellent for decarbonizing the curved walls of the combustion chamber. To avoid

GENERAL MAINTENANCE

damaging the valve seats in the head, always first insert the valves in their guides.

Remove *all* traces of carbon from the interior surfaces and do not forget the sparking plug hole and the exhaust port(s). If a curved rifler is used to clean up the port channels, be particularly careful not to allow the pointed end of the rifler to scratch the valve seats. Carbon deposits having been removed, it is permissible, though not really necessary, to polish a *cast-iron* type head with fine emery cloth, but do this *before* removing the valves, and afterwards clean all abrasive particles away with paraffin. Also scrape all carbon deposits from the heads of the valves.

With an aluminium-alloy head fitted to a "Bullet" engine, never use emery cloth or any other abrasive to clean the combustion chamber, and

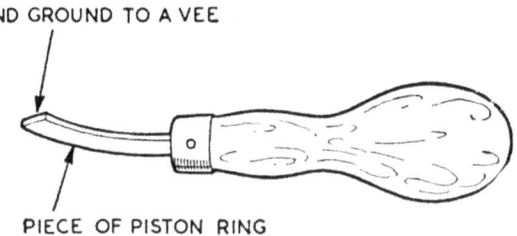

FIG. 71. A USEFUL TOOL FOR CLEANING PISTON-RING GROOVES

in no circumstances attempt to remove carbon by immersing the head in a hot caustic-soda or potash solution. Results will be disastrous.

Decarbonizing the Piston. With the comparatively soft aluminium-alloy piston, be careful when removing the carbon. *Do not use emery cloth*, but only a blunt knife, a proprietary scraper, or a blunt screwdriver. Do not attempt to remove carbon from the piston skirt or the lands between the rings. A little carbon is sometimes deposited on the inside of the piston, and this should be carefully scraped off. If a screwdriver is used, be careful not to allow the screwdriver shank to bump against the piston skirt.

Inspect the piston-ring grooves for carbon deposits; scrape any deposits off, using a proprietary scraper or a home-made tool such as that shown in Fig. 71. Do not forget to scrape carbon off the backs of the rings. Having decarbonized the piston and rings, wash them thoroughly in clean paraffin. Refit the rings by slipping them over the piston, using preferably the method shown in Fig. 70.

Testing Big- and Small-end Bearings. When the piston is removed the opportunity should always be taken of ascertaining whether any serious wear has developed in the big-and small-end bearings of the connecting-rod. The assembly is shown in Fig. 68. Appropriate instructions are on pages 136-7.

To Remove the Valves. As has been stated on page 107, the valves should be removed for inspection when decarbonizing, and *if necessary* both valves should be ground-in. On the O.H.V. singles the valves are, of course, housed in the cylinder head, the removal of which has already been dealt with. Split collets are used for valve-spring anchorage, and hardened end-caps are fitted to both valve stems (*see* Fig. 72). The tools shown in Fig. 73 are necessary for removing and grinding-in the valves. These

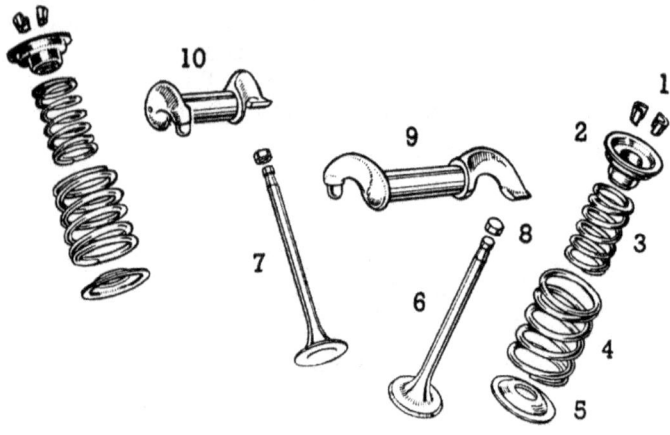

FIG. 72. THE OVERHEAD VALVE ASSEMBLY (ALL ENGINES)

1. Split collet
2. Outer collar for valve spring
3. Inner valve spring
4. Outer valve spring
5. Valve-spring inner collar
6. Exhaust valve
7. Inlet valve
8. Valve stem end-cap
9. Exhaust rockers
10. Inlet rockers

(*The Enfield Cycle Co., Ltd.*)

proprietary items can be obtained from any reputable accessory firm (*see* page 88).

Before attempting to remove the valves it is advisable first to remove the hardened end-cap 8 (Fig. 72) from each valve stem. Often the end-cap becomes stuck on the valve stem, especially in the case of the exhaust valve. To remove a stuck end-cap, prise it off with a screwdriver, or alternatively grip the cap in a vice and pull the head away.

With the cylinder head stripped of the overhead rockers, rocker-bearing caps, and valve stem end-caps, remove each valve in the following manner. Place the forked end of the valve-spring compressor squarely on the valve-spring outer collar and the pointed end of the screw in the centre of the valve head. Then turn the tommy bar clockwise until the valve-spring is compressed sufficiently to enable the split collet to be removed. These split collets often become stuck and a sharp tap should be delivered on the forked end of the valve-spring compressor. It should never be necessary to apply excessive force to compress the springs. When the collet is removed the duplex valve-spring and its upper collar can be withdrawn, and the valve pulled away from its guide. If a valve does not slide easily through the valve guide, remove any slight burrs on the end of the valve stem with a carborundum stone, otherwise there is some risk of damaging the valve guide. The inlet and exhaust valves are not interchangeable, having different size stems and different grade steel.

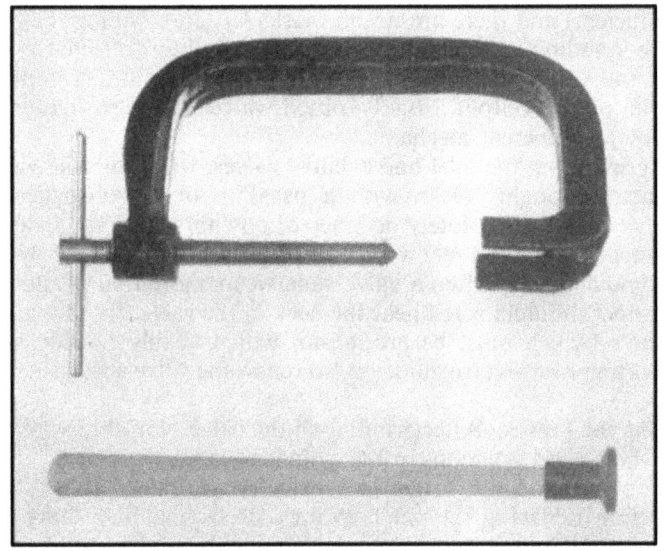

FIG. 73. TWO USEFUL PROPRIETARY TOOLS FOR THE VALVES
Above is shown a sturdy valve-spring compressor and below a suction-type valve grinding tool.

Keep all split collets, collars, and springs paired up with the respective valves.

Grinding-in the Valves. Should an inspection of the valves reveal pitting of the valve faces or seats, the valves will have to be ground-in. Deal with each valve in the following manner. Clean both the valve face and its seat in the cylinder head. Smear with a piece of rag or the finger tip, a thin film of fine grinding paste (coarse at first if dealing with a valve and seat in poor condition) on the valve face; replace the valve in its guide minus the valve spring.

When using the valve grinding tool shown in Fig. 73, it is advisable to moisten the suction pad. Only a light pressure on the tool is required and care must be taken not to rock the valve, particularly if the valve guide is somewhat worn. Rotate the valve about *a third of a turn* in one direction and then an equal amount in the opposite direction, pausing every few oscillations to raise the valve from its seat and turn it one-third to a quarter of a revolution. Cease grinding-in when no "cut" can be felt (and the valve begins to "sing") and put some more paste on the bevelled edge of the valve face if, after cleaning the valve in paraffin, some pitting is still visible.

Continue grinding-in until both the valve face and seat have a matt metallic surface uniformly over an appreciable depth (line contact is not really sufficient) and there are no pit marks left after wiping the paste off. Excessive grinding-in after a good seating has been effected eventually leads to the valves becoming "pocketed," which causes a considerable decline in power output. Badly pitted valves or seats require to be refaced by a competent mechanic.

After grinding-in the inlet and exhaust valves, wipe both the valves and their seats thoroughly clean with a paraffin- or petrol-soaked rag to ensure that there is absolutely no trace of any abrasive left. Examine the valve guides for wear and renew if much play exists, otherwise slow-running will become difficult. Often a valve stem wears more than its guide does, and a distinct shoulder is felt near the neck of the valve. In this case fitting a new valve (which must be ground-in) will probably remedy slackness without fitting a new valve guide. Also renew the valve springs if weak.

Refitting the Valves. After grinding-in the valves you should reassemble them in the correct positions in the cylinder head.

On all engines do not forget to replace the hardened valve stem end-caps. Before replacing the valve springs, check that they have not lost their tension, if possible comparing them with a new spring. Loss of tension, due mainly to heat, sometimes occurs after several thousand miles, and the free length of the valve springs is reduced. This necessitates renewal and where such renewal is, or soon will be, required, it is obviously wise to effect valve-spring renewal during decarbonizing procedure.

Smear the valve stems with oil and replace them in their guides. Then refit the valve springs and outer collars, being careful not to mix up the inlet and exhaust components. Next compress each valve spring and refit the split collet, making certain that it "beds down" properly. The application of a little grease to the inside of a split-collet enables it to stick on the valve stem until the duplex spring is released, and thereby facilitates reassembly. To ensure the split collet bedding down, hold a box spanner over the outer collar and tap sharply. Do not forget to replace the valve stem end-caps.

After Reassembly. It is an excellent plan to test the seats by pouring some petrol into the ports and watching for leakage past the valves. Petrol should not creep past the valves until after a considerable time has elapsed. If it does, then this is sure proof that the valves have not been sufficiently ground-in and the remedy is (horrible thought!) to remove and continue grinding-in. *The ultimate test of good valve seating is engine compression.*

Replacing the Piston. Fit a new circlip into one of the piston-boss annular grooves, using a small pair of snipe-nose pliers; see that the circlip beds down snugly and is fully expanded (a loose circlip can ruin the bore). If the gudgeon-pin is not a push fit in the piston bosses (it rarely is), it is a good plan to warm up the piston in a bowl of boiling water before fitting it to the small-end of the connecting-rod.

With the crankcase mouth protected by a cloth and the piston held in its normal position, start the gudgeon-pin into the piston-boss hole opposite to where the circlip has been fitted. Before fitting the gudgeon-pin, make sure that it is the correct way round (*see* page 116) and smear it liberally with some clean engine oil. Then tap in the pin holding the piston firmly on the opposite side when using a soft-nose hammer or small mallet. If the gudgeon-pin is a tight fit, press the pin in, using the tool shown in Fig. 69, or a proprietary tool such as the Terry. As soon as the gudgeon-pin contacts the circlip already fitted, fit a new circlip on the other side.

To Replace the Cylinder Barrel (1946-55 Models G, J, J2; 1956-7 350 c.c. "Clippers"). The following procedure is recommended—

1. Check that the joint faces of the cylinder barrel and the crankcase are scrupulously clean (*see* page 115) and fit a new cylinder-base washer (21, Fig. 65) to the crankcase face, after smearing it lightly with some jointing compound. Make absolutely sure that the small hole in the base washer registers exactly with the oil-feed hole leading to the rear of the cylinder bore.

2. Turn the engine over slowly so that the piston is just past B.D.C.

3. Smear the piston (especially the rings) and the bore of the cylinder barrel with some clean engine oil, and space the ring gaps so that they are at 120 degrees to each other. With a split-skirt piston, see that no gap is in the immediate vicinity of the split in the skirt.

4. Holding the cylinder barrel vertically over the crankcase studs and piston, with one hand, with the other one offer up the piston to the barrel mouth. If difficulty is experienced in holding the piston and barrel steady, it is best to obtain assistance or to tie up the barrel to the frame top-tube with some stout string. Keep the barrel and piston absolutely square to each other and squeeze the rings by hand or with a proprietary metal strap (without disturbing the ring-gap position) as the piston slowly enters the bore. If a ring sticks, use no force, or ring breakage will result.

5. When the cylinder barrel has bedded right down on the base washer, turn the engine over slowly to verify that the piston is quite free.

6. Fit and tighten evenly and in a diagonal order the five nuts (19,

Fig. 65) securing the cylinder base to the crankcase. One of these nuts must be fitted to the stud inside the valve chest (*see* Fig. 62).

7. Reconnect the exhaust-valve lifter control cable.

To Replace the Cylinder Barrel (1954-8 250 c.c. "Clippers"). Follow the previous instructions (sub-paragraphs 1-6) for 1956-7 350 c.c. "Clippers" but disregard sub-paragraph 7 referring to the exhaust-valve lifter.

To Replace the Cylinder Barrel (1949-58 350 c.c., 500 c.c. "Bullets"; 1958 350 c.c. "Clipper"). Use the following procedure—

1. Follow the 1956-7 "Clipper" instructions (sub-paragraphs 1-5) given on page 123.

2. Fit the $\frac{1}{4}$ in. nut and washer shown at 22 in Fig. 67 and tighten the nut (over the tappet chest) firmly but not dead tight. Reserve final tightening until the cylinder head has been replaced.

3. Proceed immediately with the replacing of the cylinder head (page 126), so that the sleeve nuts 18 on the five long crankcase-studs 19, securing the head and barrel, can be firmly tightened down.

Assembling Cylinder Head and Rocker-box (1946-55 Models G, J, J2; 1956-7 350 c.c. "Clippers"). Referring to Fig. 65 assemble the head and overhead-valve mechanism in the following manner—

1. Check that the joint faces of the cylinder head and cylinder barrel are absolutely clean, and turn the engine so that the piston is at T.D.C. with both tappets right down.

2. To avoid oil leakage it is important to see that each push-rod cover-tube joint (*see* Fig. 74) is perfect. Two metal ferrules 23 (Fig. 65) are screwed into the bottom face of the cylinder head and mate with two female Hallite washers 22 located in the push-rod holes on the upper face of the cylinder barrel. It is advisable to renew both washers and coat their sides with some gold size or shellac.

3. Renew the copper gasket 16. If the old gasket is in good condition and you decide to fit it to the cylinder-barrel spigot, first anneal it by heating it to a red heat and then plunging it into cold water. Before fitting the cylinder-head gasket to the barrel-face, smear both its sides with a thin film of jointing compound.

4. Replace the cylinder head (with valves fitted) on the cylinder barrel and fit the four $\frac{5}{16}$ in. nuts and washers 13 (sleeve nuts only on 250 c.c. "Clippers") to the inverted cylinder-head studs 14.

5. Tighten down the four cylinder-head securing nuts evenly, firmly, and in a diagonal order, to prevent the risk of head distortion. After fitting new Hallite washers to the push-rod cover-tube joints always apply pressure first of all to the two head-securing nuts on the *timing side*. This will compress the Hallite washers and bring even pressure to bear on the copper gasket. Further final tightening of the four cylinder-head securing

GENERAL MAINTENANCE

nuts will be necessary when engine assembly is complete and the engine has been warmed up.

6. Replace (if previously removed) in its original position the lower one-piece bearing caps 11, after checking that the oil-feed holes for the rocker shafts are unobstructed. Also fit and tighten the central stud 10.

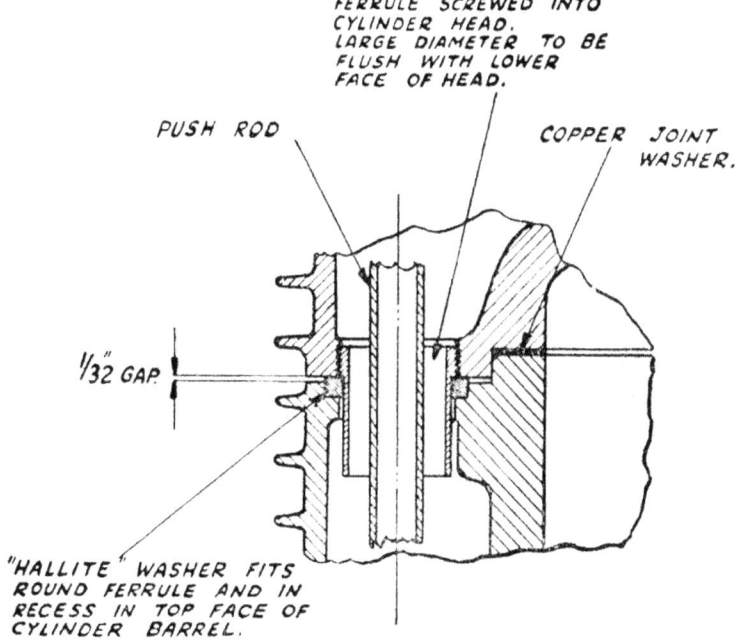

FIG. 74. SECTIONAL DRAWING SHOWING DETAILS OF PUSH-ROD COVER-TUBE JOINTS

Not applicable to "Bullet" and 1958 350 c.c. "Clipper" models.

(*The Enfield Cycle Co., Ltd.*)

Check that both valve stem end-caps (8, Fig. 72) are in position and tap them to ensure their being bedded down squarely.

7. Oil both ends of the push-rods 12, and fit the rods (the exhaust rod has a collar) in their correct positions (with their adjustable ends at the bottom); also lay the overhead-rocker shafts (*see* Fig. 72) in their respective lower bearing-caps, with the ball ends of the inner rocker-arms engaging the inlet and exhaust push-rod cupped upper-ends. Oil both rocker shafts liberally before assembly.

8. Fit the upper rocker-bearing caps 8, 9, (in their original positions) and fit and tighten evenly, firmly, and diagonally the eight $\frac{1}{4}$ in. nuts and washers 7. Make sure that the upper and lower bearing-caps are truly

aligned, and after tightening down the cap nuts verify that both rocker shafts move freely; if stiff, tap the end of each shaft smartly with a hammer.

9. Adjust both tappets as described on page 104 so that there is an inlet and exhaust valve clearance of 0·002 in. and 0·004 in. respectively. Also check the exhaust-valve lifter adjustment (*see* page 105).

10. Fit the oil-sealing gasket 6 (renew unless intact) and replace the rocker-box cover 4, securing it with the central nut and washer 5. Also replace the tappet-chest cover and washer 17.

11. Reconnect the oil-feed pipe 1 to the rocker-box and crankcase, and tighten the two union nuts 2, 3 very securely. Before replacing the pipe blow through it to make sure it is unobstructed.

12. Kick the engine over quickly several times to circulate oil and to ascertain that everything is satisfactory. Also fit the sparking plug so as to blank off the plug hole. It is assumed that the plug has been cleaned and checked for correct gap (*see* pages 93–5).

13. Proceed with the final assembly of the engine, exhaust system, petrol tank, etc., as described on page 128.

Assembling Cylinder Head and Rocker-box (1954-8 250 c.c. "Clippers").

Assemble the components exactly as just described for the 350 c.c. "Clippers." When replacing the two push-rods, be careful not to mix them up. It is assumed that you have marked them for identification (*see* page 111). When adjusting the tappets, set them so that the clearance for both valves is *nil* (*see* page 104).

Assembling Cylinder Head and Rocker-box (1949-58 350 c.c., 500 c.c. "Bullets"; 1958 350 c.c. "Clipper").

Referring to Figs. 66, 67, assemble the head and overhead valve mechanism as follows—

1. Check the joint faces of the cylinder head and barrel for absolute cleanliness, and turn the engine so that the piston is at T.D.C. with both tappets right down.

2. Fit a new copper and asbestos gasket 23 to the cylinder-barrel face, after applying some jointing compound to both sides of the gasket. Should you replace the old gasket, anneal it before fitting it (*see* page 124, sub-paragraph 3).

3. Replace the cylinder head (complete with valves) vertically on to the cylinder barrel, and fit the four long sleeve-nuts, washers 18 to the crankcase studs 19 projecting right into the rocker-boxes. Also fit the nut and washer to the crankcase stud projecting from the near-side of the cylinder head close to the sparking-plug hole. Fit also the nut and washer 20 to the cylinder-barrel stud protruding from the off-side of the cylinder head. Tighten down firmly all six nuts, being careful to tighten them evenly and in a diagonal sequence to avoid the risk of causing distortion.

4. Tighten down firmly the ¼ in. nut 22 (above the tappet chest), fitted during the replacement of the cylinder barrel (*see* page 124, sub-paragraph 2). It is advisable to check all seven nuts again for tightness after warming up the engine (*see* page 128).

5. Fit the two lower bearing-caps 16 for the overhead rockers, in their original positions, after first verifying that their oil-feed holes are clear. Also check that both valve stem end-caps (8, Fig. 72) are in position; tap them to ensure that they are squarely bedded down.

6. Replace in their correct positions the inlet and exhaust push-rods 17. Before doing so, oil both ends of each rod. Do not forget that the *inlet* rod is the shorter of the two and that the adjustable ends must face downwards. Also lay the two overhead-rocker shafts (*see* Fig. 72) in their respective lower bearing-caps, with the ball ends of the inner rocker-arms engaging the cupped upper-ends of the inlet and exhaust push-rods. Before assembling the rockers, oil both shafts liberally.

7. Fit in their original positions the two upper bearing-caps 15, and afterwards fit the eight ¼ in. nuts and washers 14 securing both rocker-housing assemblies to the cylinder head. Firmly, progressively, and in a diagonal order, tighten down the eight cap-securing nuts. Be quite sure before tightening down each pair of bearing caps that the two caps are in perfect alignment. After tightening is completed, check that both overhead-rocker shafts are able to move quite freely; if stiff, tap the end of each shaft sharply with a hammer.

8. Adjust the inlet and exhaust tappets as described on page 104 so that both valves have a clearance of *nil*. Afterwards replace the tappet-chest washer and cover on the chest (which is integral with the crankcase).

9. Fit the decompressor unit 13 to the cylinder head, not omitting to replace the copper washer between the head and the body of the unit. Reconnect the control cable to the handlebars and adjust for backlash (*see* page 106).

10. Replace the inlet and exhaust rocker-box covers 9, 10, together with their oil-sealing gaskets 26. Unless intact, renew these gaskets. The application of some jointing compound is desirable. Secure each rocker-box cover with three long sleeve nuts 11 and one short sleeve nut 12. The correct position for the shorter nut is referred to on page 112, sub-paragraph 4.

11. Reconnect the two-way oil-feed pipe 6 to the crankcase and the separate rocker-boxes; tighten firmly the union nut 7 securing the pipe to the crankcase, and the two union-screws 8 (with washers) securing the banjo ends of the composite pipe to the rocker-boxes.

12. Turn the engine over smartly several times with the kick-starter to check that everything is in order and to circulate oil. Afterwards blank off the sparking-plug hole by fitting the plug. It is assumed to have been cleaned and correctly gapped (*see* pages 93–5).

13. Complete the assembly of the engine, exhaust system, petrol tank, etc. in accordance with the appropriate instructions given on page 128.

Final Engine Assembly (All Models). Reconnect the h.t. lead to the sparking plug, after checking that its rubber insulation is sound. Fit a new copper washer if the old washer is badly flattened. On the 1956-8 350 c.c. "Clippers" and all "Bullets" models, reconnect the engine steady stay and tighten the nuts at both ends very tightly. On no account should these nuts be firmly tightened before finally bolting down the cylinder head.

If not already done, clean and inspect the carburettor (*see* pages 30-1). Ease the throttle and air slides into the mixing chamber of the assembled carburettor, and fit the carburettor to the inlet-port face, after fitting a new flange-washer; the addition of some jointing compound is beneficial. Before replacing the carburettor, check its flange for truth (*see* page 31). Tighten down firmly and evenly both carburettor-flange securing nuts, but avoid excessive tightening, as this sometimes distorts the carburettor body slightly and causes the throttle slide to stick. If the slide does stick, ease off the two nuts a fraction.

If an air filter is fitted, clean it (*see* page 34) and reconnect it to the carburettor air-intake. Two types of connexion are used (*see* sub-paragraphs 3, 1, pages 109, 111).

Replace as a unit the exhaust pipe and silencer (duplicated on 1946-55 Model J2), and if you have to tap the pipe home into the exhaust port, be most careful not to dent it at the bend. Tighten the nuts securing the exhaust system to the frame very securely. If the exhaust pipe is very sooty, it is a good plan before fitting the pipe and silencer to stand the unit upright, with the silencer-end plugged, and pour some paraffin through the other end, using a funnel. This will loosen most of the soot and carbon, and on starting the engine, the exhaust gases will do the rest.

Rechecking Engine Nuts for Tightness. Before replacing the petrol tank on 1949-58 "Bullet" models it is advisable to run up the engine and recheck, and if necessary tighten, all cylinder barrel and head securing-nuts. Some nuts, particularly the sleeve nuts inside the rocker-boxes, are not accessible when the petrol tank is replaced. It is suggested that a small auxiliary petrol-tank be temporarily connected to the carburettor for warming-up purposes and that the rocker-box covers be removed when the engine is quite hot. When checking the above-mentioned nuts, it is a good plan to check for tightness all other external nuts, especially the nuts securing the overhead rocker-bearing caps, oil and petrol pipe unions, etc.

On the 1946-55 Models G, J, J2 and all "Clipper" models the cylinder head and barrel nuts, being below the head, are fully accessible, and therefore rechecking of the nuts can be done after fitting the petrol tank as described on the opposite page.

Having rechecked engine nuts for tightness with the engine warmed up it is desirable to recheck the tappet adjustment (*see* page 104) at a convenient opportunity when the engine is *cold*.

GENERAL MAINTENANCE 129

Replacing the Petrol Tank. On the 1946-55 Models G, J, J2 a rubber pad is on the top of each of the four tank-supports. Position the petrol tank, and insert from below the four steel bolts, each having one rubber pad and a steel washer fitted as shown in Fig. 64. As mentioned on page 108, renew the rubber pads if perished or damaged. Tighten all four bolts evenly and reasonably tightly.

On the 1949-58 "Clipper" and "Bullet" models, position the petrol tank and replace and tighten the two transverse bolts, one at the front and one at the rear. See that the distance tube and rubber buffer-sleeve are fitted (in this order) over the front transverse bolt before the bolt is inserted, also check that all washers are fitted in their correct positions.

IGNITION AND VALVE TIMING

Ignition Timing. Some motor-cyclists imagine that by advancing the timing they will automatically obtain greater speed. The timing recommended by the engine manufacturers is the maximum advance permissible. A further advance in the timing submits the big-end bearing to undue stresses and spoils the flexibility of the engine; it is also likely to cause some spitting-back through the carburettor. Always employ the correct ignition timings which are given in Table VI.

If for a reason a Lucas "Magdyno," a Lucas SR-1 magneto (1956-8 "Bullets"), or a Lucas or Miller contact-breaker (250, 350 c.c. coil-ignition "Clippers") is removed (*see* page 103), or the driving pinion is freed or extracted from its tapered shaft, it is necessary to retime the ignition. This should be done as described on pages 130-4.

TABLE VI

IGNITION TIMINGS FOR 1946-58 ENGINES

Royal Enfield Engine	Maximum Ignition-Advance Permitted
1946-54 Model G	$\frac{3}{8}$ in. before T.D.C. (lever fully advanced)
1946-8 Model J	$\frac{5}{16}$ in. before T.D.C. (lever fully advanced)
1946-55 Model J2	$\frac{5}{16}$ in. before T.D.C. (lever fully advanced)
1949-55 "350 Bullet"	$\frac{1}{4}$ in. before T.D.C. (lever fully advanced)
1953-5 "500 Bullet"	$\frac{5}{16}$ in. before T.D.C. (lever fully advanced)
1956-8 "350 Bullet"	$\frac{7}{16}$ in.-$\frac{1}{2}$ in. before T.D.C. (A.I.A. fully advanced)
1956-8 "500 Bullet"	$\frac{5}{16}$ in.-$\frac{3}{8}$ in. before T.D.C. (A.I.A. fully advanced)
1954-8 "250 Clipper"	$\frac{1}{64}$ in. before T.D.C. (A.I.A. fully retarded)
1956-7 "350 Clipper"	$\frac{3}{8}$ in. before T.D.C. (lever fully advanced)
1958 "350 Clipper"	$\frac{7}{16}$ in.-$\frac{1}{2}$ in. before T.D.C. (A.I.A. fully advanced)

Note: In the above table, "lever" refers, of course, to the ignition lever on the handlebars, and "A.I.A." is an abbreviation for automatic-ignition-advance mechanism.

Timing the Ignition (All Lucas "Magdyno" Models). Before checking the ignition timing, or retiming the ignition, always clean the contacts (where necessary) and check that the gap between them, with the contacts fully open, is 0·012-0·015 in. (*see* pages 96-7). An incorrect gap affects the timing to some extent. It is assumed here that the "Magdyno" is bolted down; if it is not, attend to this (*see* page 103). It is, in any case, assumed that the "Magdyno" driving pinion has been removed with the extractor referred to on page 103.

Turn the engine slowly *forward* until the piston is at the top of the compression stroke, with both valves fully closed. Next move the ignition lever on the handlebars *outwards* to the fully advanced position; keep it in this position until retiming is completed. See that the stop-screw in the magneto cam-plate is in the end of the slot and that the plate is not sticking. If the control lever is slack, tighten the lever nut before proceeding further.

Turn the engine slowly *backwards* (by means of the rear wheel with third or top gear engaged) until the piston has descended a distance below T.D.C. corresponding exactly to the maximum ignition-advance (*see* Table VI). To find true T.D.C., where the cylinder head has *not* been removed, use a simply-made T.D.C. indicator. Screw the body of an old sparking plug into the plug hole. Then insert a piece of thick wire, or thin rod, bent over at one end for safety, through the hole in the centre of the plug body. Then mark with some red adhesive plastic, or scratch with a thin file a nick on the wire immediately above the top of the hole, when slightly rocking the crank produces no piston movement.

Make another mark $\frac{5}{16}$ in. (or whatever is the correct ignition-advance) above the first mark, and when turning the engine backwards to obtain the correct piston position for timing, allow the second mark to occupy the position of the first (T.D.C.) mark. Should the cylinder head be removed for decarbonizing, the best method is to lay a straight-edge across the top of the barrel and take vertical measurement with a steel rule. This gives a very precise timing.

Some owners prefer to retime the ignition by taking degree measurements of crankshaft rotation, using a degree disc, but this is quite unnecessary for normal purposes.

Having obtained the correct position of the piston when the spark should occur with the ignition lever fully advanced, turn the magneto shaft by hand (in its normal direction of rotation) so that the contacts of the contact-breaker are just beginning to open; the best method of determining the point at which the contacts "break" is to insert a small slip of thin cellophane or tissue-paper between the contacts and gently pull on this as the contact-breaker cam is slowly turned; immediately the slip is freed, stop moving the magneto shaft to which the cam is fitted. Replace the "Magdyno" driving pinion on the tapered end of the magneto shaft and, being careful not to turn the engine, tap it home lightly, using a box spanner and light hammer to direct even pressure on the pinion boss. Lock the pinion to the shaft by fitting and tightening the lock-nut. When doing this, it is advisable to engage a gear and lock the rear wheel so as to prevent the engine turning. Before replacing the timing-case cover and washer (see page 136), it is advisable to recheck the ignition timing.

Timing the Ignition (1956-8 "Bullets" with Lucas Magneto). The 1956-8 "Bullets" with a Lucas SR-1 rotating-magnet magneto (see Fig. 58) have an automatic-ignition-advance (A.I.A.) device into which the magneto driving-pinion is built. The pinion is mounted on a smooth taper on the magneto shaft and is secured by a nut (R.H. thread). When the engine is stationary the A.I.A. device automatically keeps the ignition fully retarded.

Before checking the ignition timing or retiming the ignition, always clean the contacts (if necessary) and check, and if necessary adjust, the gap (0·010 in.-0·012 in.) between them, with the contacts at maximum break. It is assumed here that the magneto, if previously removed, has been replaced, but that the timing cover has been removed (see page 134) and the driving pinion (with embodied A.I.A. device) extracted by unscrewing the nut which pulls the pinion off.

Turn the engine slowly *forward* until the piston is exactly at the top of the compression stroke, with both valves fully closed. Next rotate the two halves of the A.I.A. coupling relatively to each other, against the springs (i.e., into the fully-advanced position); with a piece of wire hold it in this position.

Now turn the engine slowly *backward* (by means of the rear wheel with third or top gear engaged) until the piston has moved down from T.D.C. a distance corresponding exactly to the maximum ignition-advance permitted and specified in Table VI. Insert a piece of wire through the sparking plug hole (as described on page 130) for finding the true T.D.C. position and the point of maximum ignition-advance.

Having obtained the piston position corresponding to the maker's timing, turn the magneto shaft and cam *forward* until the contacts of the contact-breaker are beginning to break, using the method referred to on page 130. Then replace the driving pinion and A.I.A. device, tap them home (see page 130), and afterwards firmly retighten the nut, being careful not to turn the engine when doing so. Then remove the piece of wire locking the A.I.A. device. Finally recheck the ignition timing (with the timing cover and washer removed) by removing the cover (see Fig. 58) from the magneto and holding the rotor in the fully-advanced position. If timing is correct, replace the timing cover and washer.

250 c.c. "Clipper" Ignition Timing (1954-8). A centrifugal type automatic-ignition-advance (A.I.A.) device is incorporated at the back of the Miller or Lucas contact-breaker, having a range of approximately $12\frac{1}{2}$

degrees on the half-speed shaft, corresponding to 25 degrees on the engine shaft. The maximum permitted ignition-advance is 30 degrees, so that, with the A.I.A. fully retarded, the contacts must open when the piston is 5 degrees or about $\frac{1}{64}$ in. before T.D.C.

Timing the Ignition (250 c.c. "Clippers" with Miller Equipment). On 1954 to early 1955 coil-ignition models it is not necessary to remove the timing cover and contact-breaker driving pinion to retime the ignition, as the contact-breaker cam can be moved as required on its shaft. The following procedure is necessary.

Switch off the ignition and after cleaning the contacts (if necessary) check and if necessary adjust the gap (0·015 in.–0·018 in.) between the contacts of the contact-breaker as described on page 99. Unscrew and remove the centre screw which secures the cam to the contact-breaker shaft. Next free the cam by screwing a $\frac{5}{16}$ in. B.S.F. bolt into the threaded hole. Slacken the two small screws securing the contact-breaker base plate, and adjust the plate so that it is centrally positioned in its slots. Afterwards tighten both screws.

Jack the motor-cycle up on its stand (use packing if necessary to raise the rear wheel clear of the ground). Engage third or top gear and slowly rotate the engine by turning the rear wheel until the piston is below T.D.C. (on the compression stroke) a distance exactly equal to the maximum ignition-advance permitted (*see* Table VI). To find the true T.D.C. and subsequent timing position, use a piece of thick wire or thin rod inserted as described on page 130.

Now switch on the ignition and rotate the cam *clockwise* (as viewed from the near-side) until the ignition warning-lamp lights up. Continue slowly to rotate the cam clockwise until the lamp just goes out, indicating that the contacts have just separated and broken the primary circuit. Secure the cam to its shaft by delivering a sharp tap endwise, and lock in position by firmly tightening the cam securing-screw. See that the engine is not turned until the cam is firmly locked. Recheck the ignition timing by causing the ignition warning-lamp to go out, and verifying the position of the piston below T.D.C. when this happens.

Should the ignition timing be slightly out, correct by loosening the two screws which secure the contact-breaker base-plate to its housing, and turn the plate clockwise to retard the timing, or anti-clockwise to advance it. An adjustment range of plus or minus about 6 degrees is provided by the slots in the plate.

Timing Ignition (250, 350 c.c. "Clippers" with Lucas Equipment). On late 1955–8 coil-ignition models it is necessary (if the driving pinion has been removed) to replace the pinion after adjusting the timing so that it is approximately correct, and then to make a final precision adjustment by slackening the clamping bolt and turning the contact-breaker housing as required; the housing is clamped on to the contact-breaker bracket which is bolted to the top of the crankcase.

If the contact-breaker drive has been dismantled, clamp the contact-breaker housing so that the name on the cover is approximately *horizontal*. Clean the contacts (if necessary) and then check and if necessary adjust the gap (0·015 in.-0·018 in.) between them. Turn the engine *forward*

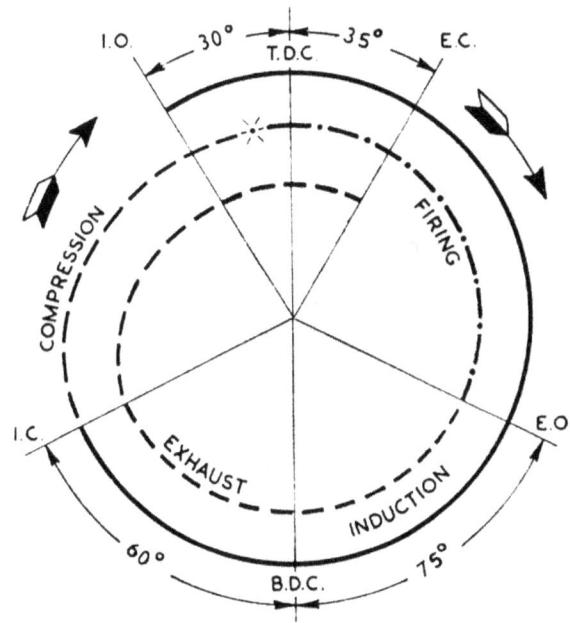

FIG. 75. VALVE TIMING DIAGRAM FOR ALL 1946-58 ENGINES EXCEPT THE 1953-8 500 c.c. "BULLET" ENGINES

On 1953-8 500 c.c. "Bullet" engines the valve timing is as shown above, except that the inlet valve opens 40 degrees before T.D.C. and closes 70 degrees after B.D.C.

until the piston is exactly at T.D.C. on the compression stroke, with both valves closed. Then turn the engine slowly backwards (by means of the rear wheel with third or top gear engaged) until the piston has descended a distance exactly equal to the maximum ignition-advance (on full retard) specified in Table VI. Insert a piece of wire or rod through the plug hole as described on page 130, to find true T.D.C. and the subsequent lower position for correct timing. Without moving the engine, turn the contact-breaker shaft and cam until the contact-breaker points are beginning to break (*see* notes on page 130).* Then replace the driving

* An alternative method of finding the exact moment of contact opening is to switch on the ignition and observe the warning lamp or ammeter.

pinion on the shaft taper, and again check the maximum opening of the contacts. Recheck the ignition timing and make the final close adjustment by slackening the clamping bolt securing the contact-breaker housing and rotating the housing slightly until the correct ignition-setting is obtained. Finally replace the timing cover and washer.

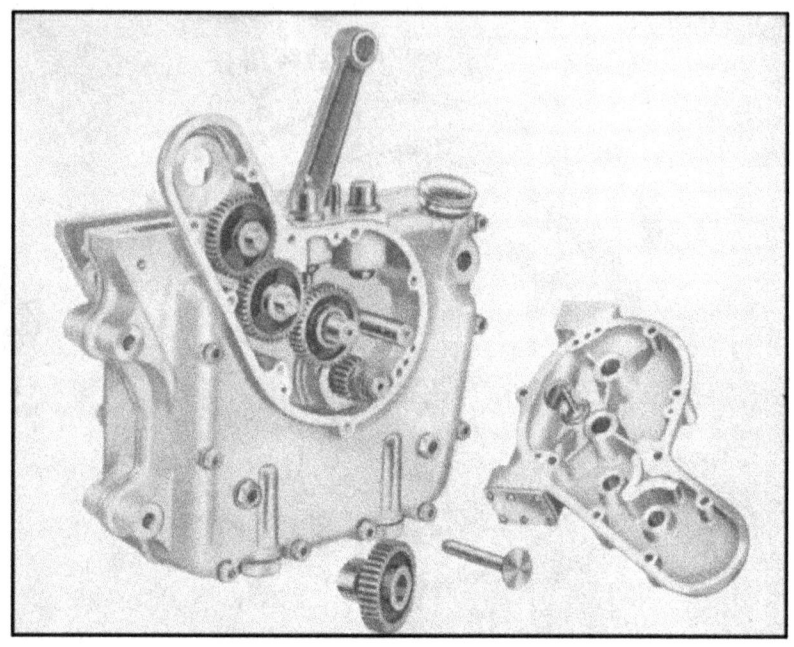

FIG. 76. ROYAL ENFIELD CRANKCASE WITH TIMING COVER REMOVED, SHOWING TIMING GEARS (ALL 1946-58 ENGINES)
The exhaust camwheel and flat-base tappet are shown removed.

Valve Timing. The correct valve timing for all 1946-58 Royal Enfield engines is shown diagrammatically in Fig. 75. Under no circumstances attempt to alter this timing which has been determined by the Redditch designers after much research and calculation. If for any reason you wish to check the valve timing, using the crankshaft degree-disc method, note that this must be done with a valve clearance of 0·005 in., except on the 1953-8 "Bullet" engines and the 1956-8 350 c.c. "Clipper" engines; here the valve clearance should be 0·012 in. The valve clearances required for normal running are those specified in Table IV on page 104.

To Remove Timing Cover (All Engines). Lay a drip-tray beneath the engine to collect the engine oil which drains off when the timing cover is removed. Remove as a unit the exhaust pipe and silencer (duplicated on

Model J2). Now remove the nine small screws which secure the timing cover to the timing case. Slacken off the screws evenly and be careful not to lose the nine oil-sealing washers. Then carefully withdraw the timing cover and its washer. If the cover is stiff, tap it gently with a mallet.

Removing and Replacing the Timing Gears. The removal of the timing

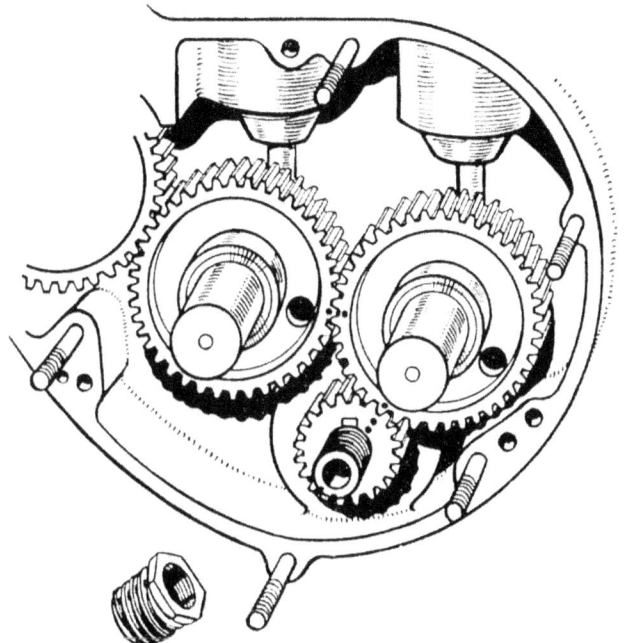

FIG. 77. THE DOT SYSTEM OF MARKING THE TIMING GEARS USED ON ALL ROYAL ENFIELD ENGINES
(*The Enfield Cycle Co., Ltd.*)

cover exposes the complete gear train (*see* Fig. 76) comprising the inlet and exhaust camwheels (with integral cams), and the two intermediate gears (for the magneto or contact-breaker drive). All gears can readily be removed if desired. But do not remove unnecessarily the worm-shaft and integral lock-nut which secure the engine pinion. To remove the pinion from the engine shaft, unscrew the worm-shaft, using service tool (Part No. E5451) on the hexagon behind the worm; it has a *left-hand thread*. Extract the pinion by inserting a flat chisel, or a similar tool, behind the pinion and tapping the tool gently.

A dot system of marking the two camwheels is employed (*see* Fig. 77). When replacing the timing gears, turn the engine so that the piston is at top-dead-centre and replace the exhaust camwheel so that its two dots are exactly opposite to the two dots on the crankshaft pinion. Similarly replace the inlet camwheel so that its single dot registers exactly with the single dot on the exhaust camwheel. Valve timing *must* then be as indicated in the timing diagram shown in Fig. 75, assuming that the tappet clearances are adjusted correctly for timing (not normal running) purposes.

To Replace Timing Cover. When doing this, see that the joint washer is located properly over the oil holes. It is not advisable to use jointing compound, but both sides of the washer should be smeared with some grease. Use a new washer unless the old one is perfect. Make sure that the cork or rubber plug is positioned in the pump-worm hole; if damaged in any way, renew the plug to ensure oil being fed to the big-end at the correct pressure.

It is important to turn the engine slowly forward while replacing the timing cover; this helps the pump worm to engage the pump spindle, and thereby avoids the risk of damage occurring. Before fitting the timing cover, clean the filter chamber with some clean engine oil, Tighten down the nine screws evenly and firmly, and do not omit the nine oil-sealing washers. After fitting the timing cover, check the functioning of the oil pump by running-up the engine, removing the oil filler-cap, and observing the flow of oil through the relief valve. Note that it may be several minutes before the oil flows back in any quantity. Afterwards replace the exhaust pipe(s) and silencer(s).

THE ENGINE BEARINGS

The bearings on the crankshaft and connecting-rod assembly (*see* Fig. 68) are of robust design and provided you keep the oil tank topped-up with a plentiful supply of oil, and change the oil regularly (*see* page 41), you are unlikely to experience any bearing trouble for a very long period. Careless driving tactics, however, have a considerable effect on the wear of engine bearings. Avoid allowing the engine to labour with top gear engaged, running on full bore for excessive periods, and being impatient during the running-in period (*see* page 14).

The Small-end Bearing. The connecting-rod small-end (*see* Fig. 68) has a carobronze bush, except on "Bullet" models where the small-end of the RR56 light-alloy connecting-rod is bored to give a direct bearing surface for the large-diameter gudgeon-pin. After long usage, the eye of the connecting-rod can be bored oversize to receive a bush, but this is rarely necessary.

With the engine cold, the fully-floating gudgeon-pin should be a free working fit in the small-end bearing, and a push fit in the piston bosses. When you have occasion to remove the cylinder barrel, insert the gudgeon-pin in the small-end and check for any "rock" in the bearing. No appreciable play is permissible.

GENERAL MAINTENANCE

The Big-end Bearing. This comprises a hardened chrome-steel bush pressed into the big-end eye of the connecting-rod, and a mild-steel white-metalled floating bush (*see* Fig. 68). When you remove the cylinder barrel, check for play in the big-end bearing by firmly gripping the connecting-rod, with the rod at B.D.C., and attempting to push-and-pull it downwards and upwards, preferably with the oil film dispersed. A very slight degree of "shake" is permissible, but there should be no marked up and down movement. Under favourable circumstances the big-end bearing can be expected to remain serviceable for up to 30,000-40,000 miles, but it is impossible to specify any definite mileage.

The Main-shaft Bearings. On Models G, J, J2, "1954-7 Clippers," heavy-duty caged-roller bearings are used for both main-shafts, the outer

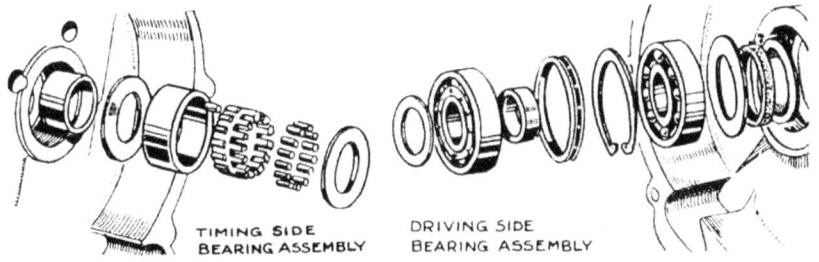

FIG. 78. SHOWING (RIGHT) THE DRIVING SIDE, AND (LEFT) THE TIMING SIDE ENGINE MAIN-SHAFT BEARING ASSEMBLIES

The above arrangement applies to all pre-1956 "Bullet" engines.

(*The Enfield Cycle Co., Ltd.*)

races being shrunk into the crankcase and the rollers running direct on the main-shafts.

On early "Bullet" engines two ball bearings are provided on the driving side and one single-row roller bearing on the timing side. The later "Bullet" engines have one ball and one roller bearing on the driving side, and a single-row caged-roller bearing on the timing side as shown in Fig. 78. On 1956-8 "Bullets," however, the timing-side bearing comprises a double-row roller bearing. A small degree of end-float is permissible, but no appreciable up-and-down movement should exist on attempting to "rock" the main-shafts up and down.

The Camwheel Bearings. The camwheels have internal bronze-bushes running on fixed spindles in the timing case, and should last for thousands of miles without attention.

Renewing Engine Bearings. When the engine begins to run somewhat roughly and inspection shows that there is appreciable "shake" in the main and big-end bearings, it is advisable to remove the cylinder, cylinder barrel, "Magdyno" (or magneto or contact-breaker), the timing cover, its contents, etc., and remove the crankcase from the frame. This should then be delivered or dispatched to the Enfield Cycle Co., Ltd., or to one of their authorized repairers, so that new bearings can be fitted, and the crankcase rebushed where necessary. Dismantling and rebuilding the crankshaft assembly is a skilled job involving accurate alignment of the flywheels and main-shafts, and the use of special tools and appliances; the work is rather beyond the ability of the average motor-cyclist and is beyond the scope of this maintenance handbook. Should you attempt this and similar repair work, you are advised to obtain a copy of the appropriate Workshop Maintenance Manual from an Enfield dealer.

TO REMOVE CRANKCASE AND GEARBOX

To Remove the Crankcase Assembly (1946-55 Models G, J, J2). Firstly remove the cylinder head and cylinder barrel as described on pages 109 and 114 respectively. Disconnect the h.t. cables to the Lucas "Magdyno." Place a drip-tray beneath the oil-bath chain case and remove the cover from the chain case. To do this, remove the nut securing the near-side footrest, detach the latter, also the rear-brake pedal, and pull the cover clear. Remove the engine sprocket (splined to the drive shaft and secured by a large lock-nut and washer), the primary chain, and the clutch sprocket.

To dismantle the clutch, unscrew the three clutch-spring pins and withdraw the spring cap, the three springs, the distance tubes, the clutch front plate, the outer retaining spring, and the assembly of driven and driving plates. Now remove the large circlip and withdraw the clutch sprocket from the clutch centre. To remove the clutch centre it is necessary to use the Royal Enfield extractor (Part No. E5414). The clutch centre is mounted on splines on the gearbox main-shaft and is secured by a nut with right-hand thread. Remove the small screw which secures the rear half of the oil-bath chain case to the gearbox securing bolts. Now withdraw the rear half of the chain case.

Support the crankcase by inserting some strong packing (e.g., a box) beneath it, and then remove the bolts holding the engine to its mounting plates. Finally ease the crankcase assembly carefully out of the frame ready for further dismantling and bearing renewal.

Instructions for removing the timing gears and the Lucas "Magdyno" are given on pages 134 and 103 respectively. Piston removal is dealt with on page 115.

To Remove the Crankcase and Gearbox (1949-55 350 c.c. 500 c.c. "Bullets"). The crankcase and gearbox are bolted together and must be removed as a single unit. First remove the cylinder head and cylinder barrel as described on pages 111 and 114 respectively. Disconnect the four h.t. leads to the Lucas "Magdyno." Next lay a drip-tray below the oil-bath chain case and remove the cover; to do this, remove the single bolt securing it. Now remove the engine sprocket, the primary chain, the clutch assembly, and the oil-bath chain case rear half.

An endless-type chain is provided, and it is therefore necessary to remove the two sprockets and the chain simultaneously. The procedure for removing the engine sprocket, the clutch assembly and the clutch sprocket is the same as for Models G, J, J2 (*see* second paragraph in the previous section). Remove the three nuts securing the rear half of the oil-bath chain case to the crankcase, and withdraw the rear half of the chain case. Remove the secondary chain.

Place a box or other suitable packing beneath the rear-fork pivot lug, to support the machine, and insert additional packing beneath the crankcase to remove its weight when freed from the frame. Remove the two front engine-plates, and disconnect the stand spring and remove the centre stand. Completely remove the attachment plates below the gearbox and remove the stud securing these plates to the base of the frame seat-tube. Remove the nuts holding the fixed half of the rear mudguard to the gearbox. Finally pull the crankcase and gearbox forward and turn slightly to the off-side until the unit is completely withdrawn.

For instructions on removing the timing gears and the Lucas "Magdyno," see pages 135 and 103 respectively. Piston removal is referred to on page 115.

To Remove Crankcase and Gearbox (1956-8 350 c.c., 500 c.c. "Bullets"; 1958 350 c.c. "Clipper"). The crankcase and gearbox are bolted together; remove as a unit. First disconnect the stop-tail lamp leads at the socket provided, and remove the rear mudguard and the dualseat. Then remove the petrol tank as described on page 108. Disconnect the horn and earth wires from the rectifier and then proceed to remove the cylinder head and cylinder barrel as described on pages 111 and 114 respectively.

Lay a drip-tray beneath the oil-bath chain case and remove the chain-case cover after unscrewing its single securing-bolt. Remove the three nuts holding the alternator to the lugs within the chain case and remove the alternator stator; be careful with the three small distance-pieces. Remove the large hexagon securing the rotor to its shaft and remove the rotor. Next remove simultaneously the engine sprocket, the endless primary chain, and the clutch sprocket. Appropriate instructions for doing this are those given in the section for removing the crankcase assembly on Models G, J, J2 (*see* page 138). Remove the three nuts securing the rear half of the chain case and withdraw the latter.

Remove the tools and the battery (*see* Fig. 34) from the container on the near-side of the machine. Remove the guard for the secondary chain, and also the short guard at the gearbox end; disconnect the spring link and remove the secondary chain.

Allow the machine to rest on the centre stand, but insert a box or other suitable packing beneath the crankcase to take its weight. Remove the $\frac{5}{16}$ in. studs from the engine front mounting-plates, and also remove the $\frac{5}{16}$ in. stud from below the gearbox. Loosen the $\frac{1}{2}$ in. stud farther along, and disconnect the spring for the centre stand. Now remove the off-side footrest and carefully ease the engine and gearbox unit out of the frame from the off-side. The removal of the piston and timing gears are dealt with on pages 115 and 135 respectively.

To Remove the Crankcase and Gearbox (1956-7 350 c.c. "Clippers"). Remove the cylinder head and cylinder barrel as described on pages 109 and 123 respectively. Disconnect the l.t. cables to the Lucas "Magdyno." Remove the footrests, the footrest rod, and the centre stand.

Place a drip-tray beneath the oil-bath chain case and remove the chain-case cover. Then remove the engine sprocket, the primary chain, the clutch sprocket, the rear half of the chain case (*see* instructions on page 138 for Model G), and the secondary chain.

Insert some substantial packing beneath the crankcase and remove the top and bottom bolts securing the rearmost points of the rear engine plates to the frame. Remove the front engine-plate bolts and carefully ease the crankcase out, complete with the gearbox and the rear engine-plates. The removal of the piston "Magdyno," and timing gears are dealt with on pages 115, 103 and 135 respectively.

To Remove the Crankcase Assembly (1954-8 250 c.c. "Clippers"). First remove the cylinder head and cylinder barrel as described on pages 111 and 114 respectively. Undo the adjuster nut from the rear of the brake rod and allow the rear-brake pedal to drop down. Next remove the footrest and disconnect the three l.t. electric leads; they are coloured (*see* Figs. 52-3) to facilitate correct replacement.

Place a drip-tray beneath the oil-bath chain case and remove the cover from the case. Now proceed with the dismantling of the clutch. Remove the three spring-studs, washers and clutch springs. Remove the clutch plates, the sprocket, and the short push-rod which has a flat head. Remove the spring link and take off the primary chain. Removal of the spring link is facilitated by removing the tensioning slipper (*see* Fig. 84) below the chain lower-run. Remove the clutch centre, using the Royal Enfield extractor (Part No. E5414). Remove the alternator rotor from the engine near-side main-shaft, and extract the sprocket from the shaft. Then remove the rear half of the oil-bath chain case after removing the three socket screws and locking washers.

With the machine on its centre stand, and some strong packing inserted under the crankcase to take its weight, remove the bolts from one front engine-mounting plate and withdraw the plate. Remove both bolts from the rear engine-mounting plate. Loosen the gearbox securing nuts so as to permit some small movement of the rear engine-plate. Finally, ease the crankcase carefully sideways and forwards until it clears the frame and can be placed on the bench for attention. The removal of the timing gears, the contact-breaker unit, and the piston are dealt with on pages 135, 103, 115 respectively.

CARE OF THE TRANSMISSION

The transmission comprises (front to rear): the primary chain, the clutch, the gearbox, the secondary chain, and the cush-drive rear hub (dealt with in the next section).

Clutch Control Adjustment. To prevent clutch slip or drag (both serious nuisances), it is essential always to keep the clutch correctly adjusted. The clutch springs themselves are not adjustable for tension. Sufficient free movement (about $\frac{1}{16}$ in.), however, must be maintained in the clutch control, otherwise the plates of the multi-plate clutch (four plates on most machines) will not be pressed firmly against each other when the clutch is engaged, and the consequent slip will damage or ruin the cork or fabric inserts.

On a new machine, or where the plates have had new inserts fitted, some initial bedding-down of the inserts occurs; this often results in the essential free movement in the clutch control being taken up during the first few hundred miles. Thereafter, after covering about 250 miles, and subsequently at intervals of about 1,000 miles, check the adjustment of the clutch control as described in succeeding paragraphs.

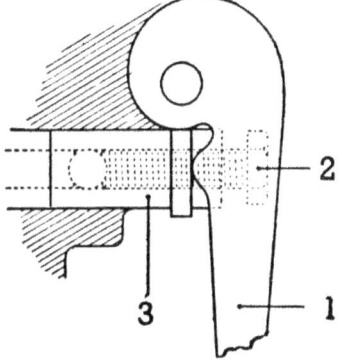

FIG. 79. CLUTCH CONTROL ADJUSTMENT
Applies to 1946–55 Models G, J, J2; 1956-7 350 c.c. "Clippers."
(*The Enfield Cycle Co., Ltd.*)

To Adjust the Clutch Control (1946-55 Models G, J, J2; 1956-7 350 c.c. "Clippers"). To adjust the direct-type of operating lever shown in Fig. 79, first detach the lever 1 from the control cable and hinge it back to give access to the adjuster screw 2 and the sleeve 3. The lever 1 should have a free movement of about $\frac{1}{16}$ in. To increase the movement, turn the adjuster screw 2 anti-clockwise. To reduce the movement, turn it clockwise. As may be observed in the sketch, no lock-nut is provided. When the lever 1 is positioned, and the control lever is connected up, the screw 2 and the sleeve 3 are automatically locked by the lever.

To Adjust the Clutch Control (1949-53 350 c.c., 500 c.c. "Bullets"). Referring to Fig. 80, first slacken the clamping screw 1. Next hold the end of the operating lever 2, turning it with a slight pressure towards the right. Then position the operating arm 3 as required until a free movement of about $\frac{1}{16}$ in. exists in the control cable after retightening the

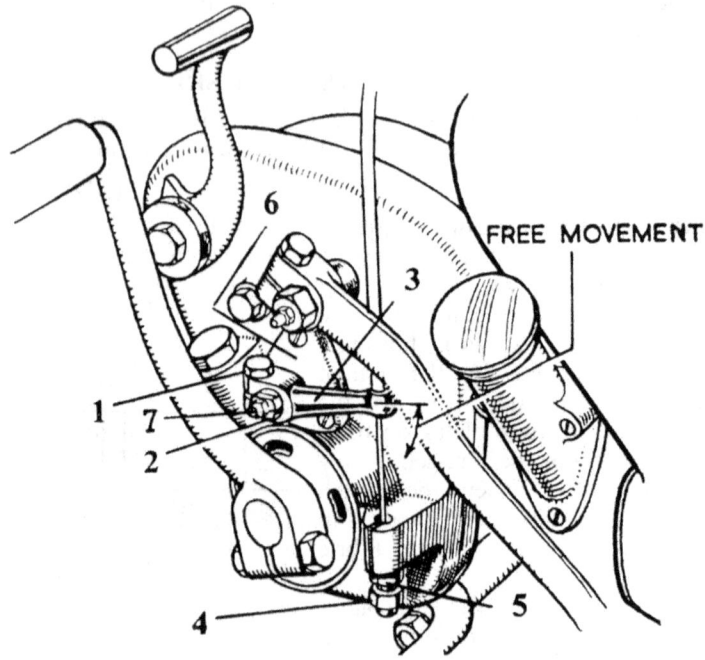

FIG. 80. CLUTCH-CONTROL ADJUSTMENT
Applies to 1949 to early 1954 350 c.c., 500 c.c. "Bullets."
(*The Enfield Cycle Co., Ltd.*)

clamping screw 1. When making the clutch-control adjustment, it is important to observe the following two points—

1. Position the arm 3 so that it is approximately square with the clutch cable, disengaged. The length of the inner cable beneath the lever can be effectively adjusted by means of the adjusting screw 4 and the lock-nut 5.

2. Position the arm 3 endwise on the operating worm 7 so that its inner face is about $\frac{1}{8}$ in. from the small triangular oil-retaining cap 6. Avoid a clearance exceeding $\frac{1}{8}$ in., otherwise there is a risk of the arm 3 fouling the crank of the kick-starter pedal.

To Adjust the Clutch Control (1954-8 350 c.c., 500 c.c. "Bullets"; 1958 350 c.c. "Clipper"). On early 1954 "Bullets" an exposed-type clutch operating-lever (Fig. 80) is provided; should a clutch-control adjustment become necessary, effect this as for the 1949–53 "Bullets."

Late 1954-7 "Bullets" and 1958 350 c.c. "Clipper" have an enclosed-type clutch control with dual adjustment. Referring to Fig. 81, to adjust the clutch control, first remove the two metal-discs from the gearbox

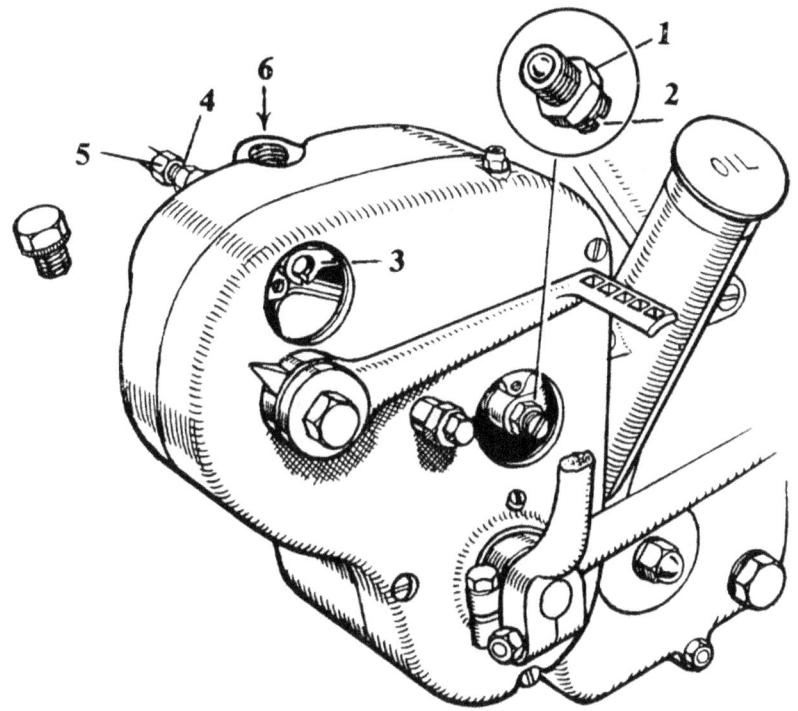

FIG. 81. CLUTCH CONTROL ADJUSTMENT
Late 1954-7 350 c.c., 500 c.c. "Bullets," 1958 "350 Clipper."
(*The Enfield Cycle Co., Ltd.*)

end-cover. Then effect any major adjustment necessary by slackening the lock-nut 1 (accessible through the lower inspection-hole) and with a screwdriver screwing the slotted adjuster-screw 2 inwards or outwards until there is a free movement of about $\frac{1}{16}$ in. at the cable end of the clutch operating-lever 3. You can check this movement through the upper inspection hole.

To compensate for stretch in the clutch operating-cable, or to make any minor clutch-control adjustment (after effecting a major adjustment as just described), loosen the lock-nut 4 and screw the adjuster screw 5 (behind the oil filler-plug hole 6), by means of its hexagon, in or out as required.

To Adjust the Clutch Control (1954-8 250 c.c. "Clippers"). Referring to Fig. 82, first disconnect the clutch operating-cable from the operating lever 1. Next remove the inspection cover from the off-side of the gearbox and move lever 1 (as shown in Fig. 82) so that the fork at the foot of the operating-lever spindle clears the adjuster screw 3. Then turn the adjuster screw as required until a slight clearance (say, $\tfrac{1}{16}$ in.) exists between the

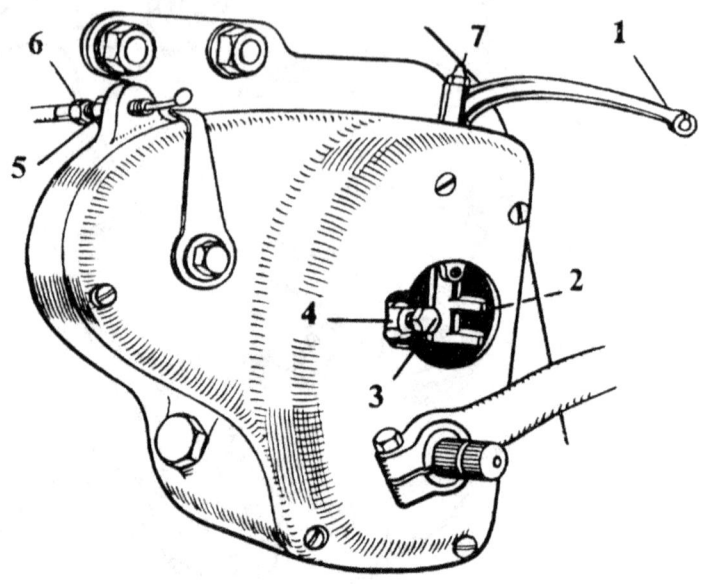

FIG. 82. CLUTCH CONTROL ADJUSTMENT
Applies to 1954-8 250 c.c. "Clippers."
(*The Enfield Cycle Co., Ltd.*)

shoulders of the adjuster sleeve 4 and the fork 2, when the lever 1 is reconnected to the clutch operating-cable. In this position the fork 2 automatically locks the adjuster screw 3.

To compensate for stretch of the clutch control-cable, or to make any minor adjustment necessary (after making a major adjustment as just described), loosen the lock-nut 5 and then turn the adjuster screw 6 as required.

If the Clutch Slips. First of all check that the clutch-control adjustment (*see* pages 141-4) is correct. If this is so, perhaps the plate inserts have become worn flush with the plates or have become burnt. The remedy here is to dismantle the clutch and have new inserts fitted to the plates. Note that where cork inserts are used (i.e., most models except the 1956-8 "Bullets") these inserts wear better when oil is present; it is advisable

GENERAL MAINTENANCE

therefore to keep the oil-bath chain case well topped-up (*see* page 47). The dismantling of the clutch assembly is dealt with in the section (*see* pages 140-1) covering the removal of the crankcase and gearbox.

As has been stated on page 141, no adjustment is provided for the clutch spring pressure and *the three screws must always be kept fully tightened.*

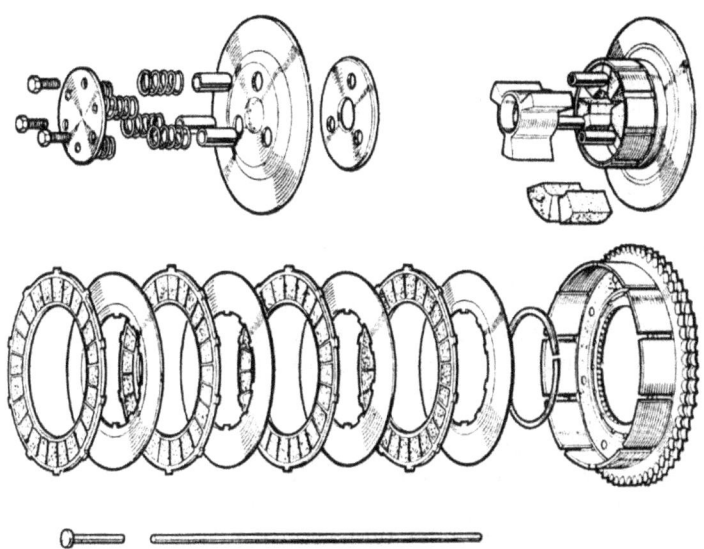

FIG. 83. THE CLUTCH SHOWN DISMANTLED

The above assembly applies to 350 c.c., 500 c.c. "Bullets," but the general layout is similar on all models. On the 250 c.c. "Clippers," however, there are only two insert plates, and one of these comprises the clutch sprocket.

(*The Enfield Cycle Co., Ltd.*)

If persistent clutch slip develops, it is advisable to renew the clutch springs as well as the clutch inserts.

Adjustment of Neutral-finder Lever. A stop-sleeve limits the forward and downward travel of the lever (provided on all except the 250 c.c. "Clippers"). Should the lever fail to locate neutral, slacken the hexagon-headed screw securing the sleeve, and turn the sleeve as required. This adjusts the position of the neutral finder at the end of its travel, the sleeve being eccentric.

Gear Control Adjustment. As the foot gear-change lever is mounted directly on the gearbox, it is impossible for the gear control to get out of adjustment. Should the gear-change lever, however, be positioned inconveniently relative to the off-side footrest, loosen the pin securing the lever to the operating mechanism on the gearbox, withdraw the lever, and replace it one serration higher or lower to enable gear changes to be made smoothly without raising the foot from the footrest.

The Four-speed Gearbox. A single striking fork operates all the gears and it is therefore quite impossible to engage two gears simultaneously, however much wear has occurred. Wear inside the gearbox takes place very slowly, always provided that the gearbox is correctly lubricated (*see* page 47). If serious gearbox trouble does develop through neglect or after a very big mileage, it is advisable to remove the complete gearbox and have it overhauled by The Enfield Cycle Co., Ltd. (*see* Preface), or by an authorized Royal Enfield repairer.

To Remove Gearbox (Models G, J, J2). Remove the oil-bath chain case, the engine sprocket, the clutch, and the secondary chain; also any items obstructing gearbox removal. Then remove the gearbox top and bottom mounting-bolts and lift the gearbox out of the frame.

To Remove Gearbox (350 c.c., 500 c.c. "Bullets"). Remove the gearbox and crankcase *together* (*see* page 139). Then remove the four $\frac{3}{8}$ in. securing nuts and withdraw the gearbox from the crankcase.

To Remove Gearbox (350 c.c. "Clippers"). Remove the gearbox and crankcase *together* (*see* page 140). Then separate the crankcase and gearbox by removing the rear engine-plates. Alternatively, if the crankcase has not been disturbed, remove the oil-bath chain case, the engine sprocket, the clutch, the secondary chain, and any items which facilitate removal of the gearbox. Then remove the top and bottom bolts on which the gearbox is mounted in the rear engine-plates. Remove the off-side rear plate. Now lift the gearbox out of the frame.

To Remove Gearbox (250 c.c. "Clippers"). Remove the oil-bath chain case, the engine sprocket, the alternator stator and rotor, the clutch, and the secondary chain. Next remove the two $\frac{5}{16}$ in. engine bolts, and the gearbox top and bottom bolts, and lift the gearbox out of the frame.

Chain Lubrication. *See* instructions on pages 47–50.

Importance of Correct Chain Tension. Always keep the primary and secondary chains correctly tensioned ($\frac{1}{4}$ in. and $\frac{1}{2}$ in. whip respectively). A slack chain is apt to rattle and jump the sprockets, while an excessively tight chain is liable to damage the chain rollers and the sprocket teeth. To check the tension of the primary chain, remove the oil-bath chain case cover or inspection cap where fitted.

Primary Chain Adjustment (1946-55 Models G, J, J2; 1956-7 350 c.c. "Clippers"). Slacken the nuts on the top and bottom bolts holding the gearbox to the engine rear mounting-plates; then pivot the gearbox as required about the bottom bolt until the chain is tensioned so that there is a total up-and-down free movement of about $\frac{1}{4}$ in., measured at the centre of the chain run (with the chain in its tightest position). Be careful to retighten the nuts on the gearbox very firmly, again recheck the primary-chain tension, and check the tension of the secondary chain.

Primary Chain Adjustment (1949 58 350 c.c., 500 c.c. "Bullets"; 1954-8 250 c.c. "Clippers"; 1958 350 c.c. "Clippers"). Remove the cover

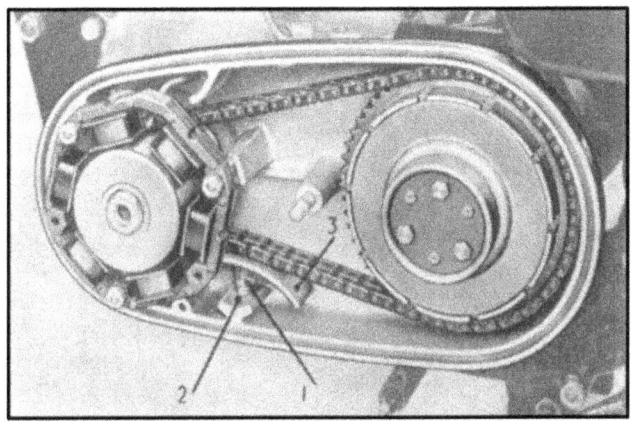

FIG. 84. SHOWING DUPLEX PRIMARY CHAIN AND THE SLIPPER-TYPE TENSIONER

The arrangement illustrated is used on all "Bullet" models and 250 c.c. "Clippers"; no alternator is, of course, fitted to pre-1956 "Bullets" with "Magdyno" lighting and ignition.

(The Enfield Cycle Co., Ltd.)

from the oil-bath chain case (*see* pages 139 and 140) to expose the duplex primary-chain and its curved slipper-type tensioner, shown in Fig. 84. Then loosen the lock-nut 1 and turn the set-screw 2 clockwise or anti-clockwise by means of its hexagon head until the slipper 3 tensions the chain such that there is a total up-and-down free movement of about $\frac{1}{4}$ in., measured at the centre of the top run of the chain (with the chain in its tightest position). Afterwards tighten the lock-nut 1 securely, and replace the cover on the oil-bath chain case.

Secondary Chain Adjustment (1946-55 Models G, J, J2). Always adjust the tension of the secondary chain after making a primary chain adjustment and when chain stretch increases whip beyond the specified limit.

To adjust the secondary chain, place the machine on its rear stand and loosen both rear-wheel spindle nuts. Then after slackening the lock-nuts, turn the set-screws in the rear-fork ends until the chain has a total up-and-down free movement of about ½ in., measured at the centre of the chain lower-run (with the chain in its tightest position).

It is most important when turning the set-screw adjusters to screw in both set-screws exactly the same amount, to maintain the chains and wheels in true alignment. If in any doubt as to the latter, check the alignment of the front and rear wheels as described on page 150. After making the

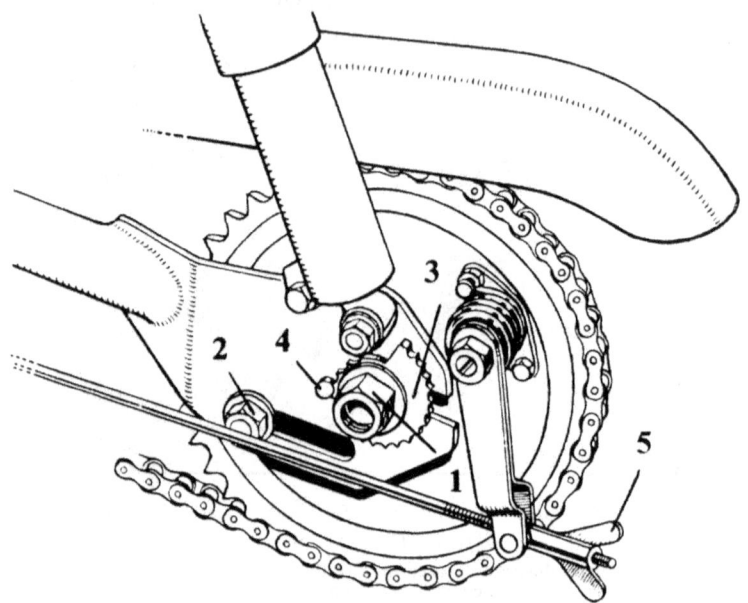

FIG. 85. ADJUSTMENT OF THE SECONDARY CHAIN AND REAR BRAKE ON MODELS WITH "SWINGING ARM" REAR SUSPENSION
(*The Enfield Cycle Co., Ltd.*)

required adjustment, retighten the lock-nuts on both set-screws very firmly, and also check the adjustment of the rear brake (*see* page 155).

Secondary Chain Adjustment (1949-58 350 c.c., 500 c.c. "Bullets"; 1954-8 250 c.c., 350 c.c. "Clippers"). On all machines with "swinging arm" rear suspension the tension of the secondary chain should be checked *with both wheels resting on the ground and the rider seated.*

Referring to Fig. 85, to adjust the tension of the secondary chain, slacken both rear-wheel spindle nuts 1 and the brake anchor-nut 2. Then turn the cam plates 3 until there is a total-up-and-down free movement of the chain (in its tightest position) of about ½ in., measured at the centre of the chain lower-run.

Assuming that both cam plates have the same notches engaging the pegs 4 in the rear-fork ends, chain and wheel alignment should automatically be correct. Should slight frame-distortion exist (as the result of a crash), it may be found that correct wheel-alignment (*see* page 150) can be obtained only by adjusting the cam plates so that different notches

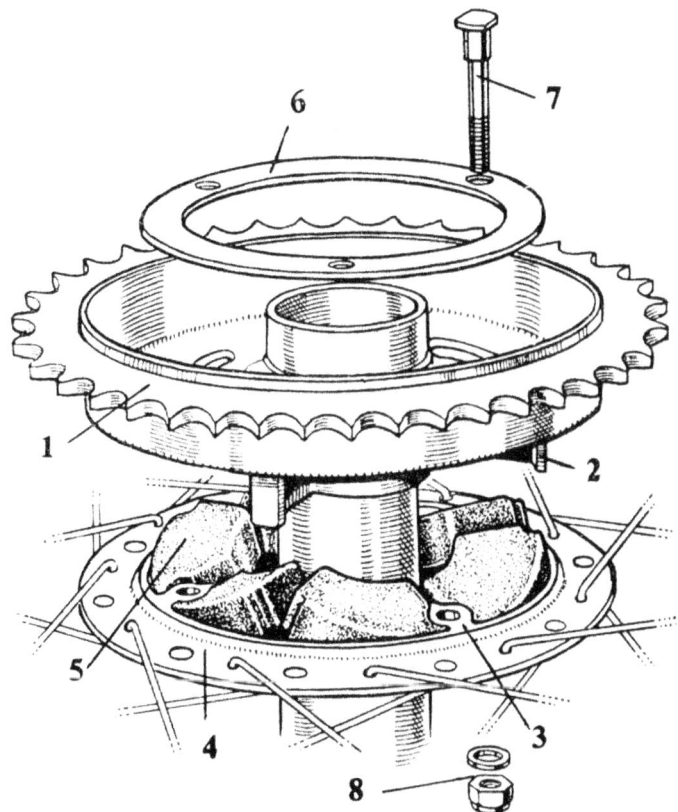

FIG. 86. FITTING RUBBER BLOCKS TO THE CUSH-DRIVE REAR HUB
(*The Enfield Cycle Co., Ltd.*)

contact the pegs in the rear-fork ends. In this instance it is desirable to check the alignment of the chain run as well as wheel-alignment.

After adjusting the tension of the secondary chain, be sure to tighten both rear-wheel spindle nuts 1 securely, retighten the anchor nut 2, and check whether a rear-brake adjustment (*see* page 155) is needed.

Chain Stretch. It is desirable to renew at once a primary or secondary chain when its stretch exceeds a quarter of an inch per foot. To check for stretch, close up a foot length of the chain, measure the exact length, pull the links apart, and again measure the chain length. The difference between the two lengths is, of course, the amount of chain stretch.

When Fitting a Chain. Always make quite sure that the spring link is fitted so that its *open end faces away from the direction of chain movement*. This is important because a chain (particularly a secondary chain) coming adrift when travelling fast can be highly dangerous.

The Cush-drive Rear Hub (All Models). The transmission smoothness on all Royal Enfields is largely due to the incorporation of the patent cush-drive rear hub; this smooths out engine impulses at all speeds, reduces any tendency for snatch in the secondary chain, and minimizes wear of the chains and rear tyre.

As may be seen in Fig. 86, the back of the brake drum 1 (with integral sprocket) has three metal vanes 2. Three similar vanes 3 are provided on the inside of the cush-drive hub shell 4. Six equal-size blocks of solid rubber 5 are placed in the hub shell, one on each side of each vane, and the three vanes on the back of the brake drum each fit between a pair of these rubber blocks. Thus the assembly comprises a rubber block and a vane alternately.

No adjustment of the cush-drive is necessary, but it is advisable about every 10,000 miles to remove the rear wheel, complete with sprocket and brake drum (*see* page 154), and inspect the cush-drive. If worn, renew the rubber blocks 5 and the lock-ring 6.

When replacing or renewing the rubber blocks, position them in the hub shell so that they lean against each other (*see* Fig. 86) and provide a lead for the metal vanes. Smear some soap (not oil) on the vanes 2 at the back of the brake drum, and insert the vanes between the pairs of rubber blocks. Then with a mallet deliver a sharp blow at the brake-drum centre until the vanes go fully down between the blocks. Now replace the lock-ring 6, insert the three bolts 7, and fit the washers and nuts 8. Tighten the latter firmly.

WHEELS, BRAKES, AND TYRES

Wheel Alignment. To obtain maximum tyre life and good steering, it is essential that the front and rear wheels are kept truly aligned. Unless frame distortion exists (a rare fault), moving the rear wheel backwards in order to take up stretch in the secondary chain will not upset wheel-alignment, except on the 1946-55 Models G, J, J2 which have a set-screw adjustment, instead of twin cam-plates on the rear-wheel spindle. As mentioned on page 147, it is essential to screw in both set-screws exactly the same amount. If uneven wear of the tyre treads suggests misalignment of the wheels, check the alignment.

On a solo model, place a straight-edge or a board alongside the two wheels. It should touch the tyres at four points when the handlebars are placed in their normal position and the machine is jacked up on its stand. If the rear tyre is of larger section than the front one, due allowance must be made for this. Some riders use a taut piece of string attached to an anchorage post for checking wheel alignment. Where a sidecar is fitted, the sidecar should generally toe-in to the extent of about ½ in. (*see* Fig. 87). A suitable adjustment can readily be made. With a sidecar alignment, also check the vertical alignment and if necessary adjust the seat-pillar

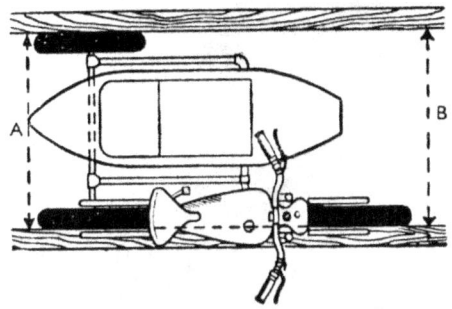

FIG. 87. CHECKING WHEEL ALIGNMENT ON A SIDECAR
If wheel alignment is correct, dimention B should
be about ½ in. less than dimension A.

connexion until the motor-cycle leans *outwards* about 1 in., measured at handlebar clinch-bolt height. Always observe carefully the fitting instructions issued by the sidecar manufacturers.

The Wheel Bearings. On all models the front and rear hubs have single-row deep-groove journal races, and the bearings require no attention other than occasional lubrication (*see* page 51).

To Remove Front Wheel (All Models). On 1946-55 Models G, J, J2, and the 1954-8 250 c.c. "Clippers" raise the front wheel well clear of the ground by placing the machine on its stand and inserting suitable packing (e.g., a strong box) beneath the engine. On 1949-58 350, 500 c.c. "Bullets," and the 1956-8 350 c.c. "Clippers," place the machine on its centre stand which is sufficiently close to the centre of gravity of the machine for the motor-cycle to rest on both the stand and the rear wheel, when the front wheel is removed.

To remove the front wheel, slacken off the front-brake cable adjustment and disconnect the cable (two on 1955-8 "Bullets") from the handlebar control and from the brake-cam operating lever(s); also remove the four nuts securing the two caps to the bases of the telescopic-fork legs. Then lift the front of the machine (unnecessary where packing has been inserted beneath the engine), and the wheel will fall away.

Removing Quickly-detachable Rear Mudguard. On all models a quickly-detachable rear mudguard is provided to facilitate tyre repairs and the removal of the rear wheel. Mudguard removal should be effected in the following manner—

On 1946-55 Models G, J, J2 slacken the two nuts securing the mudguard

Fig. 88. Rear View of 1953-5 500 c.c. "Swinging-arm" "Bullet" Showing Chain Adjustment, Mudguard Attachment, Brake Adjustment, Rear Suspension, etc.

The 1956-8 "Bullets" have a slightly modified frame, and the 1958 version has a quickly-detachable rear wheel (with full-width light-alloy hub) fitted as standard, instead of the non-detachable type wheel shown.

(bottom) slotted stays to the rear part of the frame, and also loosen the two nuts securing the slotted lugs at the front end of the mudguard to the frame. Then lift the mudguard off after first disconnecting the lead to the tail lamp.

On the 1949-55 350, 500 c.c. "Bullets" and the 1954-8 250, 350 c.c. "Clippers," referring to Fig. 88, to remove the mudguard slacken the four nuts 2 and 8 (one pair on each side of the machine), and lift the mudguard off to the rear. This does not disturb the dualseat (where fitted), but should it be desired to remove the latter it is only necessary to remove the two nuts 1 (one on each side) securing the dualseat, and lift the dualseat off.

On the 1956-8 350, 500 c.c. "Bullets," remove the two nuts securing the dualseat support-bracket and the front ends of the lifting handles to the tops of the Armstrong shock-absorber attachment brackets. Then lift off the dualseat, together with the rear part of the mudguard, after first seeing that the lead to the tail lamp is disconnected.

To Remove Rear Wheel (Not Quickly-detachable Type). First remove the rear mudguard as previously described. Next remove the nut (7, Fig. 88) from the pin securing the brake anchor-plate; also remove the adjuster wing-nut (4, Fig. 88) from the rear-brake rod. Disconnect the secondary chain by removing its spring link; and disconnect the speedometer driving cable (4, Fig. 28). Then slacken the rear-wheel spindle nuts 5, and slide the rear wheel out of the slotted fork-ends. Tilt the wheel slightly, if necessary to enable the brake anchor-pin to disengage from its slot.

When replacing the rear wheel on "swinging-arm" models (*see* Fig. 88), push it forward so that the cam-plates 3 are hard up against the pegs 6 in the fork ends; on other models see that the hub spindle abuts the set-screws in the fork ends. This will ensure correct chain adjustment and wheel alignment. *See also* Fig. 89.

Knock-out Spindle on Rear Wheel (1946-55 Models G, J, J2; 1949-53 350 c.c., 500 c.c. "Bullets"; 1956-8 350 c.c. "Clippers"). On these models having a rear wheel which is not of the quickly-detachable type it is possible to repair a puncture very quickly *without removing the rear wheel*, thanks to the provision of a knock-out spindle. To remove an inner tube with the wheel in position, use the following procedure. First remove the rear mudguard (*see* appropriate paragraph on page 152). Next remove the nut from the off-side of the rear-wheel spindle and tap the spindle out of the other side. This leaves the wheel mounted on a tubular spindle attached to the near-side fork end. Now slightly spring apart the rear fork-ends, and slide out the knurled distance-piece between the hub and the off-side fork end. Then slip the inner tube carefully through the gap left on the off-side. With the distance-piece and solid rear-wheel spindle removed, it is important not to impose any strain on the rear wheel.

To Remove Rear Wheel (Quickly-detachable Type). Available as an optional extra on many 1956-8 models, and fitted as standard equipment on 1957-8 "Bullets," the quickly-detachable rear wheel (with full-width light-alloy cush-drive hub permits the main portion of the rear wheel to be removed without disturbing the secondary chain, the brake drum (and integral sprocket), the rear brake rod, and the brake anchorage bolt. To remove the wheel proceed as below.

Jack the motor-cycle up on its centre stand and remove the mudguard as described on this page. Referring to Fig. 89, next unscrew the long bolt 1, applying a spanner to its hexagonal head, and withdraw this bolt together with the adjuster cam for the secondary chain. It is advisable to mark the cam to ensure its being replaced in its original position. Slide the distance collar 2 out of the rear-fork end, and lift away the speedometer-drive gearbox 3 which may be left attached to the driving cable 4. Also remove (to prevent damage) the spacing collar and felt washer behind the speedometer-drive gearbox. Now pull the main portion of the wheel

FIG. 89. REMOVING THE QUICKLY-DETACHABLE REAR WHEEL
(*The Enfield Cycle Co., Ltd.*)

across to the off-side of the machine to disengage the driving pins from the cush-drive shell and fixed portion of the hub. Then lift the wheel clear of the motor-cycle.

Reverse the foregoing procedure when replacing the wheel. When fitting the speedometer-drive gearbox, be sure that its internal driving dogs engage with the slots in the end of the hub barrel. Also before tightening the long bolt 1, see that the speedometer-drive gearbox is positioned so that there is no sharp bend in the driving cable 4.

To Remove Rear Wheel with Brake Drum, etc. (Quickly-detachable Type). To remove the rear wheel complete with brake drum, integral sprocket, etc., first disconnect the secondary chain by removing its spring link; also remove the brake cover-plate anchor nut and the wing nut from the brake rod. Unscrew the long bolt (1, Fig. 89) two to three turns, and the near-side spindle nut the same number of turns. Disconnect the speedometer-gearbox driving cable (4, Fig. 89) and slide the complete wheel out of the rear-fork ends. Tilt the wheel as required to enable the end of the brake-shoe pivot pin to disengage from the slot in the rear-fork end.

Front Brake Adjustment. To adjust the front brake for shoe wear and cable stretch, turn the self-locking knurled adjuster-nut mounted low down on the near-side of the front forks as required.

The 1955-8 350, 500 c.c. "Bullets" fitted with full-width light-alloy front hubs have dual front brakes, and a knurled adjuster-nut is mounted on each side of the front forks. The pull on the two cables is automatically compensated for by a pivoted compensating-lever attached to the handlebar control; in consequence, precisely the same adjustment of both knurled adjuster nuts is not essential, but it is desirable to keep the two adjusters adjusted to approximately the same extent.

Rear Brake Adjustment. Referring to Fig. 88, to adjust the rear brake, turn the wing nut 4 on the threaded end of the brake rod as required. Before doing this, however, see that the rear-brake pedal is set in the best position for convenient operation. If necessary, adjust by means of the pedal-stop provided. To lower or raise the position of the pedal, loosen the lock-nut 9 and turn the adjustable stop 10 anti-clockwise or clockwise respectively as required.

To Ensure Powerful Braking. Always keep the front and rear brakes adjusted so that the brake shoes are in close contact with the drums and yet do not bind when the brakes are released. When adjusting the brakes, test for free rotation of both wheels by spinning them with the wheels raised clear of the ground.

Brake Shoes and Linings. The internal-expanding brakes have drums or inserts (light-alloy hubs) which are free from any tendency for scoring, and the shoes are lined with a special woven material which wears very slowly. Note that somewhat more rapid wear occurs on the lining of the leading shoe than on the other, because of its servo action. The brake-cam spindles are able to float slightly in their cover-plate housings, to provide some degree of shoe centralization and good circumferential contact with the drums or inserts.

If Grease Gets on the Linings. Remove the brake shoes and scrape and wash the linings in petrol. Excessive lubrication of the wheel hubs (*see* page 51) is the usual cause of greasy linings which greatly impairs braking efficiency. Normally the linings should have a polished appearance; do not rough them up with a file. After cleaning and assembling a front or rear brake, run the motor-cycle in second gear for half a mile or so to burn off any grease which remains.

To Obtain Good Tyre Mileage. It is essential to keep the wheels correctly aligned (*see* page 150) and the pressures in the tyres correct. Do not brake fiercely, accelerate violently, or indulge in stunt cornering. Also go easy on the clutch, remove flints or small stones embedded in the tyre treads, and do not allow paraffin or oil to get on the covers.

Maintaining Correct Tyre Pressures. Over-inflation causes vibration, strains the cover, and can cause concussion bursts; under-inflation causes

TABLE VII

TYRE PRESSURES FOR 1946–58 MODELS (SOLO)

(Shown in lb per sq in.)

Royal Enfield Model	Front Tyre	Rear Tyre	Rear Tyre (Pillion)
Model G	18	22	34
Model J	18	18	30
Model J2	18	18	30
350 c.c. "Bullet"*	18	22	32
500 c.c. "Bullet"*	18	20	32
350 c.c. "Clipper"*	18	22	34
250 c.c. "Clipper"	18	26	38

* Where 3·00–21 in. and 4·00–19 in. tyres are fitted to 350, 500 c.c. "Bullets," the correct tyre-pressures for front and rear tyres are 21 lb per sq in. and 16 lb per sq in. respectively. 1958 models (except 250 c.c.) have 3·25–19 in. tyres, and correct pressures (solo) are 20 and 24 lb per sq in.

TABLE VIII

TYRE PRESSURES FOR 1946–58 MODELS (SIDECAR)

(Shown in lb per sq in.)

Royal Enfield	Front Tyre	Rear Tyre	S/C Tyre
Model J	20	24†	16
Model J2	20	24†	16
500 c.c. "Bullet"	22	25†	16

† If a pillion passenger is carried in addition to the sidecar passenger (not recommended), increase the pressure in the rear tyre to 32–34 lb per sq in. Note that on the 1958 500 c.c. "Bullet" with 3·25–19 in. rear tyre the correct inflation pressure (with sidecar) is 30 lb per sq in.

a tendency for tyres to creep, rolling, instability of steering, and cracking of the cover. Therefore, check the tyre pressures weekly with a suitable pressure gauge (*see* page 89). The correct tyre pressures for 1946–58 Royal Enfields are given in Tables VII and VIII. It is assumed that the rider is of average weight. A slight increase in the pressure for the rear tyre is advised where a rider is above average weight or where heavy equipment is carried.

STEERING HEAD AND SUSPENSION

Steering Head Adjustment (All Models). Basically the steering head adjustment is similar on all 1946-58 models, but there are some variations in regard to the arrangement of the clamping bolts. An adjustment is seldom called for, provided the ball bearings are adequately lubricated (*see* page

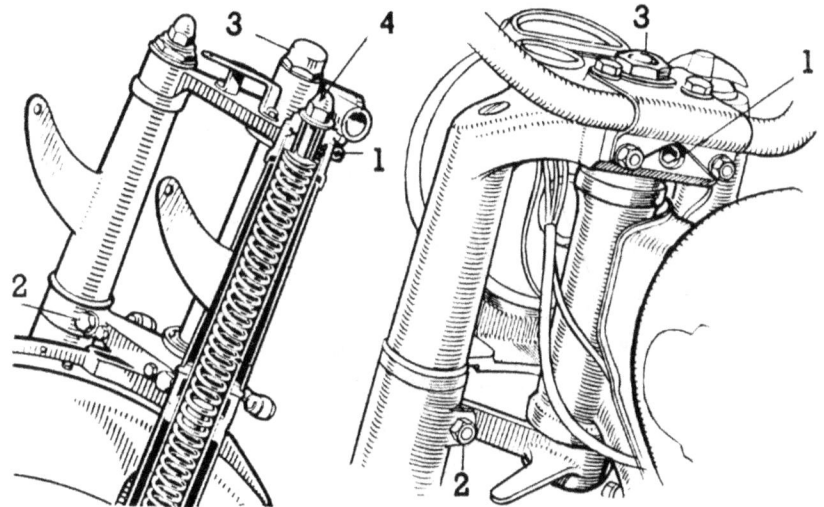

FIGS. 90 AND 91. STEERING HEAD ADJUSTMENT

Applies (left) to 1946-50 Models G, J, J2, and the 1949 350 c.c. "Bullet"; (right) to the 1954-8 350, 500 c.c. "Bullets" and 250, 350 c.c. "Clippers."

(*The Enfield Cycle Co., Ltd.*)

51), but if some play is felt, it is advisable to make an immediate adjustment; unless this is done the ball bearings are liable to become damaged, and vibration will occur. Check for play by attempting to "shake" the handlebars or, better still, by placing one hand near the centre of the handlebars and with the other hand on the front tyre, attempting to turn the wheel against its normal direction of rotation.

Referring to Figs. 90 to 92, to take up play in the two ball-bearings first place some suitable packing beneath the engine crankcase to take weight off the front wheel, unless the latter is already clear of the ground. Next slacken the head-clip clamp bolt or wedge bolt 1. If a wedge bolt is fitted (*see* Fig. 91), slacken the bolt with the special key inserted into the internal hexagon. Also loosen the two clamp bolts 2 securing the main tubes of the front-fork legs to the fork crown (*see* Figs. 90 and 91) or to the fork head (*see* Fig. 92). It is *not* necessary to slacken the two clamp bolts 5 (shown in Fig. 92) securing the main tubes of the fork legs to the fork crown. Then take up all play in the steering-head bearings by tightening down the large plated nut 3 (behind the speedometer) on top of the

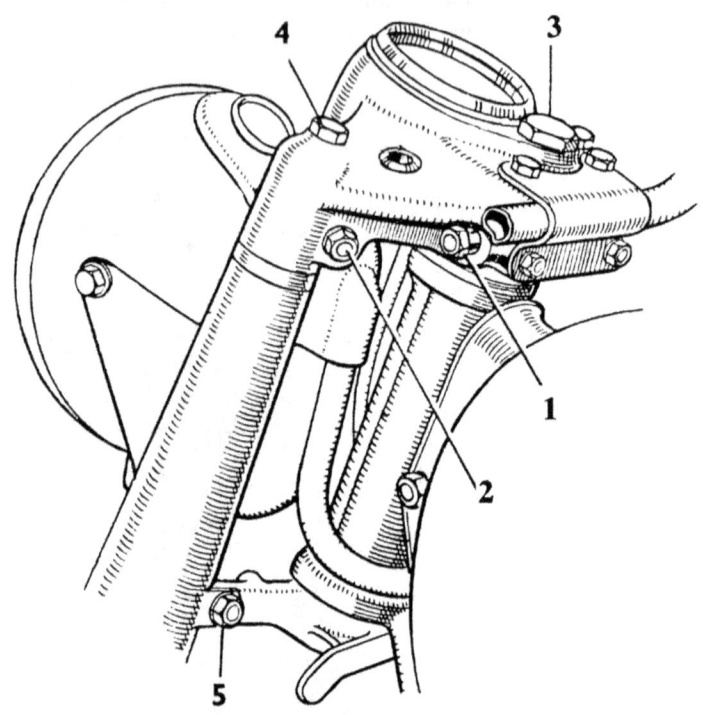

FIG. 92. STEERING HEAD ADJUSTMENT
Applies to 1951-5 Models G, J, J2; 1950-3 350, 500 c.c. "Bullets."
(*The Enfield Cycle Co., Ltd.*)

fork head or "casquette" (1954-8 "Bullets" and "Clippers"). Tighten down this nut very gradually and while doing so, make frequent checks for play.

See that all perceptible play is eliminated from the ball bearings, but also make quite sure there is no stiffness in the steering; with a slight push, the front wheel should swing over to full lock. After correctly adjusting the steering head, be careful to retighten the three clamp bolts 1 and 2 securely.

The Telescopic Front Forks (All Models). Note that on all 1954 and subsequent models the ammeter, lighting switch, and parking bulbs (*see*

Fig. 43) are held in place in the light-alloy "casquette" by rubber surrounds. No adjustment to the front forks is necessary except slackening off very occasionally some clamp bolts when a steering-head adjustment (*see* page 157) is called for.

Where the legs of the front forks are fitted with drain plugs (*see* Fig. 27) it may at long intervals be advisable to top-up the fork legs with damping oil as described on page 51. On forks with legs not fitted with drain plugs, replenishment of the legs is not necessary unless the forks require dismantling. Dismantling of the telescopic front-forks should normally not be necessary until a very big mileage has been completed, when in some instances oil seepage and wear of internal oil seals and bearings may necessitate stripping-down the forks to renew the worn parts. For appropriate instructions, see the maker's official Instruction Book, or Workshop Maintenance Manual.

The Rear Suspension Units ("Bullets" and "Clippers"). In the event of the springing becoming too "soft," it is possible with 1949-53 "Bullets" to replenish the Royal Enfield Mk. I suspension-units with damping oil (*see* page 51). On late 1954-8 "Bullets" and all "Clippers" the proprietary units require no maintenance whatever. To obtain access to the inside of the proprietary suspension-units for the removal of the springs, remove each unit from the frame, press down the top cover, and remove the split collar. You can renew the springs and the rubber bushes, but any further internal maintenance should be entrusted to the makers or an authorized repairer. Generally speaking, dismantling of suspension-units is rarely called for.

The "Swinging Arm" ("Bullets" and "Clippers"). *See* page 54 for lubrication instructions. Make no attempt to remove the arm for **any** reason unless you have the special expander required to spread the side members of the frame.

INDEX

Accessory firms, 88
Air filter, 33-4
Alignment, wheel, 150
Alternators, 61
Ammeter, 60
Automatic timing control, 101
Auxiliary oil pump, 45

Battery—
 charging, 62
 filler, 65
 first filling, 67
 topping-up, 63-5
Big-end bearing, 137
Brake—
 adjustment, 155
 lubrication, 53-4
Brushes, dynamo, 57
Bulbs, renewing, 76-9

Camwheel bearings, 137
Carbon removal, 118-19
Carburettor—
 dismantling, 28-30
 inspecting, 30-1
 principles, 17-23
 tuning, 23-8
Centre-stand, greasing, 55
Chain—
 stretch, 149
 tension, 146
Changing gear, 10
Chromium, cleaning, 91
Cleaning—
 commutator, 58
 contacts, 99
 machine, 91
 sparking plugs, 93-5
Clutch—
 control adjustment, 141-4
 slip, 144
Coil, 102-3
Colloidal graphite, 15
Commutator, cleaning, 58
Compensated voltage control, 59-60

Contact-breaker—
 gap, 96-9
 lubrication, 46
Contacts, cleaning, 99
Controls, use of, 3-7
Crankcase and gearbox removal, 138-41, 146
Crankcase breather, 41, 43
Cush-drive rear hub, 150
Cylinder—
 barrel removal, 114, 123-4
 head removal, 109-14, 124-7

Decarbonizing, 107
Decompressor, 105-7
Dipper switch, oiling, 55
Drain plugs, front forks, 52
Dynamo—
 brushes, 57
 removal, 6

Enamelled parts, cleaning, 91
Engine—
 bearings, 136-8
 nuts, tightness of, 128
 oils, 36
Exhaust—
 flame, 24
 valve lifter, 4, 105

Felt filter, cleaning, 43
Filter, air, 33-4
Focusing headlamp, 74
Foot gear-change, greasing, 54
Front forks, 51-2, 159
Front-wheel removal, 151
Fuel consumption, high, 28

Gap—
 contact-breaker, 96-9
 sparking plug, 93
Gear changing, 10-12
Gearbox—
 lubrication, 47
 removal, 138-41, 146

Gear control adjustment, 145
Generators, types of, 56
Greases, suitable, 50
Grinding-in valves, 121

HANDLEBAR controls, oiling, 53
Headlamps, 68–74
Hill climbing, 11
Horn, electric, 79
H.T. pick-up, 102
Hub lubrication, 51
Hydrometer, use of, 65

IGNITION—
 timing, 129–34
 trouble, diagnosing, 86

JET needle, 20, 27

LICENCES, 2
Light-unit assembly, 72
Linings, brake, 155
Lubrication—
 centre stand, 55
 chart, 48
 dipper switch, 55
 foot gear-change, 54
 front forks, 51–2
 gearbox, 47
 handlebar controls, 53
 "Magdyno," 45
 magneto, 46
 primary chain, 47
 secondary chain, 48
 sidecar chassis, 55
 speedometer drive, 53
 steering head, 51
 "swinging arm," 54
 wheel hubs, 51

"MAGDYNO" lubrication, 45
Magneto lubrication, 46
Main jet, 20, 25, 28, 30
Maintenance, items for, 89
"Monobloc" carburettor principles, 22–3
Moving off, 9

NEUTRAL finder, 5, 12, 145

OBSTRUCTION, pilot jet, 27

Oil-bath chain case, 47
Oil—
 circulation, 37–9
 consumption, increased, 44
 filter, cleaning, 43
 leakage, gearbox, 47
 pump, 39–41, 44
 tank, 35, 41, 43

PARKING machine, 13
Petrol—
 tank removal, 108, 129
 taps, 7
Pilot-air screw, 20, 26
Pilot jet, 20, 26, 27
Piston—
 removing, 115, 123
 rings, 116–18
 seizure, 15
Preliminaries, 1
Primary chain—
 adjustment, 146–7
 lubricating, 47

REAR-suspension units, 54, 159
Rear wheel removal, 152–5
Rectifiers, 61
Red reflector, 2
Riding position, 3
Rocker-box lubrication, 41
Running-in, 14, 35

SECONDARY chain—
 adjustment, 147–9
 lubrication, 48
Short circuits, avoiding, 56
Sidecar chassis, greasing, 55
Slip-ring, "Magdyno," 102
Slow-running, bad, 27
Small-end bearings, 136
Spares and repairs, 88
Sparking plugs, 92–6
Specific gravity, battery, 65–6
Speedometer drive, lubricating, 53
Spring arm, removing, 100
Starting engine, 8–9
Steering—
 damper, 13
 head adjustment, 157
 head lubrication, 51

INDEX

Stopping—
  engine, 13
  machine, 13
Storage battery, 67
Sump, draining, 41
"Swinging-arm" pivot, 54
Switch positions, 4, 73

TAIL lamps, 74–5
Tappet adjustment, 103–5
Terminals, dynamo and C.V.C. unit, 58
Throttle—
  cut-away, 22, 26
  stop, 20, 26
Timing case, draining, 42
Timing cover, replacing, 45
Tools, 89–90

Topping-up battery, 63–5
Tyre pressures, 155–7

UPPER cylinder lubricant, 15

VALVE timing, 134–6
Valves—
  removing, 120
  replacing, 122

WARMING up engine, 36
Wheel—
  alignment, 150
  bearings, 151
Wiring—
  details, 86
  diagrams, 80–5

AUTOBOOKS WORKSHOP MANUALS

ALFA ROMEO GIULIA 1300, 1600, 1750, 2000 1962-1978 WSM
BMW 1600 1966-1973 WSM
BMW 2000 & 2002 1966-1976 WSM
BMW 2500, 2800, 3.0 & 3.3 1968-1977 WSM
BMW 316, 320, 320i 1975-1977 WSM
BMW 518, 520, 520i 1973-1981 WSM
FIAT 1100, 1100D, 1100R & 1200 1957-1969 WSM
FIAT 124 1966-1974 WSM
FIAT 124 SPORT 1966-1975 WSM
FIAT 125 & 125 SPECIAL 1967-1973 WSM
FIAT 126, 126L, 126 DV, 126/650 & 126/650 DV 1972-1982 WSM
FIAT 127 SALOON, SPECIAL & SPORT, 900, 1050 1971-1981 WSM
FIAT 128 1969-1982 WSM
FIAT 1300, 1500 1961-1967 WSM
FIAT 131 MIRAFIORI 1975-1982 WSM
FIAT 132 1972-1982 WSM
FIAT 500 1957-1973 WSM
FIAT 600, 600D & MULTIPLA 1955-1969 WSM
FIAT 850 1964-1972 WSM
JAGUAR E-TYPE 1961-1972 WSM
JAGUAR MK 1, 2 1955-1969 WSM
JAGUAR S TYPE, 420 1963-1968 WSM
JAGUAR XK 120, 140, 150 MK 7, 8, 9 1948-1961 WSM
LAND ROVER 1, 2 1948-1961 WSM
MERCEDES-BENZ 190 1959-1968 WSM
MERCEDES-BENZ 220/8 1968-1972 WSM
MERCEDES-BENZ 220B 1959-1965 WSM
MERCEDES-BENZ 230 1963-1968 WSM
MERCEDES-BENZ 250 1968-1972 WSM
MERCEDES-BENZ 280 1968-1972 WSM
MG MIDGET TA-TF 1936-1955 WSM
MINI 1959-1980 WSM
MORRIS MINOR 1952-1971 WSM
PEUGEOT 404 1960-1975 WSM
PORSCHE 911 1964-1973 WSM
PORSCHE 911 1970-1977 WSM
RENAULT 16 1965-1979 WSM
RENAULT 8, 10, 1100 1962-1971 WSM
ROVER 3500, 3500S 1968-1976 WSM
SUNBEAM RAPIER, ALPINE 1955-1965 WSM
TRIUMPH SPITFIRE, GT6, VITESSE 1962-1968 WSM
TRIUMPH TR2, TR3, TR3A 1952-1962 WSM
TRIUMPH TR4, TR4A 1961-1967 WSM
VOLKSWAGEN BEETLE 1968-1977 WSM

VELOCEPRESS AUTOMOBILE BOOKS & MANUALS

ABARTH BUYERS GUIDE
AUSTIN-HEALEY 6-CYLINDER WSM
AUSTIN-HEALEY SPRITE & MG MIDGET 1958-1971 WSM
BMW 600 LIMOUSINE FACTORY WSM
BMW 600 LIMOUSINE OWNERS HAND BOOK & SERVICE MANUAL
BMW ISETTA FACTORY WSM
BOOK OF THE CARRERA PANAMERICANA - MEXICAN ROAD RACE
COMPLETE CATALOG OF JAPANESE MOTOR VEHICLES
DIALED IN - THE JAN OPPERMAN STORY
FERRARI 250/GT SERVICE AND MAINTENANCE
FERRARI 308 SERIES BUYER'S AND OWNER'S GUIDE
FERRARI BERLINETTA LUSSO
FERRARI BROCHURES AND SALES LITERATURE 1946-1967
FERRARI BROCHURES AND SALES LITERATURE 1968-1989
FERRARI GUIDE TO PERFORMANCE
FERRARI OPP, MAINTENANCE & SERVICE H/BOOKS 1948-1963
FERRARI OWNER'S HANDBOOK
FERRARI SERIAL NUMBERS PART I - ODD NUMBERS TO 21399
FERRARI SERIAL NUMBERS PART II - EVEN NUMBERS TO 1050
FERRARI SPYDER CALIFORNIA
FERRARI TUNING TIPS & MAINTENANCE TECHNIQUES
HENRY'S FABULOUS MODEL "A" FORD
HOW TO BUILD A FIBERGLASS CAR
HOW TO BUILD A RACING CAR
HOW TO RESTORE THE MODEL 'A' FORD
IF HEMINGWAY HAD WRITTEN A RACING NOVEL
JAGUAR E-TYPE 3.8 & 4.2 WSM
LE MANS 24 (THE BOOK THAT THE FILM WAS BASED ON)
MASERATI BROCHURES AND SALES LITERATURE
MASERATI OWNER'S HANDBOOK
METROPOLITAN FACTORY WSM
MGA & MGB OWNERS HANDBOOK & WSM
OBERT'S FIAT GUIDE
PERFORMANCE TUNING THE SUNBEAM TIGER
PORSCHE 356 1948-1965 WSM
PORSCHE 912 WSM
SOUPING THE VOLKSWAGEN
TRIUMPH TR2, TR3, TR4 1953-1965 WSM
VEDA ORR'S NEW REVISED HOT ROD PICTORIAL
VOLKSWAGEN TRANSPORTER, TRUCKS, STATION WAGONS WSM
VOLVO 1944-1968 ALL MODELS WSM

BROOKLANDS BOOKS & ROAD TEST PORTFOLIOS (RTP)

AC CARS 1904-2009
ALFA ROMEO 1920-1933 ROAD TEST PORTFOLIO
ALFA ROMEO 1934-1940 ROAD TEST PORTFOLIO
BRABHAM RALT HONDA THE RON TAURANAC STORY
BUGATTI TYPE 10 TO TYPE 40 ROAD TEST PORTFOLIO
BUGATTI TYPE 10 TO TYPE 251 ROAD TEST PORTFOLIO
BUGATTI TYPE 41 TO TYPE 55 ROAD TEST PORTFOLIO
BUGATTI TYPE 57 TO TYPE 251 ROAD TEST PORTFOLIO
DELAHAYE ROAD TEST PORTFOLIO
FERRARI ROAD CARS 1946-1956 ROAD TEST PORTFOLIO
FIAT 500 1936-1972 ROAD TEST PORTFOLIO
FIAT DINO ROAD TEST PORTFOLIO
HISPANO SUIZA ROAD TEST PORTFOLIO
HONDA ST1100/ST1300 PAN EUROPEAN 1990-2002 RTP
JAGUAR MK1 & MK2 ROAD TEST PORTFOLIO
LOTUS CORTINA ROAD TEST PORTFOLIO
MV AGUSTA F4 750 & 1000 1997-2007 ROAD TEST PORTFOLIO
TATRA CARS ROAD TEST PORTFOLIO

VELOCEPRESS MOTORCYCLE BOOKS & MANUALS

AJS SINGLES & TWINS 250cc THRU 1000cc 1932-1948 (BOOK OF)
AJS SINGLES 1955-65 350cc & 500cc (BOOK OF)
AJS SINGLES 1945-60 350cc & 500cc MODELS 16 & 18 (BOOK OF)
ARIEL 1939-1960 4 STROKE SINGLES (BOOK OF)
ARIEL LEADER & ARROW 1958-1964 (BOOK OF)
ARIEL MOTORCYCLES 1933-1951 WSM
ARIEL PREWAR MODELS 1932-1939 (BOOK OF)
BMW M/CYCLES R26 R27 (1956-1967) FACTORY WSM
BMW M/CYCLES R50 R50S R60 R69S (1955-1969) FACTORY WSM
BSA BANTAM (BOOK OF)
BSA ALL FOUR-STROKE SINGLES & V-TWINS 1936-1952 (BOOK OF)
BSA OHV & SV SINGLES - 250cc 1954-1970 (BOOK OF)
BSA OHV & SV SINGLES 1945-54 250-600cc (BOOK OF)
BSA OHV SINGLES 350 & 500cc 1955-1967 (BOOK OF)
BSA PRE-WAR MODELS TO 1939 (BOOK OF)
BSA TWINS 1948-1962 (BOOK OF)
BSA TWINS 1962-1969 (SECOND BOOK OF)
CATALOG OF BRITISH MOTORCYCLES (1951 MODELS)
DOUGLAS PRE-WAR ALL MODELS 1929-1939 (BOOK OF)
DOUGLAS POST-WAR ALL MODELS 1948-1957 FACTORY WSM
DUCATI 160cc, 250cc & 350cc OHC MODELS FACTORY WSM
HONDA 50 ALL MODELS UP TO 1970 INC MONKEY & TRAIL (BOOK OF)
HONDA 90 ALL MODELS UP TO 1966 (BOOK OF)
HONDA MOTORCYCLES 125-150 TWINS C/CS/CB/CA WSM
HONDA MOTORCYCLES 250-305 TWINS C/CS/CB WSM
HONDA MOTORCYCLES C100 SUPER CUB WSM
HONDA MOTORCYCLES C110 SPORT CUB 1962-1969 WSM
HONDA TWINS & SINGLES 50cc THRU 305cc 1960-1966 (BOOK OF)
HONDA TWINS ALL MODELS 125cc THRU 450cc UP TO 1968 (BOOK OF)
INDIAN PONYBIKE, BOY RACER & PAPOOSE ILL PARTS LIST & SALES LIT
LAMBRETTA ALL 125 & 150cc MODELS 1947-1957 (BOOK OF)
LAMBRETTA LI & TV MODELS 1957-1970 (SECOND BOOK OF)
MATCHLESS 350 & 500cc SINGLES 1945-1956 (BOOK OF)
MATCHLESS 350 & 500cc SINGLES 1955-1966 (BOOK OF)
NORTON 1932-1947 (BOOK OF)
NORTON 1938-1956 (BOOK OF)
NORTON DOMINATOR TWINS 1955-1965 (BOOK OF)
NORTON MODELS 19, 50 & ES2 1955-1963 (BOOK OF)
NORTON MOTORCYCLES 1957-1970 FACTORY WSM
NORTON PREWAR MODELS 1932-1939 (BOOK OF)
NSU QUICKLY ALL MODELS 1953-1963 (BOOK OF)
ROYAL ENFIELD SINGLES & V TWINS 1937-1953 (BOOK OF)
ROYAL ENFIELD SINGLES 1946-1962 (BOOK OF)
ROYAL ENFIELD 736cc INTERCEPTOR FACTORY WSM
ROYAL ENFIELD 250cc & 350cc SINGLES 1958-1966 (SECOND BOOK OF)
SUZUKI 50cc & 80cc UP TO 1966 (BOOK OF)
SUZUKI T10 1963-1967 FACTORY WSM
SUZUKI T20 & T200 1965-1969 FACTORY WSM
TRIUMPH PRE-WAR MOTORCYCLE 1935-1939 (BOOK OF)
TRIUMPH MOTORCYCLES 1937-1951 WSM
TRIUMPH MOTORCYCLES 1945-1955 FACTORY WSM
TRIUMPH TWINS 1956-1969 (BOOK OF)
VELOCETTE ALL SINGLES & TWINS 1925-1970 (BOOK OF)
VESPA 1951-1961 (BOOK OF)
VESPA 125 & 150cc & GS MODELS 1955-1963 (SECOND BOOK OF)
VESPA 90, 125 & 150cc 1963-1972 (THIRD BOOK OF)
VESPA GS & SS 1955-1968 (BOOK OF)
VINCENT MOTORCYCLES 1935-1955 WSM

PLEASE VISIT OUR WEBSITE
www.VelocePress.com
FOR A DETAILED DESCRIPTION
OF ANY OF THESE TITLES